Computer Test Bank

Prentice Hall
Physical Science

Concepts in Action
With Earth and Space Science

PEARSON

Prentice Hall

Needham, Massachusetts
Upper Saddle River, New Jersey

Computer Test Bank

Prentice Hall
Physical Science
Concepts in Action
With Earth and Space Science

ISBN 0-13-069974-8

1 2 3 4 5 6 7 8 9 10   07 06 05 04 03

About the Computer Test Bank

The *Computer Test Bank* for *Physical Science: Concepts in Action* helps you create customized tests for your classes. You can design tests to reflect your particular teaching emphasis by editing questions or adding your own. Create alternate forms of the same test by letting the software scramble the questions or even the answer choices within a question. You can also create tests for one chapter or for any combination of chapters, as well as for midterm and final exams.

The *Computer Test Bank* book is a printed version of all the questions available on the *Computer Test Bank* CD-ROM. The *Computer Test Bank* is organized by chapter and question type. It is a convenient reference source that allows you to review the available questions without a computer.

Question Organization

Within each chapter, the test questions are organized by question type and correlated to objectives from the Teacher's Edition. The questions are provided in a variety of formats, including multiple choice, modified true or false, completion, short answer, using science skills, and essay. In total, the *Computer Test Bank* contains over 2000 questions.

Every question is correlated to the objectives, which are found in the Teacher's Edition by referencing the chapter number, section, and objective number. A difficulty level of L1 or L2 is also assigned to each question. L1 questions are more basic, while L2 questions are intended for all students. The *Computer Test Bank* refers to this information as *objective* (OBJ) and *difficulty* (DIF). The objective and difficulty level information is also printed, along with the answer keys, in this book.

When building a test or quiz, you can select questions by objective, difficulty level, or both. This allows you to quickly customize tests to meet the specific objectives you've taught and different ability levels of your students.

Quick Start Instructions

Install the *Computer Test Bank* software by double-clicking the setup.exe program on the disk and following the prompts. After installation, start the **Exam***View* software by finding the **Exam***View* icon and opening the program. The Startup menu will appear every time you start **Exam***View,* unless you turn it off. The Startup menu has five options:

- Create a new test using the QuickTest Wizard
- Create a new test
- Open an existing test
- Create a new question bank
- Open an existing question bank

Selecting the QuickTest Wizard will provide you with detailed instructions on how to automatically generate a test. You will be asked to choose which chapters' question banks to use and how many questions of each question type to include in the test. The software will then randomly select the correct number of questions from the question banks you chose and format the test for printing. It will even include a custom answer key for the test.

For more information on the other test and question bank options, please refer to the User's Guide included with the CD-ROM.

Need Help?

Stuck at any point? Simply call our toll-free HELP hotline (1-800-234-5TEC) for continuous and reliable support.

Name _____ Class _____ Date _____

Chapter 1   Science Skills

Multiple Choice

Identify the letter of the choice that best completes the statement or answers the question.

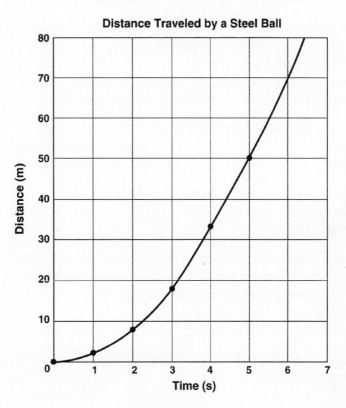

Figure 1-1

_____ 1. What type of graph is represented by Figure 1-1?
a.   bar graph   c.   circle graph
b.   line graph   d.   none of the above

_____ 2. What is a system of knowledge and the methods used to find that knowledge?
a.   science   c.   measurement
b.   technology   d.   curiosity

_____ 3. How are science and technology related?
a.   Technology is a branch of natural science.
b.   Science is a branch of technology.
c.   Advances in science may lead to advances in technology and vice versa.
d.   Science and technology are not related.

_____ 4. Which of the following is NOT a branch of natural science?
a.   life science   c.   physical science
b.   Earth and space science   d.   social science

____ 5. How does Earth science overlap with life science?
   a.   Earth science involves the study of Earth's rocks.
   b.   Earth science involves the study of systems that may include living organisms.
   c.   Earth science involves the study of the composition of matter.
   d.   Earth science does not overlap with life science.

____ 6. Which of the following is NOT one of the main ideas of physical science?
   a.   The universe is very old and very large.
   b.   Forces cause changes in motion.
   c.   Energy can be transferred from one form to another, but it can never be destroyed.
   d.   One of the main branches of natural science is biology.

____ 7. What are the building blocks of all matter?
   a.   forces   c.   magnetic fields
   b.   atoms   d.   kinetic and potential energy

____ 8. In which step of the scientific method is information obtained through the senses?
   a.   drawing conclusions   c.   analyzing data
   b.   making observations   d.   revising a hypothesis

____ 9. What happens when the data in an investigation do not support the original hypothesis?
   a.   The scientist gives up and starts an investigation on a new topic.
   b.   The data must be incorrect and are thrown out.
   c.   The hypothesis will be revised.
   d.   The data are altered so that they support the original hypothesis.

____ 10. What is a statement that summarizes a pattern found in nature?
   a.   a scientific law   c.   a scientific theory
   b.   a fact   d.   a hypothesis

____ 11. Which of the following statements is true about scientific theories?
   a.   Scientific theories become scientific laws.
   b.   Scientific theories are never proven.
   c.   Scientific theories become hypotheses.
   d.   Scientific theories summarize patterns found in nature.

____ 12. What is a physical or mental representation of an object or an event?
   a.   a theory   c.   a model
   b.   a hypothesis   d.   a scientific law

____ 13. Why are scientific models important?
   a.   They prove scientific theories.
   b.   They help visualize things that are very complex, very large, or very small.
   c.   They make it harder to understand things.
   d.   They never change.

_____ 14. What is the most important safety rule?
   a. Never work with chemicals.
   b. Always use unbreakable glassware.
   c. Always follow your teacher's instructions and textbook directions exactly.
   d. Never do experiments that involve flames or hot objects.

_____ 15. Which of the following is an example of a safe laboratory procedure?
   a. tying back long hair and loose clothing
   b. eating or drinking from laboratory glassware
   c. touching hot objects with your bare hands
   d. testing an odor by directly inhaling the vapor

_____ 16. How is 0.00025 written in scientific notation?
   a. 25×10^{-5}
   b. 2.5×10^{4}
   c. 0.25×10^{-3}
   d. 2.5×10^{-4}

_____ 17. Which of the following conversion factors would you use to change 18 kilometers to meters?
   a. 1000 m/1 km
   b. 1 km/1000 m
   c. 100 m/1 km
   d. 1 km/100 m

_____ 18. What is 1 centimeter equal to?
   a. 100 meters
   b. 1/10 of a millimeter
   c. 10 millimeters
   d. 100 millimeters

_____ 19. There are 1660 megawatts of wind-generated electricity produced globally every year. This amount is equivalent to
   a. 1,660,000 watts
   b. 1,660,000 kilowatts
   c. 16,600,000 watts
   d. 166,000 kilowatts

_____ 20. Timers at a swim meet used four different clocks to time an event. Which recorded time is the most precise?
   a. 55 s
   b. 55.2 s
   c. 55.25 s
   d. 55.254 s

_____ 21. Which of the following clocks offers the most precision?
   a. a clock with only one hand to measure the hour
   b. a clock with only one hand to measure the minutes
   c. a clock with a hand to measure the hour and a hand to measure the minutes
   d. a clock with a hand to measure the hour, a hand to measure the minutes, and a hand to measure the seconds

_____ 22. On the Celsius scale, at what temperature does water boil?
   a. 0°
   b. 212°
   c. 100°
   d. 32°

_____ 23. Approximately how many kelvins are equal to 60°F?
   a. 439
   b. 212
   c. 902
   d. 289

_____ 24. The type of graph used to show how a part of something relates to the whole is a
   a.   circle graph   c.   line graph
   b.   bar graph   d.   direct proportion

_____ 25. What is the relationship in which the ratio of the manipulated variable and the responding variable is constant?
   a.   inverse proportion   c.   slope
   b.   direct proportion   d.   interdependent

_____ 26. How do scientists communicate the results of investigations?
   a.   by publishing articles in scientific   c.   by exchanging e-mails
        journals
   b.   by giving talks at scientific conferences   d.   all of the above

_____ 27. How do scientists who speak different languages make their data understandable to one another?
   a.   They all use different systems of measurement.
   b.   They all use SI.
   c.   They communicate through a universal translator.
   d.   They all must speak French.

_____ 28. What is a peer review?
   a.   a process in which only close friends of a scientist review the scientist's work
   b.   a process in which scientists examine other scientists' work
   c.   a process in which scientists copy other scientists' work
   d.   a process in which scientists keep their work secret

_____ 29. Why are peer reviews important?
   a.   Scientists receive questions and criticism from their peers.
   b.   Data are checked for accuracy.
   c.   Scientists receive comments and suggestions from other scientists.
   d.   all of the above

_____ 30. If the relationship between the manipulated variable and the responding variable is a direct proportion, what will a line graph of this relationship look like?
   a.   a straight line   c.   a jagged line
   b.   a curved line   d.   none of the above

Completion

Complete each sentence or statement.

31. The SI base unit of mass is the _____.

32. A measurement must include both a number and a(an) _____.

33. An experiment in which only one variable, the manipulated variable, is changed at a time is called a(an) _____.

Name _____ Class _____ Date _____

34. An organized plan for gathering, organizing, and communicating information is called a(an) _____.

35. A(An) _____ is a way of organizing data that is used to show changes that occur in related variables.

36. Computers are an example of _____ that helps people solve problems.

37. The two main areas of physical science are physics and _____.

38. Natural science is divided into life science, Earth and space science, and _____.

39. The _____ is the variable that changes in response to the manipulated variable.

40. A(An) _____ is a statement that summarizes a pattern found in nature.

41. A(An) _____ explains a pattern found in nature.

42. A flight simulator that helps astronauts prepare for a shuttle launch is an example of a(an) _____.

43. Because lab activities can involve hazardous materials, it is always important to read and understand any _____ that must be followed.

44. A(An) _____ makes it easier to understand things that are too small, too large, or too hard to observe directly.

45. In scientific notation, $(8.2 \times 10^4 \text{ m}) \times (3.7 \times 10^2 \text{ m})$ equals _____.

46. In an experiment, 0.014 seconds equals _____ milliseconds.

47. _____ is the closeness of a measurement to the actual value being measured.

48. A temperature of 68°F is equal to _____ kelvins.

49. In an experiment, if doubling the manipulated variable results in a doubling of the responding variable, the relationship between the variables is a(an) _____.

50. The three values—10.714 m, 12.821 m, and 13.646 m—have the same number of _____.

Short Answer

51. What is the single most important laboratory safety rule?

52. Why do scientists speak at conferences and write articles in scientific journals?

53. What is a peer review?

54. What are the major branches of natural science?

55. What is a hypothesis?

56. What is a scientific theory?

57. Why do scientists use models?

58. When a number in a measurement is converted from kilometers to meters, does the number get larger or smaller?

59. How many significant figures will the answer to the calculation 65.25×37.4 have?

60. What is the temperature at which water freezes, expressed in Fahrenheit, Celsius, and kelvins?

61. Explain how technology and science are related.

62. What type of graph would be the best to use to compare the levels of lead contamination in six water wells?

63. What is the relationship between two variables if the product of the variables is constant?

64. The study of an organism that lived 10 million years ago would most likely fall under which two branches of natural science?

65. Describe a main idea of physical science that deals with space and time.

Essay
On a separate sheet of paper, write an answer to each of the following questions.

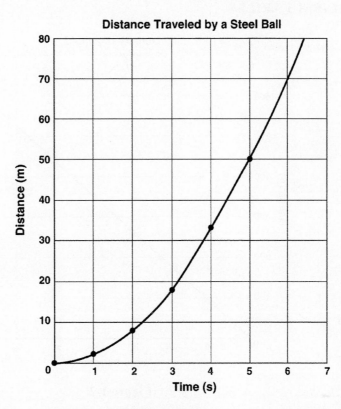

Figure 1-1

66. Use Figure 1-1 to describe how the steel ball moved during the experiment. Average speed is calculated by dividing total distance by time. Did the steel ball speed up, slow down, or remain at the same speed throughout the experiment?

67. What is the difference between a scientific law and a scientific theory?

68. Describe some of the main ideas of physical science.

69. Describe a possible order of steps of a scientific method used in an investigation.

70. Explain how peer reviews are important in either supporting a hypothesis or revising a hypothesis.

Name _____ Class _____ Date _____

Other

USING SCIENCE SKILLS

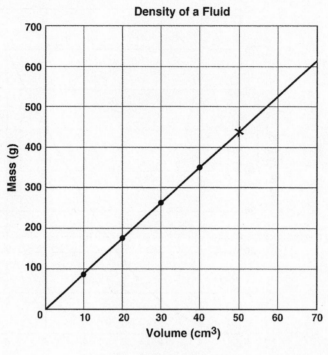

Figure 1-2

71. **Analyzing Data** What is the slope of the line shown in Figure 1-2?

72. **Controlling Variables** In Figure 1-2, what is the responding variable?

73. **Analyzing Data** In Figure 1-2, what is the relationship between mass and volume?

74. **Using Tables and Graphs** In Figure 1-2, what quantity does the slope represent?

75. **Analyzing Data** In Figure 1-2, what metric units are represented by values on the plotted line?

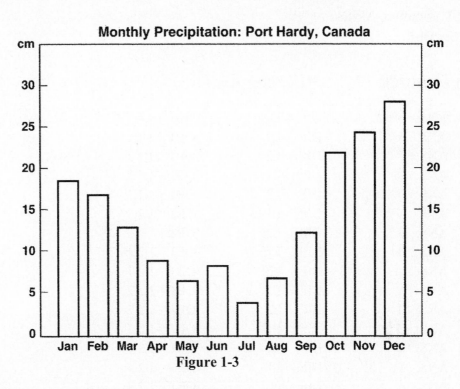

Figure 1-3

76. **Using Tables and Graphs** What measurements are compared in Figure 1-3?

77. **Analyzing Data** In Figure 1-3, which month had the highest amount of precipitation?

78. **Inferring** Why might the data in Figure 1-3 be important to share with a scientist studying agriculture trends in Port Hardy?

79. **Using Tables and Graphs** Use Figure 1-3 to determine the approximate total annual precipitation.

80. **Analyzing Data** In Figure 1-3, how many meters of precipitation were recorded during January?

Chapter 1 Science Skills
Answer Section

MULTIPLE CHOICE

1.	ANS: B	DIF: L1	OBJ: 1.4.1		
2.	ANS: A	DIF: L1	OBJ: 1.1.1		
3.	ANS: C	DIF: L2	OBJ: 1.1.1		
4.	ANS: D	DIF: L1	OBJ: 1.1.2		
5.	ANS: B	DIF: L2	OBJ: 1.1.2		
6.	ANS: D	DIF: L1	OBJ: 1.1.3		
7.	ANS: B	DIF: L2	OBJ: 1.1.3		
8.	ANS: B	DIF: L1	OBJ: 1.2.1		
9.	ANS: C	DIF: L2	OBJ: 1.2.1		
10.	ANS: A	DIF: L1	OBJ: 1.2.2		
11.	ANS: B	DIF: L2	OBJ: 1.2.2		
12.	ANS: C	DIF: L1	OBJ: 1.2.3		
13.	ANS: B	DIF: L2	OBJ: 1.2.3		
14.	ANS: C	DIF: L1	OBJ: 1.2.4		
15.	ANS: A	DIF: L2	OBJ: 1.2.4		
16.	ANS: D	DIF: L1	OBJ: 1.3.1		
17.	ANS: A	DIF: L2	OBJ: 1.3.1		
18.	ANS: C	DIF: L1	OBJ: 1.3.2		
19.	ANS: B	DIF: L2	OBJ: 1.3.2		
20.	ANS: D	DIF: L1	OBJ: 1.3.3		
21.	ANS: D	DIF: L2	OBJ: 1.3.3		
22.	ANS: C	DIF: L1	OBJ: 1.3.4		
23.	ANS: D	DIF: L2	OBJ: 1.3.4		
24.	ANS: A	DIF: L2	OBJ: 1.4.1		
25.	ANS: B	DIF: L1	OBJ: 1.4.2		
26.	ANS: D	DIF: L1	OBJ: 1.4.3		
27.	ANS: B	DIF: L2	OBJ: 1.4.3		
28.	ANS: B	DIF: L1	OBJ: 1.4.4		
29.	ANS: D	DIF: L2	OBJ: 1.4.4		
30.	ANS: A	DIF: L2	OBJ: 1.4.2		

COMPLETION

31. ANS:
kilogram
kg
DIF: L1   OBJ: 1.3.2

32.	ANS: unit	DIF: L2	OBJ: 1.3.2
33.	ANS: controlled experiment	DIF: L2	OBJ: 1.2.1

34. ANS: scientific method   DIF: L1   OBJ: 1.2.1
35. ANS: line graph   DIF: L1   OBJ: 1.4.1
36. ANS: technology   DIF: L1   OBJ: 1.1.1
37. ANS: chemistry   DIF: L2   OBJ: 1.1.2
38. ANS: physical science   DIF: L1   OBJ: 1.1.2
39. ANS: responding variable   DIF: L1   OBJ: 1.4.2
40. ANS: scientific law   DIF: L1   OBJ: 1.2.2
41. ANS:
    scientific theory
    theory
    DIF: L2   OBJ: 1.2.2
42. ANS:
    scientific model
    model
    DIF: L2   OBJ: 1.2.3
43. ANS:
    safety rules
    safety procedures
    DIF: L2   OBJ: 1.2.4
44. ANS:
    scientific model
    model
    DIF: L1   OBJ: 1.2.3
45. ANS: 3.0×10^7 DIF: L2   OBJ: 1.3.1
46. ANS: 14   DIF: L1   OBJ: 1.3.2
47. ANS: Accuracy   DIF: L1   OBJ: 1.3.3
48. ANS: 293   DIF: L2   OBJ: 1.3.4
49. ANS: direct proportion   DIF: L2   OBJ: 1.4.2
50. ANS: significant figures   DIF: L2   OBJ: 1.3.3

SHORT ANSWER

51. ANS: Always follow your teachers instructions and textbook directions exactly.
    DIF: L1   OBJ: 1.2.4
52. ANS: to communicate with other scientists about the results of their investigations
    DIF: L1   OBJ: 1.4.3
53. ANS: a process in which scientists examine other scientists' work
    DIF: L1   OBJ: 1.4.4
54. ANS: Earth and space science, life science, and physical science
    DIF: L1   OBJ: 1.1.2
55. ANS: a proposed answer to a question   DIF: L1   OBJ: 1.2.1
56. ANS: a well-tested explanation for a set of observations or results
    DIF: L1   OBJ: 1.2.2
57. ANS: to help understand things that are too difficult to observe directly
    DIF: L1   OBJ: 1.2.3
58. ANS: larger   DIF: L1   OBJ: 1.3.1

59. ANS: three   DIF: L1   OBJ: 1.3.3
60. ANS: 32°F, 0°C, and 273 K   DIF: L1   OBJ: 1.3.4
61. ANS: Science is a system of knowledge, while technology is the practical application of that knowledge to the solving of problems.
   DIF: L2   OBJ: 1.1.1
62. ANS: a bar graph   DIF: L2   OBJ: 1.4.1
63. ANS: an inverse proportion   DIF: L2   OBJ: 1.4.2
64. ANS: life science and Earth and space science
   DIF: L2   OBJ: 1.1.2
65. ANS: The universe is very old (about 13.7 billion years old) and very large (7.0×10^{26} meters in diameter).
   DIF: L1   OBJ: 1.1.3

ESSAY

66. ANS: The steel ball started out slowly. Then it continued to speed up throughout the experiment.
   DIF: L2   OBJ: 1.4.2
67. ANS: A scientific law is a statement that summarizes a pattern found in nature, without attempting to explain it. A scientific theory explains the pattern.
   DIF: L2   OBJ: 1.2.2
68. ANS: Possible answers: The universe is very large and very old. A small amount of the universe is matter. Matter on Earth usually is either a solid, liquid, or gas. All matter is made of atoms. Forces cause changes in motion. Energy can be transferred from one form or object to another, but it can never be destroyed.
   DIF: L2   OBJ: 1.1.3
69. ANS: Possible answer: 1) make observations, 2) ask questions, 3) develop a hypothesis, 4) test the hypothesis, 5) analyze data, 6) draw conclusions, 7) revise hypothesis.
   DIF: L2   OBJ: 1.2.1
70. ANS: In peer reviews, scientists review and question other scientists' data. Scientists also help determine if the data is accurately reported. If the review finds errors in the data, in the conclusions, or in the experimental procedures, the hypothesis may need to be revised.
   DIF: L2   OBJ: 1.4.4

OTHER

71. ANS: 8.8 g/cm³   DIF: L2   OBJ: 1.4.1
72. ANS: mass   DIF: L2   OBJ: 1.4.2
73. ANS: a direct proportion   DIF: L2   OBJ: 1.4.2
74. ANS: the density of the fluid   DIF: L2   OBJ: 1.4.1
75. ANS: g/cm³   DIF: L2   OBJ: 1.3.2
76. ANS: monthly precipitation in centimeters
   DIF: L1   OBJ: 1.3.2
77. ANS: December   DIF: L1   OBJ: 1.4.1
78. ANS: The precipitation data might provide insight into agriculture growth trends.
   DIF: L1   OBJ: 1.4.3

79. ANS: approximately 165 cm   DIF: L1   OBJ: 1.4.1
80. ANS: about 18 cm, which equals 0.18 meters
     DIF: L1   OBJ: 1.3.2

All rights reserved.

© Pearson Education, Inc., publishing as Pearson Prentice Hall.

Physical Science Chapter 1   13

Name _____ Class _____ Date _____

Chapter 2   Properties of Matter

Multiple Choice
Identify the letter of the choice that best completes the statement or answers the question.

____ 1. Which of the following are pure substances?
  a. solutions
  b. compounds
  c. homogeneous mixtures
  d. colloids

____ 2. Which of the following is NOT a pure substance?
  a. milk
  b. oxygen
  c. water
  d. carbon dioxide

____ 3. A substance that is made up of only one kind of atom is a(an)
  a. compound.
  b. homogeneous mixture.
  c. element.
  d. solution.

____ 4. If an unknown substance CANNOT be broken down into simpler substances, it is
  a. a compound.
  b. an element.
  c. made of one kind of atom.
  d. both b and c

____ 5. What is the symbol for aluminum?
  a. AL
  b. Al
  c. Au
  d. A

____ 6. The symbol for gold is
  a. Au.
  b. Al.
  c. Gl.
  d. Go.

____ 7. If a material contains three elements joined in a fixed proportion, it is a(an)
  a. mixture.
  b. solution.
  c. atom.
  d. compound.

____ 8. Water is a compound because it
  a. can be broken down into simpler substances.
  b. always has two hydrogen atoms for each oxygen atom.
  c. is made of water atoms joined together.
  d. both a and b

____ 9. Which of the following is a mixture?
  a. carbon dioxide
  b. silicon
  c. silicon dioxide
  d. sand

____ 10. Which of the following is a characteristic of a mixture?
  a. has varying properties
  b. has a fixed composition
  c. contains only pure substances
  d. both a and b

____ 11. A mixture that appears to contain only one substance is a(an)
  a. homogeneous mixture.
  b. heterogeneous mixture.
  c. compound.
  d. element.

____ 12. Which of the following is a heterogeneous mixture?
a. water in a swimming pool   c. a jar of mixed nuts
b. sugar water   d. stainless steel

____ 13. A mixture can be classified as a solution, suspension, or colloid based on the
a. number of particles it contains.   c. color of its particles.
b. size of its largest particles.   d. size of its smallest particles.

____ 14. You are about to open a container of soy milk but notice that there are instructions to "shake well before serving." The soy milk is most likely a
a. solution.   c. colloid.
b. pure substance.   d. suspension.

____ 15. Which of the following is malleable?
a. glass   c. ice
b. pottery   d. gold

____ 16. Which of the following has the highest viscosity?
a. corn syrup   c. water
b. milk   d. orange juice

____ 17. A substance has a melting point of 0°C and a boiling point of 100°C. The substance is most likely
a. water.   c. gold.
b. hydrogen.   d. table salt.

____ 18. A material that is malleable and conducts electricity is most likely
a. wood.   c. a metal.
b. ice.   d. motor oil.

____ 19. What physical properties of nylon and leather make them good materials to use for shoelaces?
a. high density and low conductivity   c. hardness and durability
b. durability and flexibility   d. low viscosity and flexibility

____ 20. Which of the following materials is useful for making molds because it has a low melting point?
a. wood   c. clay
b. metal   d. wax

____ 21. Filtration can be used to separate mixtures based on
a. their boiling points.   c. their melting points.
b. their densities.   d. the size of their particles.

____ 22. What method can be used to separate parts of a liquid mixture when the entire mixture can pass through a filter?
a. filtration   c. straining
b. distillation   d. screening

____ 23. When a physical change in a sample occurs, which of the following does NOT change?
a. shape   c. volume
b. mass   d. composition

Name _____ Class _____ Date _____

_____ 24. Which of the following is a physical change?
  a. sawing a piece of wood in half
  b. burning a piece of wood
  c. rust forming on an iron fence
  d. a copper roof changing color from red to green

_____ 25. Flammability is a material's ability to burn in the presence of
  a. hydrogen.   c. oxygen.
  b. nitrogen.   d. carbon dioxide.

_____ 26. A substance that has high reactivity
  a. easily combines chemically with other substances.
  b. burns in the presence of water.
  c. displaces dissolved oxygen.
  d. has a high boiling point.

_____ 27. Which of the following is NOT a clue that a chemical change has occurred?
  a. change in color   c. formation of a precipitate
  b. production of a gas   d. change in shape

_____ 28. During which of the following chemical changes does a precipitate form?
  a. vinegar is added to baking powder   c. lemon juice is added to water
  b. lemon juice is added to milk   d. a banana ripens

_____ 29. Which of the following is a chemical change?
  a. ice melting
  b. ice being carved
  c. water boiling
  d. water breaking down into hydrogen and oxygen

_____ 30. Which of the following is a clue of a chemical change?
  a. iron changes color when heated
  b. gas bubbles form in boiling water
  c. balls of wax form when melted wax is poured into ice water
  d. a gas forms when vinegar and baking soda are mixed

Completion
Complete each sentence or statement.

31. Matter that always has exactly the same composition is classified as a(an)

    _____.

32. Pure substances are either _____ or _____.

33. An element has a fixed composition because it contains only one type of

    _____.

34. The symbols for elements have either _____ or _____ letters.

35. A compound can be made from two or more elements or other _____ joined together in a fixed composition.

36. The substances in a(an) _____ mixture are evenly distributed throughout the mixture.

37. In a(an) _____ mixture, the parts of the mixture are noticeably different from one another.

38. Fresh milk is a suspension, but homogenized milk is a(an) _____.

39. If the particles in a mixture scatter light, the mixture is either a(an) _____ or a(an) _____.

Melting and Boiling Points of Some Substances		
Substance	Melting Point	Boiling Point
Hydrogen	−259.3˚C	−252.9˚C
Nitrogen	−210.0˚C	−195.8˚C
Acetic Acid	16.6˚C	117.9˚C
Gold	1064.2˚C	2856˚C

Figure 2-1

40. Based on the information in Figure 2-1, the _____ point of nitrogen is −210.0ºC and the _____ point of nitrogen is −195.8ºC.

41. Measuring _____ can be used to test the purity of some substances.

42. If a spoon gets hot quickly when it is used to stir a pot of soup, it is probably made of _____.

43. A material used for electrical wiring would need to have good _____.

44. _____ is a process that could be used to separated dissolved particles from the liquid in a solution.

45. A(An) _____ change occurs when a material changes shape or size but the composition of the material does not change.

46. _____ properties can be observed only when the substances in a sample of matter are changing into different substances.

47. Rust forms because iron and oxygen are highly _____ elements.

48. A solid that forms and separates from a liquid mixture is a(an) _____.

49. A cake rises as it bakes because a chemical change causes _____ to be produced.

50. When a metal changes color because it has been heated, a(an) _____ change occurred. When a metal changes color because it has reacted with another substance, a(an) _____ change occurred.

Short Answer

51. How do the properties of a compound compare to the properties of the elements it contains?

52. How is the composition of a substance different from the composition of a mixture?

53. How can you change the properties of a mixture?

54. If you looked at a glass containing a solution and a glass containing a suspension, how could you tell which glass contained the suspension?

55. What is viscosity?

Melting and Boiling Points of Some Substances		
Substance	**Melting Point**	**Boiling Point**
Hydrogen	−259.3°C	−252.9°C
Nitrogen	−210.0°C	−195.8°C
Acetic Acid	16.6°C	117.9°C
Gold	1064.2°C	2856°C

Figure 2-1

56. Based on the information in Figure 2-1, which substances would be solids at 10.0°C?

57. What physical property would be important in a tool used to carve wood? Compare this property of the tool to the same property of the wood.

58. How do changes in temperature usually affect the viscosity of a liquid?

59. Explain why boiling can be used to separate water from the other compounds in seawater.

60. Give an example of a physical change that can be reversed and an example of a physical change that cannot be reversed.

61. What is flammability?

62. Is flammability a physical property or a chemical property? Explain your answer.

63. What kind of change is taking place if you see white mold growing on a strawberry?

64. What are three common clues that a chemical change has occurred?

65. How is a chemical change different from a physical change?

Essay
On a separate sheet of paper, write an answer to each of the following questions.

66. Compare the properties of water to the properties of the elements it contains.

67. Explain how you could use a physical property to test the purity of a silver coin without damaging the coin.

68. Suppose you want to separate the leaves, acorns, and twigs from a pile of soil. Filtration and distillation are two processes of separating mixtures. Explain which process you would use and why.

69. Explain why rust forms in steel tanks that hold seawater in ships. How can nitrogen be used to reduce rust in these tanks?

70. Suppose you heat a liquid and then gas bubbles are produced. With no other evidence, can you tell if a physical change or chemical change is occurring? Explain your answer.

Other

USING SCIENCE SKILLS

Properties of Three Mixtures			
	Scatters Light	**Separates into Layers**	**Can Be Separated by Filtration**
Mixture A	Yes	No	No
Mixture B	No	No	No
Mixture C	Yes	Yes	Yes

Figure 2-2

71. **Classifying** Based on the data in Figure 2-2, is Mixture C a homogeneous or heterogeneous mixture? Explain your answer.

72. **Analyzing Data** Which of the mixtures in Figure 2-2 is a solution? Explain how you know.

73. **Analyzing Data** Which of the mixtures in Figure 2-2 is a colloid? Explain how you know.

74. **Classifying** Rank the mixtures in Figure 2-2 in order of the size of their particles, starting with the mixture with the smallest particles.

75. **Predicting** Why can't Mixture B in Figure 2-2 be separated by filtration? What method might be used to separate the substances in Mixture B?

Physical Properties of Four Materials Used to Make Sculptures			
	Malleability	Hardness	Melting Point
Wax	Soft enough to be carved and molded	Soft but keeps its shape at room temperature	Low melting point
Unbaked clay	Can be molded	Soft	Very high melting point
Baked clay	Brittle after being baked at a high temperature	Hard	Very high melting point
Metal (a mixture of copper, zinc, and lead)	Can be hammered without shattering	Hard	High melting point

Figure 2-3

76. **Comparing and Contrasting** Use Figure 2-3 to compare the physical properties of clay before and after it is baked at a high temperature.

77. **Using Tables and Graphs** Which of the materials in Figure 2-3 are malleable?

78. **Comparing and Contrasting** Based on the information in Figure 2-3, compare the properties of a sculpture made from metal and a sculpture made from baked clay.

79. **Inferring** You have an object made from one of the materials listed in Figure 2-3. It changes shape when you leave it in a sunny window. Which material is the object made from? How do you know?

80. **Inferring** Which of the materials described in Figure 2-3 would be least likely to be recycled? Explain your choice.

Chapter 2   Properties of Matter
Answer Section

MULTIPLE CHOICE

1.	ANS: B	DIF: L1	OBJ: 2.1.1
2.	ANS: A	DIF: L2	OBJ: 2.1.1
3.	ANS: C	DIF: L1	OBJ: 2.1.2
4.	ANS: D	DIF: L2	OBJ: 2.1.2
5.	ANS: B	DIF: L1	OBJ: 2.1.2
6.	ANS: A	DIF: L2	OBJ: 2.1.2
7.	ANS: D	DIF: L1	OBJ: 2.1.3
8.	ANS: D	DIF: L2	OBJ: 2.1.3
9.	ANS: D	DIF: L1	OBJ: 2.1.4
10.	ANS: A	DIF: L2	OBJ: 2.1.4
11.	ANS: A	DIF: L1	OBJ: 2.1.5
12.	ANS: C	DIF: L2	OBJ: 2.1.5
13.	ANS: B	DIF: L1	OBJ: 2.1.6
14.	ANS: D	DIF: L2	OBJ: 2.1.6
15.	ANS: D	DIF: L1	OBJ: 2.2.1
16.	ANS: A	DIF: L2	OBJ: 2.2.1
17.	ANS: A	DIF: L1	OBJ: 2.2.2
18.	ANS: C	DIF: L2	OBJ: 2.2.2
19.	ANS: B	DIF: L1	OBJ: 2.2.3
20.	ANS: D	DIF: L2	OBJ: 2.2.3
21.	ANS: D	DIF: L1	OBJ: 2.2.4
22.	ANS: B	DIF: L2	OBJ: 2.2.4
23.	ANS: D	DIF: L1	OBJ: 2.2.5
24.	ANS: A	DIF: L2	OBJ: 2.2.5
25.	ANS: C	DIF: L1	OBJ: 2.3.1
26.	ANS: A	DIF: L2	OBJ: 2.3.1
27.	ANS: D	DIF: L1	OBJ: 2.3.2
28.	ANS: B	DIF: L2	OBJ: 2.3.2
29.	ANS: D	DIF: L1	OBJ: 2.3.3
30.	ANS: D	DIF: L2	OBJ: 2.3.3

COMPLETION

31. ANS:
    pure substance
    substance
    DIF: L1   OBJ: 2.1.1
32. ANS: elements, compounds   DIF: L2   OBJ: 2.1.1
33. ANS: atom   DIF: L1   OBJ: 2.1.2

34. ANS: one, two   DIF: L2   OBJ: 2.1.2
35. ANS: compounds   DIF: L2   OBJ: 2.1.3
36. ANS: homogeneous   DIF: L1   OBJ: 2.1.5
37. ANS: heterogeneous   DIF: L2   OBJ: 2.1.5
38. ANS: colloid   DIF: L2   OBJ: 2.1.6
39. ANS: suspension, colloid   DIF: L2   OBJ: 2.1.6
40. ANS: melting, boiling   DIF: L1   OBJ: 2.2.1
41. ANS: density   DIF: L2   OBJ: 2.2.1
42. ANS: metal   DIF: L1   OBJ: 2.2.2
43. ANS: conductivity   DIF: L2   OBJ: 2.2.3
44. ANS: Distillation   DIF: L1   OBJ: 2.2.4
45. ANS: physical   DIF: L1   OBJ: 2.2.5
46. ANS: Chemical   DIF: L1   OBJ: 2.3.1
47. ANS: reactive   DIF: L2   OBJ: 2.3.1
48. ANS: precipitate   DIF: L1   OBJ: 2.3.2
49. ANS:
    a gas
    carbon dioxide
    DIF: L1   OBJ: 2.3.2
50. ANS: physical, chemical   DIF: L2   OBJ: 2.3.3

SHORT ANSWER

51. ANS: They are different.   DIF: L1   OBJ: 2.1.3
52. ANS: The composition of a substance is fixed, while the composition of a mixture can vary.
    DIF: L1   OBJ: 2.1.4
53. ANS: Accept any of the following: by adding more of a substance in the mixture; by adding a new substance; by removing a substance from the mixture.
    DIF: L2   OBJ: 2.1.4
54. ANS: Accept any of the following: the suspension would appear cloudy, while the solution would be clear; the particles in the suspension would settle to the bottom, while the particles in the solution would not settle.
    DIF: L1   OBJ: 2.1.6
55. ANS: Viscosity is the tendency of a liquid to keep from flowing or its resistance to flowing.
    DIF: L1   OBJ: 2.2.1
56. ANS: acetic acid, table salt, and gold   DIF: L2   OBJ: 2.2.1
57. ANS: A tool for carving wood would need to be harder than the wood being carved.
    DIF: L1   OBJ: 2.2.3
58. ANS: The viscosity of a liquid usually decreases as the liquid is heated and increases as the liquid cools.
    DIF: L2   OBJ: 2.2.3
59. ANS: Water has a lower boiling point than the compounds dissolved in the seawater. As the water boils and changes from a liquid to a gas, the other compounds are left behind in the container.
    DIF: L1   OBJ: 2.2.4

60. ANS: For a physical change that can be reversed, accept any of the following: freezing water, melting ice, braiding hair, wrinkling clothes. For a physical change that cannot be reversed, accept any of the following: cutting hair, slicing a tomato, peeling an orange.
   DIF: L2   OBJ: 2.2.5

61. ANS: Flammability is a material's ability to burn in the presence of oxygen.
   DIF: L1   OBJ: 2.3.1

62. ANS: A chemical property; the composition of a material changes when it burns.
   DIF: L1   OBJ: 2.3.1

63. ANS: a chemical change   DIF: L2   OBJ: 2.3.2

64. ANS: a change in color, the production of a gas, and the formation of a precipitate
   DIF: L1   OBJ: 2.3.2

65. ANS: A chemical change involves a change in the composition of matter. During a physical change, the composition of matter does not change.
   DIF: L1   OBJ: 2.3.3

ESSAY

66. ANS: Water is a liquid at room temperature, does not burn, and can be used to put out fires. Oxygen and hydrogen are the elements that make up water. Both elements are gases at room temperature. Hydrogen can fuel a fire, and oxygen can keep a fire burning.
   DIF: L2   OBJ: 2.1.3

67. ANS: Silver has a known density at room temperature (10.5 g/cm^3). You can measure the density of the coin and compare it to the density of silver. If the densities of the coin and silver are the same, the coin is pure silver. If the densities of the coin and silver are different, the coin either does not contain silver or contains at least one other substance in addition to silver.
   DIF: L2   OBJ: 2.2.2

68. ANS: Filtration would be used because it is the process of separating mixtures based on the size of their particles (or pieces). A screen could be used to separate the mixture. The holes in the screen would need to be large enough to allow the soil to pass through but not the leaves, acorn, or twigs.
   DIF: L2   OBJ: 2.2.4

69. ANS: Rust forms in the tanks because oxygen dissolved in the water reacts with iron in the steel. Nitrogen gas can be pumped into the tanks. The nitrogen displaces some of the dissolved oxygen. Because nitrogen is less reactive than oxygen, less rust forms.
   DIF: L2   OBJ: 2.3.1

70. ANS: With no other evidence, the gas could be the result of either a physical or chemical change. A liquid could be changing to a gas, which is a physical change. A reaction that produces a gas could be occurring as the liquid is heated. Without testing the composition of the liquid before and after heating, there is no way to tell.
   DIF: L2   OBJ: 2.3.3

OTHER

71. ANS: A heterogeneous mixture; the mixture scatters light, separates into layers, and can be separated by filtration.
   DIF: L2   OBJ: 2.1.5

72. ANS: Mixture B; it does not scatter light, does not separate into layers, and cannot be separated by filtration.
   DIF: L2   OBJ: 2.1.6
73. ANS: Mixture A; it scatters light, does not separate into layers, and cannot be separated by filtration.
   DIF: L2   OBJ: 2.1.6
74. ANS: Mixture B, Mixture A, Mixture C   DIF: L2   OBJ: 2.1.6
75. ANS: Possible answer: Mixture B is a solution and all the particles would pass through a filter. Distillation might be used to separate the substances in Mixture B.
   DIF: L2   OBJ: 2.2.4
76. ANS: Before clay is baked, it is soft and can be molded. After clay is baked, it is hard and brittle.
   DIF: L1   OBJ: 2.2.1
77. ANS: wax, unbaked clay, and metal   DIF: L1   OBJ: 2.2.1
78. ANS: Both sculptures would be hard and would only melt at very high temperatures. The metal sculpture might be dented if it was hammered, but if the sculpture made from baked clay was hammered, it would shatter.
   DIF: L1   OBJ: 2.2.1
79. ANS: The object would have been made from wax because wax has a low melting point. It is the only material listed that would soften enough in a sunny window to change shape.
   DIF: L1   OBJ: 2.2.2
80. ANS: Baked clay; it is brittle and shatters.
   DIF: L1   OBJ: 2.2.3

Chapter 3 States of Matter

Multiple Choice
Identify the letter of the choice that best completes the statement or answers the question.

_____ 1. A gas has
   a. a definite volume but no definite shape.   c. no definite shape or definite volume.
   b. a definite shape but no definite volume.   d. a definite volume and definite shape.

_____ 2. Ninety-nine percent of all the matter that can be observed in the universe exists as
   a. gases.   c. liquids.
   b. plasmas.   d. solids.

_____ 3. Matter that has a definite volume but no definite shape is a
   a. liquid.   c. gas.
   b. solid.   d. plasma.

_____ 4. If you move a substance from one container to another and its volume changes, the substance is a
   a. solid.   c. gas.
   b. liquid.   d. solution.

Substance A

Substance B

Substance C

Figure 3-1

_____ 5. In which of the substances in Figure 3-1 are the forces of attraction among the particles so weak that they can be ignored under ordinary conditions?
   a. Substance A   c. Substance C
   b. Substance B   d. all of the above

_____ 6. Forces of attraction limit the motion of particles most in
   a. a solid.   c. a gas.
   b. a liquid.   d. both b and c

_____ 7. What is the result of a force distributed over an area?
   a. temperature   c. pressure
   b. volume   d. mass

_____ 8. Collisions of helium atoms and the walls of a closed container cause
   a. condensation.
   b. gas pressure.
   c. a decrease in volume.
   d. an overall loss of energy.

_____ 9. Which of the following factors affect the pressure of an enclosed gas?
   a. temperature
   b. volume
   c. number of particles
   d. all of the above

_____ 10. Raising the temperature of a gas will increase its pressure if the volume of the gas
   a. and the number of particles are increased.
   b. is increased, but the number of particles is constant.
   c. and the number of particles are constant.
   d. is constant, but the number of particles is increased.

_____ 11. The temperature and volume in a closed container of gas remain constant. If the number of particles of gas is increased, the gas pressure will
   a. increase.
   b. decrease.
   c. remain constant.
   d. cause a decrease in the average kinetic energy of the particles.

_____ 12. Which of the following will cause a decrease in gas pressure in a closed container?
   a. lowering the temperature
   b. reducing the volume
   c. adding more gas
   d. both a and b

_____ 13. The law that states that the volume of a gas is directly proportional to its temperature in kelvins if the pressure and the number of particles is constant is
   a. Boyle's law.
   b. Bose's law.
   c. Einstein's law.
   d. Charles's law.

_____ 14. Boyle's law states that the volume of a gas is inversely proportional to its pressure if the
   a. temperature and number of particles are constant.
   b. temperature reaches absolute zero.
   c. number of particles decreases.
   d. temperature and number of particles are doubled.

_____ 15. If the volume of a cylinder is reduced from 4.0 liters to 2.0 liters, the pressure of the gas in the cylinder will change from 100 kilopascals to
   a. 50 kilopascals.
   b. 150 kilopascals.
   c. 200 kilopascals.
   d. 400 kilopascals.

_____ 16. At a temperature of 274 K, the gas in a cylinder has a volume of 4.0 liters. If the volume of the gas is decreased to 2.0 liters, what must the temperature be for the gas pressure to remain constant?
   a. 137 K
   b. 273 K
   c. 378 K
   d. 556 K

_____ 17. What type of change occurs when water changes from a solid to a liquid?
   a. a phase change
   b. a physical change
   c. an irreversible change
   d. both a and b

_____ 18. The phase change that is the reverse of condensation is
    a.   freezing.   c.   vaporization.
    b.   sublimation.   d.   melting.

_____ 19. Temperature can be used to recognize a phase change because during the phase change, the temperature of the substance
    a.   increases.   c.   does not change.
    b.   decreases.   d.   increases and decreases.

_____ 20. During a phase change, the temperature of a substance
    a.   increases.
    b.   decreases.
    c.   stays the same.
    d.   either increases or decreases, depending on the change.

_____ 21. If a solid piece of naphthalene is heated and remains at 80°C until it is completely melted, you know that 80°C is the
    a.   freezing point of naphthalene.   c.   boiling point of naphthalene.
    b.   melting point of naphthalene.   d.   both a and b

_____ 22. The heat of fusion for water is the amount of energy needed for water to
    a.   freeze.   c.   melt.
    b.   boil.   d.   evaporate.

_____ 23. During what phase change does the arrangement of water molecules become more orderly?
    a.   melting   c.   boiling
    b.   freezing   d.   condensing

_____ 24. Which of the following statements about ice melting is true?
    a.   Energy flows from the ice to its surroundings.
    b.   Water molecules move from their fixed position.
    c.   Water molecules lose energy.
    d.   The temperature of the ice increases as it melts.

_____ 25. The phase change in which a substance changes from a liquid to a gas is
    a.   deposition.   c.   condensation.
    b.   sublimation.   d.   vaporization.

_____ 26. The phase change in which a substance changes from a solid to a liquid is
    a.   freezing.   c.   sublimation.
    b.   melting.   d.   condensation.

_____ 27. The phase change in which a substance changes from a solid to a gas or vapor without changing to a liquid first is
    a.   sublimation.   c.   evaporation.
    b.   deposition.   d.   melting.

_____ 28. The phase change in which a substance changes from a gas directly to a solid is
    a.   condensation.   c.   deposition.
    b.   evaporation.   d.   sublimation.

_____ 29. Which of the following phase changes is an endothermic change?
a.   condensation   c.   deposition
b.   vaporization   d.   freezing

_____ 30. Which of the following phase changes is an exothermic change?
a.   sublimation   c.   vaporization
b.   deposition   d.   melting

Completion
Complete each sentence or statement.

31. A(an) _____ has a definite volume and a definite shape.

32. The state of matter that exists only at extremely low temperatures is called a Bose-Einstein _____.

33. Materials can be classified as solids, liquids, or gases based on whether their shapes and _____ are definite or variable.

34. The shape of a material remains constant when it is moved from one container to another. This material is a(an) _____.

35. The _____ theory of matter states that all particles of matter are in constant motion.

36. The motion of one particle of a gas is unaffected by the motion of other particles of the gas unless the particles _____.

37. _____ between the particles of a gas and the walls of the container cause pressure in a closed container of gas.

38. The pascal is the SI unit for _____.

39. Reducing the volume of a gas _____ its pressure if the _____ of the gas and the number of particles are constant.

40. A graph representing Charles's law shows that the _____ of a gas increases at the same rate as the _____ of the gas.

41. The combined gas law describes the relationship among the _____, _____, and _____ of a gas when the number of particles is constant.

42. If you are using Charles's law to find the volume of a gas at a certain temperature, the temperature must be expressed in _____.

43. If you know the volume and pressure of a gas and the pressure changes, you can find the new volume by multiplying P_1 by V_1 and _____ this number by P_2.

44. The phase change that is the reverse of deposition is _____.

45. At sea level, water _____ at 100°C.

46. When water boils, some of its molecules have enough _____ to overcome the attraction of neighboring molecules.

47. Water boils when its vapor pressure becomes equal to _____ pressure.

48. During vaporization, a substance changes from a(an) _____ to a(an) _____.

49. Evaporation is the process that changes a substance from a liquid to a gas at temperatures below the substance's _____ point.

50. During a(an) _____ change, the system releases energy to its surroundings.

Short Answer

51. Solid, liquid, and gas are three states of matter. What are two other states of matter, and under what conditions do they exist?

52. Compare the shape and volume of solids, liquids, and gases.

53. Why is the volume of a liquid constant?

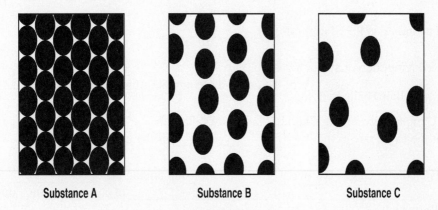

Substance A   Substance B   Substance C

Figure 3-1

54. What substance in Figure 3-1 is a solid? Explain how you know.

55. Why does the air pressure in a car's tires increase after a long drive?

56. If you push on the sides of a filled balloon, how does the gas pressure inside the balloon change? What variable did you decrease to cause this change in pressure?

57. Charles's law can be written as $\dfrac{V_1}{T_1} = \dfrac{V_2}{T_2}$. Explain what V_1 and V_2 represent.

58. If a gas has a volume of 1 L at a pressure of 200 kPa, what volume would it have when the pressure is increased to 400 kPa? Assume the temperature and number of particles are constant.

59. If gas in a sealed container has a pressure of 50 kPa at 300 K, what will the pressure be if the temperature rises to 360 K?

60. What two phase changes occur between solid water and liquid water, and at what temperature does each phase change take place?

61. Explain why boiling water in a large pot on a stove has a temperature of 100°C even if it has been boiling for an hour.

62. Describe what happens to the average kinetic energy of water molecules as water freezes.

63. Describe what happens to the arrangement of water molecules as ice melts.

64. Name and describe the phase change that occurs when dry ice is placed in an open container at room temperature.

65. How could you determine if a phase change is endothermic?

Essay
On a separate sheet of paper, write an answer to each of the following questions.

66. Use billiard balls to describe the motion of particles in a gas. Use students in a crowded hallway to describe the motion of particles in a liquid. Use an audience in a movie theater to describe the motion of particles in a solid.

67. Use breathing as an example to explain the relationship between volume and air pressure.

68. What factors affect the volume of a weather balloon as it rises through the atmosphere?

69. Why does pasta take longer to cook in boiling water at elevations above sea level?

70. Describe how water can change from a liquid to a vapor at temperatures lower than its boiling point.

Name _____ Class _____ Date _____

Other

USING SCIENCE SKILLS

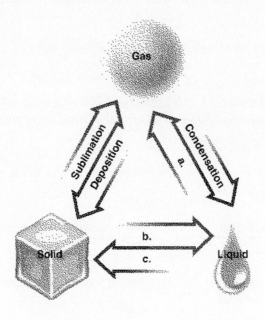

Figure 3-2

71. **Interpreting Graphics** Identify the phase changes in Figure 3-2 that are labeled a, b, and c.

72. **Interpreting Graphics** Explain why the phase changes in Figure 3-2 are shown in pairs.

73. **Comparing and Contrasting** Use the terms in Figure 3-2 to compare the phase changes that occur when water vapor changes to dew or frost.

74. **Interpreting Graphics** Describe the two phase changes represented in Figure 3-2 that can happen to a liquid.

75. **Applying Concepts** What three phase changes in Figure 3-2 are endothermic?

Boyle's Law

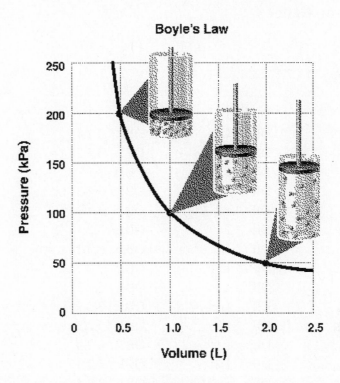

Figure 3-3

76. **Interpreting Graphics** In Figure 3-3, what is the unit used for pressure? What is the pressure when the volume is 0.5 L? What is the pressure when the volume is 1.0 L?

77. **Interpreting Graphics** In Figure 3-3, what is the manipulated variable, and what is the responding variable?

78. **Predicting** What would happen to the gas pressure in Figure 3-3 if the volume of the cylinder remained constant and temperature was the manipulated variable?

79. **Inferring** Based on Figure 3-3, compare the collisions between particles of gas and the walls of a container when the volume of gas is 1.0 L and when the volume is 2.0 L. Assume the number of particles does not change. Explain any differences in collisions.

80. **Interpreting Graphics** In Figure 3-3, if P_1 is 200 kPa and P_2 is 50 kPa, what are V_1 and V_2?

Chapter 3   States of Matter
Answer Section

MULTIPLE CHOICE

1.	ANS: C	DIF: L1	OBJ: 3.1.1
2.	ANS: B	DIF: L2	OBJ: 3.1.1
3.	ANS: A	DIF: L1	OBJ: 3.1.2
4.	ANS: C	DIF: L2	OBJ: 3.1.2
5.	ANS: C	DIF: L1	OBJ: 3.1.3
6.	ANS: A	DIF: L2	OBJ: 3.1.3
7.	ANS: C	DIF: L1	OBJ: 3.2.1
8.	ANS: B	DIF: L2	OBJ: 3.2.1
9.	ANS: D	DIF: L1	OBJ: 3.2.2
10.	ANS: C	DIF: L2	OBJ: 3.2.2
11.	ANS: A	DIF: L1	OBJ: 3.2.3
12.	ANS: A	DIF: L2	OBJ: 3.2.3
13.	ANS: D	DIF: L1	OBJ: 3.2.4
14.	ANS: A	DIF: L2	OBJ: 3.2.4
15.	ANS: C	DIF: L1	OBJ: 3.2.5
16.	ANS: A	DIF: L2	OBJ: 3.2.5
17.	ANS: D	DIF: L1	OBJ: 3.3.1
18.	ANS: C	DIF: L2	OBJ: 3.3.1
19.	ANS: C	DIF: L2	OBJ: 3.3.2
20.	ANS: C	DIF: L1	OBJ: 3.3.2
21.	ANS: D	DIF: L2	OBJ: 3.3.2
22.	ANS: C	DIF: L2	OBJ: 3.3.2
23.	ANS: B	DIF: L1	OBJ: 3.3.3
24.	ANS: B	DIF: L2	OBJ: 3.3.3
25.	ANS: D	DIF: L1	OBJ: 3.3.4
26.	ANS: B	DIF: L1	OBJ: 3.3.4
27.	ANS: A	DIF: L2	OBJ: 3.3.4
28.	ANS: C	DIF: L2	OBJ: 3.3.4
29.	ANS: B	DIF: L1	OBJ: 3.3.5
30.	ANS: B	DIF: L2	OBJ: 3.3.5

COMPLETION

31.	ANS: solid	DIF: L1	OBJ: 3.1.1
32.	ANS: condensate	DIF: L2	OBJ: 3.1.1
33.	ANS: volumes	DIF: L1	OBJ: 3.1.2
34.	ANS: solid	DIF: L1	OBJ: 3.1.2
35.	ANS: kinetic	DIF: L1	OBJ: 3.1.3
36.	ANS: collide	DIF: L2	OBJ: 3.1.3

37.	ANS: Collisions	DIF: L1	OBJ: 3.2.1
38.	ANS: pressure	DIF: L2	OBJ: 3.2.1
39.	ANS: increases, temperature	DIF: L1	OBJ: 3.2.2
40.	ANS: volume, temperature	DIF: L1	OBJ: 3.2.4
41.	ANS: temperature, volume, pressure	DIF: L2	OBJ: 3.2.4
42.	ANS: kelvins	DIF: L1	OBJ: 3.2.5
43.	ANS: dividing	DIF: L2	OBJ: 3.2.5
44.	ANS: sublimation	DIF: L2	OBJ: 3.3.1
45.	ANS: boils	DIF: L2	OBJ: 3.3.2

46. ANS:
kinetic energy
speed
DIF: L2   OBJ: 3.3.3

47.	ANS: atmospheric	DIF: L1	OBJ: 3.3.4
48.	ANS: liquid, gas	DIF: L2	OBJ: 3.3.4
49.	ANS: boiling	DIF: L2	OBJ: 3.3.4
50.	ANS: exothermic	DIF: L1	OBJ: 3.3.5

SHORT ANSWER

51. ANS: Plasma exists at extremely high temperatures, and a Bose-Einstein condensate exists at extremely low temperatures.
DIF: L2   OBJ: 3.1.1

52. ANS: Solids have a definite shape and definite volume, liquids have a definite volume but not a definite shape, and gases do not have a definite volume or a definite shape.
DIF: L1   OBJ: 3.1.2

53. ANS: The volume of a liquid is constant because forces of attraction keep the particles close together.
DIF: L1   OBJ: 3.1.3

54. ANS: Substance A; its particles are packed close together and arranged in a regular pattern.
DIF: L2   OBJ: 3.1.3

55. ANS: The constant motion of the tires on the road causes the tires and the air in the tires to warm up. The increase in temperature increases the average kinetic energy of the air in the tires. The frequency and force of collisions between particles increases, which increases the air pressure.
DIF: L1   OBJ: 3.2.2

56. ANS: The gas pressure increased because the volume of the gas was decreased.
DIF: L1   OBJ: 3.2.3

57. ANS: V_1 is the volume of a gas before a change occurs, and V_2 is the volume of a gas after a change occurs.
DIF: L1   OBJ: 3.2.4

58. ANS: The new volume would be 0.5 L.   DIF: L1   OBJ: 3.2.5

59. ANS: The new pressure would be 60 kPa.
DIF: L2   OBJ: 3.2.5

60. ANS: Melting and freezing are the two phase changes that occur between solid water and liquid water, and they both take place at 0°C.
DIF: L1   OBJ: 3.3.1

61. ANS: A phase change is taking place as water boils and changes from a liquid to water vapor. The temperature of a substance does not change during a phase change.
DIF: L1   OBJ: 3.3.2

62. ANS: As water freezes, it releases energy to its surroundings, and the average kinetic energy of the water molecules decreases.
DIF: L1   OBJ: 3.3.3

63. ANS: At the melting point of water, some molecules gain enough energy to move from their fixed positions.
DIF: L2   OBJ: 3.3.3

64. ANS: At room temperature, dry ice changes from solid carbon dioxide to carbon dioxide gas, which is an example of sublimation.
DIF: L1   OBJ: 3.3.4

65. ANS: Take the temperature measurements of the surroundings during the phase change. If the temperature decreases, the phase change is endothermic; a system absorbs energy from its surroundings during an endothermic phase change.
DIF: L2   OBJ: 3.3.5

ESSAY

66. ANS: Like a particle in a gas, a billiard ball moves in a straight line until it collides with another object. During a collision, kinetic energy can be transferred between billiard balls or particles in a gas. Students in a crowded hallway are closely packed like the particles in a liquid. The motion of the students is restricted by interactions with other students. The motion of particles in a liquid is limited by forces of attraction. The fixed positions of the audience in a movie theater are like the fixed locations of particles in solids. However, both the audience and the particles can move within or around their locations.
DIF: L2   OBJ: 3.1.3

67. ANS: The volume of the chest cavity increases as the diaphragm contracts and the rib cage is lifted. This increase in volume allows the particles in air to spread out, which lowers the air pressure in the lungs. Air rushes into the lungs because the air pressure outside the body is greater than the air pressure in the lungs. As the diaphragm relaxes and the rib cage moves down and in, the volume of the chest cavity decreases. This decrease in volume increases the air pressure, and air is forced out of the lungs.
DIF: L2   OBJ: 3.2.2

68. ANS: Temperature and air pressure affect the volume of a weather balloon. As the balloon rises, the temperature decreases, which should cause the volume of the balloon to decrease. However, pressure in the atmosphere also decreases, which should cause the volume of the balloon to increase.
DIF: L2   OBJ: 3.2.3

69. ANS: Water boils when its vapor pressure equals atmospheric pressure. Atmospheric pressure is lower at higher elevations. Therefore, the vapor pressure of water will equal atmospheric pressure at temperatures below 100°C. Pasta takes longer to cook at lower temperatures.
DIF: L2   OBJ: 3.3.3

70. ANS: Water can evaporate at temperatures lower than its boiling point. Evaporation can take place at the surface of water because some water molecules are moving fast enough to escape the liquid and become water vapor. The higher the temperature is, the faster the water molecules move, on average, and the faster evaporation takes place.
DIF: L2   OBJ: 3.3.4

OTHER

71. ANS: a. vaporization, b. melting, c. freezing
DIF: L1   OBJ: 3.3.1
72. ANS: Each pair represents the opposing endothermic and exothermic changes that occur between the same two states of matter.
DIF: L1   OBJ: 3.3.1
73. ANS: Water vapor is a gas. The phase change from water to liquid dew is called condensation. The phase change from water vapor to solid frost is called deposition.
DIF: L1   OBJ: 3.3.4
74. ANS: Vaporization is the phase change in which a liquid changes to a gas. Freezing is the phase change in which a liquid changes to a solid.
DIF: L1   OBJ: 3.3.4
75. ANS: melting, vaporization, and sublimation
DIF: L1   OBJ: 3.3.5
76. ANS: the kilopascal; 200 kPa; 100 kPa   DIF: L2   OBJ: 3.2.2
77. ANS: Volume is the manipulated variable. Pressure is the responding variable.
DIF: L2   OBJ: 3.2.2
78. ANS: The pressure would increase as the temperature increased.
DIF: L2   OBJ: 3.2.3
79. ANS: The number of collisions will increase when the volume is reduced from 2.0 L to 1.0 L because the same number of particles occupies a smaller space and will collide more often with the walls of the container.
DIF: L2   OBJ: 3.2.3
80. ANS: V_1 is 0.5 L, and V_2 is 2.0 L.   DIF: L2   OBJ: 3.2.4

Name _____ Class _____ Date _____

Chapter 4   Atomic Structure

Multiple Choice

Identify the letter of the choice that best completes the statement or answers the question.

____ 1. The Greek philosopher Democritus coined what word for a tiny piece of matter that cannot be divided?
    a. element
    b. atom
    c. electron
    d. molecule

____ 2. Democritus thought that matter was made of tiny particles
    a. of earth, air, fire, and water.
    b. that could not be divided.
    c. that could be divided.
    d. that were all round and smooth.

____ 3. If 2 grams of element X combine with 4 grams of element Y to form compound XY, how many grams of element Y would combine with 12 grams of X to form the same compound?
    a. 6 grams
    b. 12 grams
    c. 18 grams
    d. 24 grams

____ 4. According to John Dalton's observations, when elements combine in a compound,
    a. the ratio of their masses is always the same.
    b. each element contributes an equal number of atoms.
    c. their volumes are always equal.
    d. their masses are always equal.

____ 5. Which of the following is NOT part of John Dalton's atomic theory?
    a. All elements are composed of atoms.
    b. All atoms of the same element have the same mass.
    c. Atoms contain subatomic particles.
    d. A compound contains atoms of more than one element.

____ 6. Which of the following most accurately represents John Dalton's model of the atom?
    a. a tiny, solid sphere with an unpredictable mass for a given element
    b. a hollow sphere with a dense nucleus
    c. a tiny, solid sphere with predictable mass for a given element
    d. a sphere that is hollow throughout

____ 7. J.J. Thomson's experiments provided evidence that an atom
    a. is the smallest particle of matter.
    b. contains negatively charged particles.
    c. has a negative charge.
    d. has a positive charge.

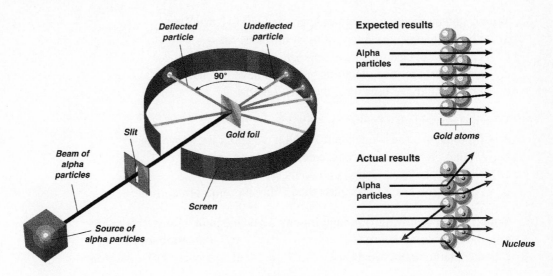

Figure 4-1

_____ 8. The diagram in Figure 4-1 shows the results of Rutherford's gold foil experiment. What caused some of the alpha particles to bounce straight back from the gold foil?
a. electrons in the gold atoms
b. negative charges in the gold atoms
c. other alpha particles
d. nuclei in the gold atoms

_____ 9. Rutherford's gold foil experiment provided evidence for which of the following statements?
a. Negative and positive charges are spread evenly throughout an atom.
b. Alpha particles have a positive charge.
c. Gold is not as dense as previously thought.
d. There is a dense, positively charged mass in the center of an atom.

_____ 10. Who provided evidence for the existence of a nucleus in an atom?
a. John Dalton
b. J.J. Thomson
c. Democritus
d. Ernest Rutherford

_____ 11. In an atomic model that includes a nucleus, positive charge is
a. concentrated in the center of an atom.
b. spread evenly throughout an atom.
c. concentrated at multiple sites in an atom.
d. located in the space outside the nucleus.

_____ 12. Which statement best describes Rutherford's model of the atom?
a. It is like an avocado with the pit representing the nucleus.
b. It is like an aquarium with swimming fish representing positive charges.
c. It is like a fried egg with the yolk representing the nucleus.
d. It is like a huge stadium with a positively charged marble at the center.

_____ 13. Which subatomic particle has a negative charge?
a. electron
b. alpha particle
c. neutron
d. proton

____ 14. Which statement about subatomic particles is NOT true?
   a. Protons and neutrons have almost the same mass.
   b. Protons and electrons have opposite charges.
   c. Unlike protons and electrons, neutrons have no charge.
   d. Protons and neutrons have the same charge.

____ 15. Which statement about subatomic particles is true?
   a. Protons, neutrons, and electrons all have about the same mass.
   b. Unlike protons or neutrons, electrons have no mass.
   c. Neutrons have no charge and no mass.
   d. An electron has far less mass than either a proton or neutron.

____ 16. Which of the following is unique for any given element?
   a. the number of neutrons   c. the number of protons
   b. the charge on the electrons   d. the mass of a neutron

____ 17. The number of protons in one atom of an element is that element's
   a. mass number.   c. atomic number.
   b. balanced charge.   d. isotope.

____ 18. To find the number of neutrons in an atom, you would subtract
   a. mass number from atomic number.   c. atomic number from electron number.
   b. atomic number from mass number.   d. isotope number from atomic number.

____ 19. Suppose an atom has a mass number of 35. Which statement is true beyond any doubt?
   a. The atom has an odd number of neutrons.
   b. The atomic number is less than 17.
   c. The atom is not an isotope.
   d. The number of protons in the nucleus does not equal the number of neutrons.

____ 20. Which statement is true about oxygen-17 and oxygen-18?
   a. They do not have the same number of protons.
   b. Their atoms have identical mass.
   c. They are isotopes of oxygen.
   d. The have the same mass number.

____ 21. In Niels Bohr's model of the atom, electrons move
   a. like balls rolling down a hill.   c. like popcorn in a popcorn popper.
   b. like planets orbiting the sun.   d. like beach balls on water waves.

____ 22. What can you assume has happened if an electron moves to a higher energy level?
   a. The atom has become more stable.   c. The electron has gained energy.
   b. The electron has lost energy.   d. The atom has lost an electron.

____ 23. How was Bohr's atomic model similar to Rutherford's model?
   a. It assigned energy levels to electrons.
   b. It described electron position in terms of the electron cloud model.
   c. It described how electrons gain or lose energy.
   d. It described a nucleus surrounded by a large volume of space.

_____ 24. Which statement accurately represents the arrangement of electrons in Bohr's atomic model?
   a. Electrons vibrate in fixed locations around the nucleus.
   b. Electrons travel around the nucleus in fixed energy levels with energies that vary from level to level.
   c. Electrons travel around the nucleus in fixed energy levels with equal amounts of energy.
   d. Electrons travel randomly in the relatively large space outside the nucleus.

_____ 25. What do scientists use to predict the locations of electrons in atoms?
   a. probability
   b. algebra
   c. geometry
   d. ratios and proportions

_____ 26. What does the electron cloud model describe?
   a. the most likely locations of electrons in atoms
   b. the precise locations of electrons in atoms
   c. the number of electrons in an atom
   d. the mass of the electrons in an atom

_____ 27. Which statement about electrons and atomic orbitals is NOT true?
   a. An electron has the same amount of energy in all orbitals.
   b. An orbital can contain a maximum of two electrons.
   c. An electron cloud represents all the orbitals in an atom.
   d. An atom's lowest energy level has only one orbital.

_____ 28. Which of the following provides the best analogy for an electron in an atomic orbital?
   a. a bee buzzing from flower to flower in a garden
   b. a bird flying high in the sky
   c. an ant crawling on the surface of a leaf
   d. a bee buzzing inside a closed jar

_____ 29. What is the difference between an atom in the ground state and an atom in an excited state?
   a. The atom in the ground state has less energy and is less stable than the atom in an excited state.
   b. The atom in an excited state has one fewer electron than the atom in the ground state.
   c. The atom in an excited state has more energy and is less stable than the atom in the ground state.
   d. The atom in an excited state has one more electron than the atom in the ground state.

_____ 30. The glowing of a neon light is caused by electrons emitting energy as they
   a. move from lower to higher energy levels.
   b. collide with other electrons.
   c. move from higher to lower energy levels.
   d. collide with the nucleus.

Completion
Complete each sentence or statement.

31. According to _____, all matter was made up of four elements: earth, air, fire, and water.

32. Unlike Democritus, Aristotle did not believe that matter was composed of tiny, indivisible _____.

33. John Dalton concluded that all the atoms of a single _____ have the same mass.

34. John Dalton observed that elements always combine in the same ratio to form a particular _____.

35. The subatomic particle that J.J. Thomson discovered has a(an) _____ charge.

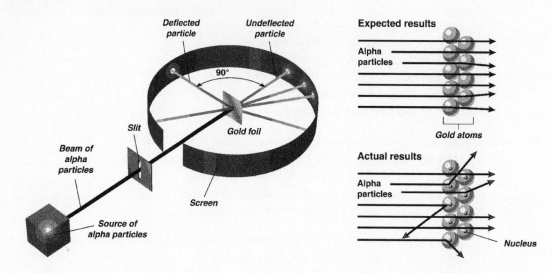

Figure 4-1

36. In Rutherford's gold foil experiment, shown in Figure 4-1, alpha particles that bounce straight back from the foil have struck _____ in the gold atoms.

37. In Rutherford's gold foil experiment, some of the _____ aimed at gold atoms bounced back, suggesting that a solid mass was at the center of the atom.

38. The results of Rutherford's gold foil experiment demonstrated that the _____ occupies a very small amount of the total space inside an atom.

39. Protons and _____ are found in the nucleus of an atom.

40. Neutrons and _____ have almost the same mass.

41. If element Q has 11 protons, its atomic _____ is 11.

42. The nuclei of isotopes contain different numbers of _____.

43. The _____ of an isotope is the sum of the number of protons and neutrons in its nucleus.

44. The difference between a sample of heavy water and regular water is that a hydrogen atom in heavy water has an extra _____.

45. In Bohr's model of the atom, _____ move in fixed orbits around the nucleus.

46. When an atom gains or loses energy, some of its _____ may move between energy levels.

47. The moving blades of an airplane propeller provide an analogy for the electron _____ model.

48. The region in which an electron is most likely to be found is called a(an) _____.

49. When all the electrons in an atom are in orbitals with the lowest possible energy, the atom is in its _____ state.

50. An atom in which an electron has moved to a higher energy level is in a(an) _____ state.

Short Answer

51. What did Democritus believe about matter?

52. How did the results of J.J. Thomson's experiments change how scientists thought about atoms?

53. What did Rutherford conclude about the location of positive charge in an atom?

54. Which of the three subatomic particles—proton, electron, or neutron—has the least mass?

55. If an atom has 32 protons and 38 neutrons, what is its mass number?

56. What scientific word comes from a Greek word meaning "uncut"? Which Greek philosopher first used the word to describe matter?

57. If an atom of an element has a mass number of 31 and 16 neutrons in its nucleus, what is the atomic number of the element?

58. If an atom of germanium has a mass number of 70 and an atomic number of 32, how many neutrons are in its nucleus?

59. Most calcium atoms have an atomic number of 20 and a mass number of 40, but some calcium atoms have a mass number of 48. What word could you use to describe these two kinds of calcium atoms?

60. In the nucleus of an atom, there are 15 protons and 16 neutrons. What is the atomic number and mass number of this isotope?

61. What can scientists measure to provide evidence that electrons can move from one energy level to another?

62. What did Bohr's model of the atom do that Rutherford's model did not?

63. How does the electron cloud model of the atom represent the locations of electrons in atoms?

64. What is the maximum number of electrons that an atomic orbital can contain?

65. How does the state of atoms in a neon light change when light is emitted?

Essay
On a separate sheet of paper, write an answer to each of the following questions.

66. Why did Rutherford propose a new model of the atom after seeing the results of the gold foil experiment?

67. A sample of calcium contains calcium-40, calcium-44, calcium-42, calcium-48, calcium-43, and calcium-46 atoms. Explain why these atoms can have different mass numbers, but they must have the same atomic number.

68. Why is Bohr's model of the atom often called the planetary model?

69. What is the difference between an orbital and the electron cloud?

70. Explain what the colors in a fireworks display reveal about the movement of electrons in atoms.

Other

USING SCIENCE SKILLS

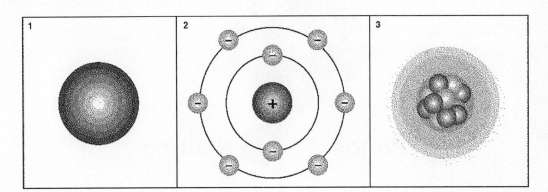

Figure 4-2

71. **Comparing and Contrasting** In Figure 4-2, what is the main difference between the atomic model in panel 1 and the model in panel 2?

72. **Comparing and Contrasting** In Figure 4-2, what is the main difference between the atomic model in panel 2 and the model in panel 3?

73. **Interpreting Graphics** Are the atomic models in Figure 4-2 arranged in the order that they were developed? Explain your answer.

74. **Using Analogies** Read the following analogy and explain how it applies to panels 1 and 2 in Figure 4-2: The atomic model in panel 1 is to the model in panel 2 as a drawing of the outside of a house is to a blueprint of the inside.

75. **Evaluating** In Figure 4-2, how is the atomic model in panel 2 helpful to your understanding of the atom? In what ways is it not helpful?

Name _____ Class _____ Date _____

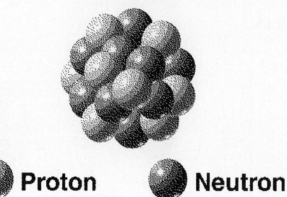

Nucleus

Proton　　　**Neutron**

Figure 4-3

76. **Analyzing Data** What subatomic particles are represented in Figure 4-3? Assuming all the particles in the nucleus are visible, what are the atomic and mass numbers of the atom shown?

77. **Inferring** Would Dalton have recognized the model of a nucleus shown in Figure 4-3? Explain your answer.

78. **Inferring** Would Rutherford have recognized the model of a nucleus in Figure 4-3? Explain your answer.

79. **Inferring** Why do you think the proton was discovered before the neutron? (*Hint:* Consider the properties of protons and neutrons.)

80. **Evaluating** Is Figure 4-3 a useful model of an atom? Explain your answer.

Chapter 4   Atomic Structure
Answer Section

MULTIPLE CHOICE

1.	ANS:	B	DIF:	L1	OBJ:	4.1.1
2.	ANS:	B	DIF:	L2	OBJ:	4.1.1
3.	ANS:	A	DIF:	L2	OBJ:	4.1.2
4.	ANS:	A	DIF:	L1	OBJ:	4.1.2
5.	ANS:	C	DIF:	L1	OBJ:	4.1.2
6.	ANS:	C	DIF:	L2	OBJ:	4.1.2
7.	ANS:	B	DIF:	L2	OBJ:	4.1.3
8.	ANS:	D	DIF:	L1	OBJ:	4.1.3
9.	ANS:	D	DIF:	L2	OBJ:	4.1.3
10.	ANS:	D	DIF:	L1	OBJ:	4.1.3
11.	ANS:	A	DIF:	L1	OBJ:	4.1.3
12.	ANS:	D	DIF:	L2	OBJ:	4.1.3
13.	ANS:	A	DIF:	L1	OBJ:	4.2.1
14.	ANS:	D	DIF:	L1	OBJ:	4.2.1
15.	ANS:	D	DIF:	L2	OBJ:	4.2.1
16.	ANS:	C	DIF:	L2	OBJ:	4.2.1
17.	ANS:	C	DIF:	L1	OBJ:	4.2.2
18.	ANS:	B	DIF:	L1	OBJ:	4.2.2
19.	ANS:	D	DIF:	L2	OBJ:	4.2.2
20.	ANS:	C	DIF:	L2	OBJ:	4.2.2
21.	ANS:	B	DIF:	L1	OBJ:	4.3.1
22.	ANS:	C	DIF:	L1	OBJ:	4.3.1
23.	ANS:	D	DIF:	L2	OBJ:	4.3.1
24.	ANS:	B	DIF:	L2	OBJ:	4.3.1
25.	ANS:	A	DIF:	L2	OBJ:	4.3.2
26.	ANS:	A	DIF:	L1	OBJ:	4.3.2
27.	ANS:	A	DIF:	L2	OBJ:	4.3.2
28.	ANS:	D	DIF:	L1	OBJ:	4.3.2
29.	ANS:	C	DIF:	L1	OBJ:	4.3.3
30.	ANS:	C	DIF:	L2	OBJ:	4.3.3

COMPLETION

31.	ANS:	Aristotle	DIF:	L1	OBJ:	4.1.1
32.	ANS:	atoms	DIF:	L2	OBJ:	4.1.1
33.	ANS:	element	DIF:	L1	OBJ:	4.1.2
34.	ANS:	compound	DIF:	L2	OBJ:	4.1.2
35.	ANS:	negative	DIF:	L1	OBJ:	4.1.3
36.	ANS:	nuclei	DIF:	L2	OBJ:	4.1.3

37. ANS: alpha particles   DIF: L1   OBJ: 4.1.3
38. ANS: nucleus   DIF: L2   OBJ: 4.1.3
39. ANS: neutrons   DIF: L1   OBJ: 4.2.1
40. ANS: protons   DIF: L2   OBJ: 4.2.1
41. ANS: number   DIF: L1   OBJ: 4.2.2
42. ANS: neutrons   DIF: L1   OBJ: 4.2.2
43. ANS: mass number   DIF: L2   OBJ: 4.2.2
44. ANS: neutron   DIF: L2   OBJ: 4.2.2
45. ANS: electrons   DIF: L1   OBJ: 4.3.1
46. ANS: electrons   DIF: L2   OBJ: 4.3.1
47. ANS: cloud   DIF: L1   OBJ: 4.3.2
48. ANS: orbital   DIF: L2   OBJ: 4.3.2
49. ANS: ground   DIF: L1   OBJ: 4.3.3
50. ANS: excited   DIF: L2   OBJ: 4.3.3

SHORT ANSWER

51. ANS: Democritus believed all matter consisted of tiny particles that could not be divided into smaller particles.
    DIF: L1   OBJ: 4.1.1
52. ANS: Scientists realized that atoms contained smaller subatomic particles.
    DIF: L1   OBJ: 4.1.3
53. ANS: Rutherford concluded that positive charge was concentrated in the nucleus of an atom.
    DIF: L1   OBJ: 4.1.3
54. ANS: electron   DIF: L1   OBJ: 4.2.1
55. ANS: 70   DIF: L1   OBJ: 4.2.2
56. ANS: atom; Democritus   DIF: L2   OBJ: 4.1.1
57. ANS: 15   DIF: L2   OBJ: 4.2.2
58. ANS: 38   DIF: L2   OBJ: 4.2.2
59. ANS: isotope   DIF: L1   OBJ: 4.2.2
60. ANS: atomic number = 15; mass number = 31
    DIF: L1   OBJ: 4.2.2
61. ANS: Scientists can measure the energy gained when electrons absorb energy and move to a higher level or the energy released when the electron returns to a lower energy level.
    DIF: L1   OBJ: 4.3.1
62. ANS: Bohr's model focused on electrons.
    DIF: L2   OBJ: 4.3.1
63. ANS: It provides a visual model of the most likely locations of electrons in an atom.
    DIF: L2   OBJ: 4.3.2
64. ANS: two   DIF: L1   OBJ: 4.3.2
65. ANS: The atoms return from an excited state to the ground state.
    DIF: L1   OBJ: 4.3.3

ESSAY

66. ANS: Thomson's model no longer explained all the available evidence. In Thomson's model, for example, positive charge spread evenly throughout the atom. Rutherford had concluded that the positive charge of an atom was concentrated in the center of the atom.
   DIF: L2   OBJ: 4.1.3

67. ANS: All the atoms of an element have the same atomic number because the atomic number equals the number of protons in an atom. If one of the atoms had a different number of protons, the atom would not be a calcium atom. The mass number can vary because it is the sum of the protons and neutrons and because isotopes of an element can have different numbers of neutrons.
   DIF: L2   OBJ: 4.2.2

68. ANS: Bohr's atomic model represents electrons as moving in fixed orbits around the nucleus like planets moving in orbit around a sun.
   DIF: L2   OBJ: 4.3.1

69. ANS: An orbital is a region of space around the nucleus where an electron is likely to be found. The electron cloud is a visual model that represents all the orbitals in an atom.
   DIF: L2   OBJ: 4.3.2

70. ANS: When fireworks explode, the heat produced by the explosions causes some electrons in atoms to move to higher energy levels. When the electrons return to lower energy levels, some of the energy is released as visible light. The colors vary because each element has a different set of energy levels.
   DIF: L2   OBJ: 4.3.3

OTHER

71. ANS: Panel 1 depicts an atom as a solid sphere without any subatomic particles. Panel 2 shows an atom that has a subatomic structure.
   DIF: L1   OBJ: 4.1.2, 4.2.1, 4.3.1

72. ANS: The main difference is the way in which electron motion is depicted. In panel 2, the movement of electrons is represented by fixed circular orbits. In panel 3, the probable locations of the moving electrons are represented by a cloud.
   DIF: L1   OBJ: 4.3.1, 4.3.2

73. ANS: Yes; they go from the simplest (the solid sphere in 1) to the most complex (the electron cloud diagram in panel 3). Students may specifically cite John Dalton in connection with panel 1 and Niels Bohr in connection with panel 2 to support their answer.
   DIF: L1   OBJ: 4.1.2, 4.3.1, 4.3.2

74. ANS: The solid ball in panel 1 is like the drawing of the exterior of a house. It provides no details about the internal structure of an atom. The model in panel 2 shows the locations of different parts of the atom within the atom and their relative sizes. It is like a blueprint that shows the size and location of rooms in a house.
   DIF: L1   OBJ: 4.1.2, 4.2.1, 4.3.1

75. ANS: It is helpful because it shows the general locations of the subatomic particles in an atom. It is not helpful because it implies that electrons travel in fixed paths around the nucleus.
   DIF: L1   OBJ: 4.1.2

76. ANS: The particles are protons and neutrons. Protons have a positive charge, while neutrons have no charge. This atom has an atomic number of 8 and a mass number of 17.
   DIF: L2   OBJ: 4.2.1

77. ANS: Dalton probably would not have recognized this model because he thought of the atom as a solid indivisible ball and had no knowledge of subatomic particles.
   DIF: L2   OBJ: 4.1.2

78. ANS: Yes; Rutherford demonstrated the existence of a nucleus, named subatomic particles with a positive charge protons, and predicted the existence of neutrons.
   DIF: L2   OBJ: 4.1.3

79. ANS: The proton has a positive charge, but the neutron has no charge. It was easier to detect the existence of a charged particle because its path could be deflected by a charged plate.
   DIF: L2   OBJ: 4.2.1

80. ANS: Students may answer yes because the model shows the composition of the nucleus of an atom. Students may answer no because the model does not include any electrons or show the position of the nucleus in the atom.
   DIF: L2   OBJ: 4.3.1, 4.3.2

Name _____ Class _____ Date _____

Chapter 5 The Periodic Table

Multiple Choice
Identify the letter of the choice that best completes the statement or answers the question.

_____ 1. Mendeleev arranged the known chemical elements in a table according to increasing
    a.   atomic number.
    b.   number of electrons.
    c.   number of protons.
    d.   mass.

_____ 2. In a periodic table, a set of properties repeats from
    a.   element to element.
    b.   group to group.
    c.   column to column.
    d.   row to row.

_____ 3. Mendeleev gave the name *eka-aluminum* to a(an)
    a.   compound containing aluminum.
    b.   mixture of aluminum and an unknown element.
    c.   unknown element he predicted would have properties similar to those of aluminum.
    d.   rare isotope of aluminum.

_____ 4. The usefulness of Mendeleev's periodic table was confirmed by
    a.   the discovery of subatomic particles.
    b.   its immediate acceptance by other scientists.
    c.   the discovery of elements with predicted properties.
    d.   the discovery of the nucleus.

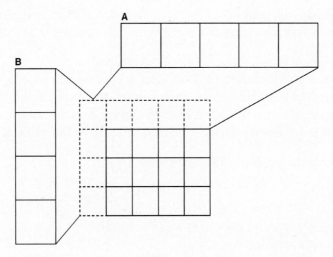

Figure 5-1

_____ 5. Figure 5-1 shows a portion of a blank periodic table. Identify the segments labeled A and B.
    a.   A and B are both periods.
    b.   A is a period and B is a group.
    c.   A and B are both groups.
    d.   A is a group and B is a period.

6. Moving from left to right across a row of the periodic table, which of the following values increases by exactly one from element to element?
   a. isotope number   c. atomic mass unit
   b. atomic number   d. mass number

7. The standard on which the atomic mass unit is based is the mass of a
   a. proton.   c. chlorine-35 atom.
   b. neutron.   d. carbon-12 atom.

8. The atomic mass of an element is
   a. the sum of the protons and neutrons in one atom of the element.
   b. double the number of protons in one atom of the element.
   c. a ratio based on the mass of a carbon-12 atom.
   d. a weighted average of the masses of an element's isotopes.

9. One-twelfth the mass of a carbon-12 atom is used to define a(an)
   a. atomic number.   c. mass number.
   b. atomic mass.   d. atomic mass unit.

10. How is the atomic mass of an element determined?
    a. Average the atomic masses of all its isotopes.
    b. Use the atomic mass of the most abundant isotope.
    c. Take a weighted average of the masses of the isotopes present in nature.
    d. Count the number of protons and neutrons in an atom of the element.

11. Which list of elements contains only metals?
    a. helium, carbon, gold   c. iodine, iron, nickel
    b. sodium, chromium, copper   d. phosphorus, nitrogen, oxygen

12. Which statement is true about the metalloid silicon?
    a. Silicon is a better conductor of an electric current than silver is.
    b. Silicon does not conduct an electric current under any conditions.
    c. Silicon's ability to conduct an electron current does not vary with temperature.
    d. Silicon is a better conductor of an electric current than sulfur is.

13. At room temperature, none of the metals are
    a. soft.   c. malleable.
    b. liquids.   d. gases.

14. Which general statement does NOT apply to metals?
    a. Most metals are ductile.
    b. Most metals are malleable.
    c. Most metals are brittle.
    d. Most metals are good conductors of electric current.

15. The column on the far left of the periodic table contains the
    a. most reactive metals.   c. least reactive nonmetals.
    b. most reactive nonmetals.   d. least reactive metals.

_____ 16. Two highly reactive elements in Period 4 are the metal potassium and the
   a.   metalloid arsenic.   c.   nonmetal bromine.
   b.   nonmetal selenium.   d.   nonmetal krypton.

_____ 17. Atoms of the most reactive elements tend to have
   a.   one or seven valence electrons.   c.   four or five valence electrons.
   b.   eight valence electrons.   d.   no valence electrons.

_____ 18. As you move from left to right across a period, the number of valence electrons
   a.   increases.   c.   increases and then decreases.
   b.   stays the same.   d.   decreases.

_____ 19. Compared with Group 1A elements, Group 7A elements have
   a.   more atoms in ground state.   c.   more isotopes.
   b.   more valence electrons.   d.   fewer valence electrons.

_____ 20. The tendency of an element to react chemically is closely related to
   a.   its atomic mass.
   b.   how tightly atoms are packed in the element.
   c.   the number of valence electrons in atoms of the element.
   d.   the ratio of protons to neutrons in atoms of the element.

_____ 21. An alkali metal has one valence electron, while an alkaline earth metal has
   a.   none.   c.   four.
   b.   two.   d.   three.

_____ 22. Which statement is NOT true about the elements fluorine, chlorine, and iodine?
   a.   They are all halogens.   c.   They are similar to noble gases.
   b.   They react easily with metals.   d.   They are all nonmetals.

_____ 23. Which of the following Group 1A elements is the most reactive?
   a.   Cs (cesium)   c.   K (potassium)
   b.   Li (lithium)   d.   Na (sodium)

_____ 24. Which of the following Group 7A elements is the most reactive?
   a.   Cl (chlorine)   c.   F (fluorine)
   b.   I (iodine)   d.   Br (bromine)

_____ 25. Among the alkali metals, the tendency to react with other substances
   a.   does not vary among the members of each group.
   b.   increases from top to bottom within the group.
   c.   varies in an unpredictable way within the group.
   d.   decreases from top to bottom within the group.

_____ 26. Which halogen is most likely to react?
   a.   Br (bromine)   c.   I (iodine)
   b.   F (fluorine)   d.   Cl (chlorine)

_____ 27. Which of the following gases emit colors when an electric current is applied?
   a.   hydrogen and helium   c.   fluorine and chlorine
   b.   helium and neon   d.   oxygen and nitrogen

____ 28. To keep them from reacting, some highly reactive elements are stored in
    a. water.   c. liquid mercury.
    b. pure oxygen.   d. argon.

____ 29. Which element is found in nature only in compounds?
    a. sodium   c. oxygen
    b. helium   d. nitrogen

____ 30. Which element is found in most of the compounds in your body except for water?
    a. iodine   c. iron
    b. potassium   d. carbon

Completion
Complete each sentence or statement.

31. When Mendeleev organized elements in his periodic table in order of increasing mass, elements with similar properties were in the same _____.

32. Mendeleev organized elements in his periodic table in order of increasing _____.

33. Mendeleev predicted that the undiscovered element he called *eka-aluminum* would have a(an) _____ melting point.

34. Mendeleev's periodic table was useful because it enabled scientists to predict properties of unknown _____.

35. The pattern of repeating properties of elements revealed in the periodic table is known as the _____.

36. Phosphorus is one block to the left of sulfur in the periodic table. The atomic number of sulfur is 16. The atomic number of phosphorus is _____.

37. The atomic mass unit (amu) is defined as one-twelfth the mass of a(an) _____-12 atom.

38. To determine the atomic mass of an element, you would take a(an) _____ average of the isotopes that make up that element.

39. Elements can be classified as metals, nonmetals, and _____.

40. Metals that grow dull when exposed to air are more _____ than metals that remain shiny.

41. The elements potassium (K), calcium (Ca), and scandium (Sc) appear from left to right in Period 4 of the periodic table. Among these elements, the most reactive is _____.

42. From left to right across a period in the periodic table, elements become less _____ and more _____ in their properties.

43. Element 3, lithium, has one valence electron, and element 4, beryllium, has two valence electrons. Element 5, boron, has _____ valence electrons.

44. Hydrogen does not have the typical properties of a metal. However, hydrogen is located above Group 1A because it has one _____.

45. In general, a(an) _____ metal will be more reactive than an alkaline earth metal in the same period.

46. The two most reactive groups of elements in the periodic table are the alkali metals and the _____.

47. Although they are called _____ lights, they can contain any noble gas.

48. Reactive elements, such as alkali metals and halogens, are found in nature only as _____.

49. Fertilizers usually contain two elements from Group 5A, which are _____ and phosphorus.

50. One way to demonstrate reactivity among the alkaline earth metals, Group 2A, is to observe what happens when they are placed in _____.

Short Answer

51. Why did Mendeleev want to make a periodic table of the elements?

52. What do the whole numbers on the periodic table represent?

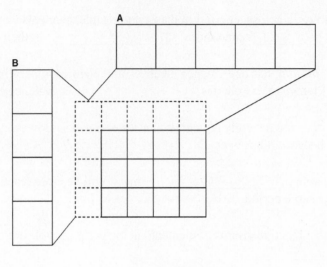

Figure 5-1

53. In which segment of Figure 5-1—A or B—will properties of the elements vary the most?

54. Selenium has six valence electrons, while rubidium has one valence electron. Identify each element as a metal or a nonmetal.

55. The elements silicon (atomic number 14) and chlorine (atomic number 17) are both in Period 3. Which is the more reactive element?

56. Sulfur is often found in nature as an element, not combined with other elements in a compound. What does this fact tell you about the reactivity of sulfur?

57. Suppose you are looking at elements in the periodic table in this order: element 23, element 24, element 25, element 26, and so on. Are you looking across a period or down a group? Explain your answer.

58. What determines an element's chemical properties?

59. On the periodic table, there are two numbers in the block for the element krypton, Kr: 36 and 83.80. What are each of these numbers, and what do they represent?

60. Boron (B), silicon (Si), germanium (Ge), and arsenic (As) are elements that have properties that fall between those of metals and nonmetals. What common label could you apply to these elements?

61. Period 5 of the periodic table begins with element 37 and ends with element 54. Consider the following elements from row 5: strontium (element 38), cadmium (element 48), iodine (element 53). Which of these elements is most likely to be a transition metal?

62. Element X has five valence electrons, element Y has one valence electron, and element Z has five valence electrons. Which two of these elements are most likely to have similar properties? Explain your answer.

63. Among the alkaline earth metals in Group 2A, which is more reactive—beryllium (element 4) or strontium (element 38)?

64. Sodium chloride is a compound of sodium and chlorine. Which of these elements is the alkali metal, and which is the halogen?

65. Why is argon gas used instead of air in light bulbs that contain a filament that is heated to glowing?

Essay
On a separate sheet of paper, write an answer to each of the following questions.

66. In a laboratory procedure, you form a useful but highly reactive compound. How could you store the compound so that it will not react?

67. In science lab, your teacher gives you two small pieces of matter and tells you that one piece is a metal and one is a nonmetal. Without changing the size or shape of the pieces, how could you test them to determine which is the metal?

68. Why were the elements gallium (Ga), scandium (Sc), and germanium (Ge) important to Mendeleev?

69. How are the octaves on a keyboard an analogy for the periods in a periodic table?

70. Although lithium and neon are both in Period 2 of the periodic table, they have very different properties. Explain how this is possible.

Name _____ Class _____ Date _____

Other

USING SCIENCE SKILLS

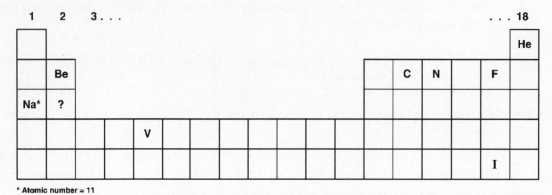

Figure 5-2

71. **Using Tables and Graphs** Which of the elements shown in Figure 5-2 are in the same period?

72. **Classifying** Which element in Figure 5-2 is a transition metal? Which is a noble gas?

73. **Using Tables and Graphs** Which elements in Figure 5-2 have the same number of valence electrons? How do you know?

74. **Comparing and Contrasting** Based on what you know about elements and the periodic table, compare and contrast the elements beryllium, Be, and iodine, I, which are shown in Figure 5-2.

75. **Inferring** Find the block labeled ? in Figure 5-2. Predict the properties of this element. What is its atomic number? How many valence electrons does it have? Which of the elements shown in Figure 5-2 will it most resemble?

Name ______________________ Class ____________________ Date ________

1A	2A	3B	4B
3 Li	4 Be		
11 Na	12 Mg		
19 K	20 Ca	21 Sc	22 Ti
37 Rb	38 Sr	39 Y	40 Zr

Figure 5-3

76. **Classifying** Classify the elements in Figure 5-3 as metals, metalloids, or nonmetals. Explain your answer.

77. **Inferring** Identify the most reactive element shown in Figure 5-3. Explain your answer.

78. **Predicting** Explain why knowing the properties of K, Ca, Sc, and Ti would allow you to predict the properties of Rb, Sr, Y, and Zr.

79. **Using Tables and Graphs** What do the numbers in the boxes in Figure 5-3 represent? What is the importance of these numbers?

80. **Comparing and Contrasting** Describe ways in which the elements in Group 1A are similar. Then describe ways in which Group 2A elements differ from elements in Group 1A.

Chapter 5   The Periodic Table
Answer Section

MULTIPLE CHOICE

1.	ANS: D	DIF: L2	OBJ: 5.1.1
2.	ANS: D	DIF: L1	OBJ: 5.1.1
3.	ANS: C	DIF: L2	OBJ: 5.1.2
4.	ANS: C	DIF: L1	OBJ: 5.1.2
5.	ANS: B	DIF: L1	OBJ: 5.2.1
6.	ANS: B	DIF: L2	OBJ: 5.2.1
7.	ANS: D	DIF: L2	OBJ: 5.2.2
8.	ANS: D	DIF: L2	OBJ: 5.2.2
9.	ANS: D	DIF: L1	OBJ: 5.2.2
10.	ANS: C	DIF: L1	OBJ: 5.2.2
11.	ANS: B	DIF: L1	OBJ: 5.2.3
12.	ANS: D	DIF: L1	OBJ: 5.2.3
13.	ANS: D	DIF: L2	OBJ: 5.2.3
14.	ANS: C	DIF: L2	OBJ: 5.2.3
15.	ANS: A	DIF: L1	OBJ: 5.2.4
16.	ANS: C	DIF: L2	OBJ: 5.2.4
17.	ANS: A	DIF: L2	OBJ: 5.3.1
18.	ANS: A	DIF: L1	OBJ: 5.3.1
19.	ANS: B	DIF: L1	OBJ: 5.3.1
20.	ANS: C	DIF: L1	OBJ: 5.3.1
21.	ANS: B	DIF: L2	OBJ: 5.3.1
22.	ANS: C	DIF: L2	OBJ: 5.3.1
23.	ANS: A	DIF: L1	OBJ: 5.3.2
24.	ANS: C	DIF: L1	OBJ: 5.3.2
25.	ANS: B	DIF: L2	OBJ: 5.3.2
26.	ANS: B	DIF: L2	OBJ: 5.3.2
27.	ANS: B	DIF: L1	OBJ: 5.3.3
28.	ANS: D	DIF: L2	OBJ: 5.3.3
29.	ANS: A	DIF: L2	OBJ: 5.3.3
30.	ANS: D	DIF: L1	OBJ: 5.3.3

COMPLETION

31.	ANS: column	DIF: L2	OBJ: 5.1.1
32.	ANS: mass	DIF: L1	OBJ: 5.1.1
33.	ANS: low	DIF: L2	OBJ: 5.1.2
34.	ANS: elements	DIF: L1	OBJ: 5.1.2
35.	ANS: periodic law	DIF: L2	OBJ: 5.2.1
36.	ANS: 15	DIF: L1	OBJ: 5.2.1

37.	ANS: carbon	DIF: L1	OBJ: 5.2.2
38.	ANS: weighted	DIF: L2	OBJ: 5.2.2
39.	ANS: metalloids	DIF: L1	OBJ: 5.2.3
40.	ANS: reactive	DIF: L2	OBJ: 5.2.3

41. ANS:
potassium
K
DIF: L2   OBJ: 5.2.4

42.	ANS: metallic, nonmetallic	DIF: L1	OBJ: 5.2.4
43.	ANS: three	DIF: L1	OBJ: 5.3.1
44.	ANS: valence electron	DIF: L2	OBJ: 5.3.1
45.	ANS: alkali	DIF: L1	OBJ: 5.3.2
46.	ANS: halogens	DIF: L2	OBJ: 5.3.2
47.	ANS: neon	DIF: L1	OBJ: 5.3.3
48.	ANS: compounds	DIF: L1	OBJ: 5.3.3
49.	ANS: nitrogen	DIF: L2	OBJ: 5.3.3
50.	ANS: water	DIF: L2	OBJ: 5.3.3

SHORT ANSWER

51. ANS: He wanted to organize information about the elements for a textbook he was writing.
DIF: L2   OBJ: 5.1.1

52. ANS:
atomic number
number of protons in each element
DIF: L2   OBJ: 5.2.2

53. ANS: Properties will vary the most in segment A, which is a period.
DIF: L2   OBJ: 5.2.4

54. ANS: Selenium is a nonmetal. Rubidium is a metal.
DIF: L2   OBJ: 5.3.1

55. ANS: chlorine   DIF: L2   OBJ: 5.3.2

56. ANS: Sulfur is not a highly reactive element under ordinary conditions.
DIF: L2   OBJ: 5.3.1, 5.3.2

57. ANS: across a period because the atomic number is increasing by one each time
DIF: L1   OBJ: 5.2.1

58. ANS: the number of valence electrons   DIF: L1   OBJ: 5.2.1

59. ANS: The integer, 36, is the atomic number, or number of protons in an atom of krypton. The decimal number, 83.80, is the atomic mass, which is the weighted average of the atomic masses of krypton found in nature.
DIF: L1   OBJ: 5.2.2

60. ANS: metalloids   DIF: L1   OBJ: 5.2.3

61. ANS: cadmium   DIF: L1   OBJ: 5.2.3, 5.2.4

62. ANS: Elements X and Z will have similar properties because they have the same number of valence electrons.
DIF: L1   OBJ: 5.3.1

63. ANS: strontium   DIF: L1   OBJ: 5.3.2
64. ANS: Sodium is the alkali metal, and chlorine is the halogen.
    DIF: L1   OBJ: 5.3.3
65. ANS: The heated filament will react with the oxygen in air but not with argon, which is a noble gas and hardly ever reacts.
    DIF: L1   OBJ: 5.3.3

ESSAY

66. ANS: You could store the compound in a jar filled with a noble gas such as argon. Students may also recall that reactive elements are stored under oil.
    DIF: L2   OBJ: 5.3.1
67. ANS: You could see which piece conducts an electric current or which piece is a better conductor of heat.
    DIF: L2   OBJ: 5.2.3
68. ANS: Mendeleev predicted the properties of these undiscovered elements from data in his periodic table. When the elements were discovered, their actual properties were found to be a close match to those Mendeleev had predicted. Their discovery provided evidence of the usefulness of Mendeleev's periodic table.
    DIF: L1   OBJ: 5.1.2
69. ANS: Answers should include a discussion of properties that repeat at regular intervals.
    DIF: L2   OBJ: 5.2.1
70. ANS: Lithium is an alkali metal in Group 1A. Alkali metals are the most reactive metals. Neon is a noble gas in Group 8A. Noble gases are highly unreactive nonmetals.
    DIF: L2   OBJ: 5.3.1, 5.3.2

OTHER

71. ANS: Be, C, N, and F   DIF: L1   OBJ: 5.2.1
72. ANS: V; He   DIF: L1   OBJ: 5.2.3
73. ANS: F and I; they are in the same group in the periodic table.
    DIF: L1   OBJ: 5.3.1
74. ANS: Beryllium is a reactive metal with two valence electrons. Iodine is a highly reactive nonmetal with seven valence electrons.
    DIF: L1   OBJ: 5.2.3, 5.3.1, 5.3.2, 5.3.3
75. ANS: 12; 2; beryllium   DIF: L1   OBJ: 5.3.2
76. ANS: These elements are all metals. The elements in Groups 1A and 2A are the alkali metals and alkaline earth metals, respectively. The elements in Groups 3B and 4B are transition metals.
    DIF: L2   OBJ: 5.2.3
77. ANS: Rubidium; Group 1A alkali metals are the most reactive metals, and the reactivity of elements in Group 1A increases from top to bottom.
    DIF: L2   OBJ: 5.2.4, 5.3.1, 5.3.2

78. ANS: When elements are arranged in a periodic table in order of increasing atomic number, the properties of elements repeat from period to period so that elements in the same group have similar properties.
    DIF: L2   OBJ: 5.2.1
79. ANS: Atomic numbers; an atomic number is the number of protons and the number of electrons in an atom. The periodic table is organized in order by increasing atomic number. No two elements have the same atomic number.
    DIF: L2   OBJ: 5.2.2
80. ANS: The elements in Group 1A, the alkali metals, are soft and extremely reactive. Atoms of these elements have a single valence electron. Elements in Group 2A have two valence electrons. The alkaline earth metals are harder, less reactive, and have higher melting points than the alkali metals in the same period.
    DIF: L2   OBJ: 5.2.1, 5.3.2, 5.3.3

Chapter 6   Chemical Bonds

Multiple Choice
Identify the letter of the choice that best completes the statement or answers the question.

_____ 1. Which of the following groups contain three elements with stable electron configurations?
     a. lithium, krypton, argon   c. xenon, neon, boron
     b. argon, neon, barium   d. helium, xenon, neon

_____ 2. Typically, atoms gain or lose electrons to achieve
     a. an exchange of energy.   c. a stable electron configuration.
     b. ionization.   d. vaporization.

_____ 3. In an electron dot diagram, the symbol for an element is used to represent
     a. the nucleus.   c. the nucleus and valence electrons.
     b. the nucleus and all electrons.   d. the nucleus and all non-valence
                                           electrons.

Figure 6-1

_____ 4. Study the electron dot diagrams for lithium, carbon, fluorine, and neon in Figure 6-1. Choose
     the statement that correctly identifies the most stable of the elements.
     a. Lithium is the most stable element because it has to lose only one electron to achieve a
         stable configuration.
     b. Carbon is the most stable element because it can form four bonds.
     c. Fluorine is the most stable element because it has to gain only one electron to achieve a
         stable configuration.
     d. Neon is the most stable element because its highest occupied energy level is filled.

_____ 5. Ionization energies tend to
     a. decrease from left to right across a period.
     b. increase from the top of a group to the bottom.
     c. increase from left to right across a period.
     d. decrease from the bottom of a group to the top.

_____ 6. The formation of an ionic bond involves the
     a. transfer of electrons.   c. transfer of protons.
     b. transfer of neutrons.   d. sharing of electrons.

_____ 7. Which of the following statements correctly describes the substance with the formula KI?
   a. Molecules of potassium iodide contain one atom of potassium and one atom of iodine.
   b. There is a one-to-one ratio of potassium ions to iodide ions.
   c. Potassium iodide is a molecular compound.
   d. Potassium iodide is a polyatomic ion.

_____ 8. In the compound $MgCl_2$, the subscript *2* indicates that
   a. there are two magnesium ions for each ion of chlorine.
   b. the chloride ion is twice the size of the magnesium ion.
   c. magnesium and chlorine form a double covalent bond.
   d. there are two chloride ions for each magnesium ion.

_____ 9. Which statement best describes the properties of sodium chloride?
   a. Sodium chloride is a malleable solid.
   b. Solid sodium chloride is a good conductor of electric current.
   c. Sodium chloride has a low melting point.
   d. Liquid sodium chloride is a good conductor of electric current.

_____ 10. Which of the following is a typical property of an ionic compound?
   a. low melting point
   b. poor conductor of electric current when melted
   c. tendency to shatter when struck
   d. all of the above

_____ 11. Which of the following compounds does NOT contain molecules?
   a. H_2 c. CO_2
   b. NaCl   d. H_2O

_____ 12. When two atoms of the same nonmetal react, they often form a(an)
   a. ionic bond.   c. diatomic molecule.
   b. polyatomic ion.   d. polar molecule.

_____ 13. You see a structural formula in which the symbols for elements are connected by a long dash. You can assume that the chemical bonds in the compound are
   a. ionic.   c. metallic.
   b. covalent.   d. unstable.

_____ 14. Which of the following formulas represents a compound whose molecules contain a triple bond?
   a. $N{\equiv}N$ c. O_3
   b. $O{=}O{=}O$ d. SO_3

_____ 15. In a polar covalent bond,
   a. electrons are shared equally between atoms.
   b. a cation is bonded to an anion.
   c. electrons are transferred between atoms.
   d. electrons are not shared equally between atoms.

_____ 16. The water molecule H_2O is polar because it contains two polar single bonds and
    a.   its molecule has a linear shape.
    b.   molecules that contain polar bonds are always polar.
    c.   its molecule has a bent shape.
    d.   the attractions between water molecules are strong.

_____ 17. Water has a higher boiling point than expected because
    a.   there is so much water vapor in the atmosphere.
    b.   water molecules are not very massive.
    c.   hydrogen and oxygen form single covalent bonds.
    d.   of the strong attractions between polar water molecules.

_____ 18. Because water molecules are polar and carbon dioxide molecules are nonpolar,
    a.   water has a lower boiling point than carbon dioxide does.
    b.   attractions between water molecules are weaker than attractions between carbon dioxide molecules.
    c.   carbon dioxide cannot exist as a solid.
    d.   water has a higher boiling point than carbon dioxide does.

_____ 19. The elements most likely to form more than one type of ion are the
    a.   transition metals.   c.   halogens.
    b.   alkali metals.   d.   alkaline earth metals.

_____ 20. Fluorine, F, forms a binary ionic compound with lithium, Li. What is the name of this compound?
    a.   fluorine lithide   c.   lithium fluorine
    b.   lithium fluoride   d.   fluorine lithium

_____ 21. The name *copper(II)* indicates that a compound contains
    a.   copper ions with a 11+ charge.   c.   copper ions with a negative charge.
    b.   copper ions with a 2+ charge.   d.   two types of copper ions.

_____ 22. Which of the following statements about ions is true?
    a.   All metals form more than one type of ion.
    b.   Many transition metals can form more than one type of ion.
    c.   Halogens form more than one type of ion.
    d.   Alkali metals form more than one type of ion.

_____ 23. Beryllium, Be, and chlorine, Cl, form a binary ionic compound with a one-to-two ratio of beryllium ions to chloride ions. The formula for the compound is
    a. Be_2Cl.   c. $BeCl_2$.
    b. $2BeCl$.   d. Be_2Cl_2.

_____ 24. In the name *carbon dioxide,* the prefix of the second word indicates that a molecule of carbon dioxide contains
    a.   two carbon atoms.   c.   a polyatomic ion.
    b.   two oxygen atoms.   d.   an ionic bond.

____ 25. Which phrase best describes a metallic bond?
   a.   a bond that is formed by a metal
   b.   the attraction between a metal anion and a shared pool of electrons
   c.   a bond that forms between a metal and a nonmetal
   d.   the attraction between a metal cation and a shared pool of electrons

____ 26. Metallic bonding is similar to ionic bonding because
   a.   electrons are transferred between atoms.
   b.   electrons are shared between atoms.
   c.   the lattice that forms contains anions and cations.
   d.   there is an attraction between positively charged and negatively charged particles.

____ 27. Many metals can be drawn into thin wires without breaking because
   a.   cations are still surrounded by electrons when they shift their positions in the lattice.
   b.   metals generally have low melting points.
   c.   when a metal is struck with a hammer, the positions of the anions do not change.
   d.   electrons have fixed positions in a metallic lattice.

____ 28. Which statement about metals is true?
   a.   A metal lattice is extremely rigid.
   b.   A metal lattice has weak bonds within a metal.
   c.   Electrons in a metal lattice are free to move.
   d.   Generally, metals have a low melting point.

____ 29. An alloy that contains mainly copper and tin is
   a.   sterling silver.   c.   brass.
   b.   stainless steel.   d.   bronze.

____ 30. How does increasing the amount of carbon in steel affect its properties?
   a.   Carbon makes the lattice harder and stronger.
   b.   Carbon forms an oxide that protects the steel from rusting.
   c.   Carbon makes the steel light enough to use for airplane parts.
   d.   Carbon makes the steel softer and easier to cut.

Completion
Complete each sentence or statement.

31. In an electron dot diagram, each dot represents a(an) _____.

32. In an ionic compound, the attractions between cations and _____ hold the compound together.

33. In the binary ionic compound potassium bromide, KBr, the element that forms cations is _____.

34. The chemical formula for calcium chloride, $CaCl_2$, shows that the compound contains two _____ ions for every _____ ion.

35. KBr is the formula for an ionic compound. The fact that neither symbol is followed by a subscript means that there is a(an) _____ ratio of ions in the compound.

36. You are given the melting points of three unknown substances and asked to predict which is an ionic compound. You would select the compound with the _____ melting point.

37. The ions in solid sodium chloride are arranged in a structure called a(an) _____ lattice.

38. If there are two long dashes between two atoms in a structural formula, molecules of the compound contain a(an) _____ bond.

39. A polar covalent bond forms when _____ are not shared equally between atoms.

40. Two factors that determine whether a molecule is polar are the types of atoms in the molecule and the _____ of the molecule.

41. When cesium and fluorine react, they form an ionic compound called cesium _____.

42. A(An) _____ ion is a covalently bonded group of atoms that has a positive or negative charge.

43. In ionic compounds, the sum of the charges of all the cations and anions must be _____.

44. The compound whose formula is SO_3 is called sulfur _____.

45. The metallic bonds in a transition metal, such as tungsten, are stronger than the metallic bonds in a(an) _____ metal, such as sodium.

46. In general, the more _____ a metal has, the stronger its metallic bonds will be.

47. Among the elements potassium, lithium, and iron, the metallic bonds are likely to be strongest in _____.

48. In a metal lattice, _____ are surrounded by a pool of shared electrons.

49. In its simplest form, the alloy brass consists of zinc and _____.

50. To produce stainless steel, _____ is added to iron.

Name _____ Class _____ Date _____

Short Answer

51. In a periodic table that included electron dot diagrams, in which column would the diagrams contain more dots—Group 2A (the alkaline metals) or Group 7A (the halogens)?

52. In an electron dot diagram of rubidium, there is one dot. In an electron dot diagram of silicon, there are four dots. Which element would you expect to be more reactive?

Figure 6-1

53. Study the electron dot diagrams in Figure 6-1. Which of the elements are most likely to react and form a compound? What type of compound are they likely to form?

54. Potassium, an alkali metal, and bromine, a halogen, are both in Period 4 of the periodic table. Which element has a higher ionization energy? Explain your answer.

55. In the binary ionic compound lithium iodide, LiI, which element forms anions?

56. Are covalent bonds more likely to be found in compounds containing both metals and nonmetals or compounds containing only nonmetals?

57. Suppose a covalent compound has a relatively high boiling point compared to molecules with a similar mass. Are the molecules in the compound likely to be polar or nonpolar?

58. The molecules in compound AB are strongly polar, while the molecules in compound XY are nonpolar. Which substance probably has the higher boiling point?

59. In potassium bromide, KBr, which element forms anions?

60. In sodium chloride, NaCl, are the cations sodium ions or chloride ions?

61. How do you know that magnesium is the more metallic element in the compound magnesium oxide, MgO?

62. The structure in a metal lattice can be described as cations surrounded by a pool of shared electrons. What two properties of metals can be explained by this structure?

63. Why are metals good conductors of electric current?

64. Which material is most likely to shatter if you strike it with a hammer—sodium chloride or bronze?

65. Mixing magnesium and aluminum together produces an excellent lightweight material from which to make airplane parts. What is this type of mixture called?

Essay

On a separate sheet of paper, write an answer to each of the following questions.

66. Fluorine is the most reactive nonmetal. To fluorine's immediate right in the periodic table is neon, a noble gas that does not form chemical bonds. Explain this contrast in reactivity in terms of atomic structure.

67. How is an electron dot diagram a useful model for focusing on the chemical properties of an element?

68. Water droplets tend to have a spherical, round shape. Explain this fact in terms of the polar nature of water molecules.

69. Compare the lattice in an ionic compound, such as sodium chloride, with the lattice in a metal, such as tungsten. How do any differences affect the malleability of these solids?

70. How does the ability of metals such as copper and alloys such as steel to be drawn into wires affect the possible uses of these materials?

Other

USING SCIENCE SKILLS

Chemical Formula	Name	Type of Bond	Description of Bond
NaCl	(1)	ionic	(2)
CO_2	carbon dioxide	(3)	Atoms share pairs of valence electrons.
W	tungsten	(4)	Metal cations are attracted to the shared electrons that surround them.

Figure 6-2

71. **Using Tables and Graphs** Write a description to place in box (2) in Figure 6-2.

72. **Using Tables and Graphs** What compound name belongs in box (1) in Figure 6-2?

73. **Classifying** What type of bond belongs in box (3) in Figure 6-2?

74. **Classifying** What type of bond belongs in box (4) in Figure 6-2?

75. **Comparing and Contrasting** How are metallic bonds and ionic bonds similar? How are they different?

	Substances	Compound	Remarks
A	potassium, K, and iodine, I	KI	Iodine is a member of the halogen group; potassium is an alkali metal.
B	carbon, C, and oxygen, O	CO_2	Carbon and oxygen are both nonmetals.
C	Al, O, and H	$Al(OH)_3$	OH^- (hydroxide) is a polyatomic ion.

Figure 6-3

76. **Applying Concepts** How does the saying "Opposites attract" apply to the bonding in the compound shown in row A of Figure 6-3?

77. **Comparing and Contrasting** What kind of bond forms between the elements in row B in Figure 6-3? How is this type of bond different from the type of bond that forms between the elements in row A?

78. **Comparing and Contrasting** How are the compounds in rows A and C in Figure 6-3 similar? How are they different?

79. **Inferring** A hydroxide ion has a charge of 1–. What is the charge on the aluminum ion? Explain your answer. Use Figure 6-3 to answer this question.

80. **Predicting** Suppose you could substitute sulfur, S, for iodine in row A in Figure 6-3. What would the formula for the resulting compound be? Explain your answer.

Chapter 6   Chemical Bonds
Answer Section

MULTIPLE CHOICE

1.	ANS: D	DIF:	L2	OBJ:	6.1.1
2.	ANS: C	DIF:	L1	OBJ:	6.1.1
3.	ANS: D	DIF:	L1	OBJ:	6.1.2
4.	ANS: D	DIF:	L1	OBJ:	6.1.2
5.	ANS: C	DIF:	L2	OBJ:	6.1.3
6.	ANS: A	DIF:	L2	OBJ:	6.1.3
7.	ANS: B	DIF:	L2	OBJ:	6.1.4
8.	ANS: D	DIF:	L1	OBJ:	6.1.4
9.	ANS: D	DIF:	L2	OBJ:	6.1.5
10.	ANS: C	DIF:	L1	OBJ:	6.1.5
11.	ANS: B	DIF:	L1	OBJ:	6.2.1
12.	ANS: C	DIF:	L2	OBJ:	6.2.1
13.	ANS: B	DIF:	L1	OBJ:	6.2.1
14.	ANS: A	DIF:	L2	OBJ:	6.2.1
15.	ANS: D	DIF:	L2	OBJ:	6.2.2
16.	ANS: C	DIF:	L1	OBJ:	6.2.2
17.	ANS: D	DIF:	L1	OBJ:	6.2.3
18.	ANS: D	DIF:	L2	OBJ:	6.2.3
19.	ANS: A	DIF:	L1	OBJ:	6.3.1
20.	ANS: B	DIF:	L2	OBJ:	6.3.1
21.	ANS: B	DIF:	L2	OBJ:	6.3.1
22.	ANS: B	DIF:	L1	OBJ:	6.3.1
23.	ANS: C	DIF:	L2	OBJ:	6.3.2
24.	ANS: B	DIF:	L1	OBJ:	6.3.2
25.	ANS: D	DIF:	L1	OBJ:	6.4.1
26.	ANS: D	DIF:	L2	OBJ:	6.4.1
27.	ANS: A	DIF:	L2	OBJ:	6.4.2
28.	ANS: C	DIF:	L1	OBJ:	6.4.2
29.	ANS: D	DIF:	L1	OBJ:	6.4.3
30.	ANS: A	DIF:	L2	OBJ:	6.4.3

COMPLETION

31.	ANS: valence electron	DIF:	L1	OBJ:	6.1.1
32.	ANS: anions	DIF:	L1	OBJ:	6.1.3
33.	ANS: potassium	DIF:	L2	OBJ:	6.1.3
34.	ANS: chloride, calcium	DIF:	L1	OBJ:	6.1.4
35.	ANS: one-to-one	DIF:	L2	OBJ:	6.1.4
36.	ANS: highest	DIF:	L2	OBJ:	6.1.5

| 37. | ANS: crystal | DIF: L1 | OBJ: 6.1.5 |
| 38. | ANS: double | DIF: L2 | OBJ: 6.2.1 |

39. ANS:
electrons
valence electrons
DIF: L1   OBJ: 6.2.2

40.	ANS: shape	DIF: L2	OBJ: 6.2.2
41.	ANS: fluoride	DIF: L2	OBJ: 6.3.1
42.	ANS: polyatomic	DIF: L1	OBJ: 6.3.1
43.	ANS: zero	DIF: L1	OBJ: 6.3.2
44.	ANS: trioxide	DIF: L2	OBJ: 6.3.2
45.	ANS: alkali	DIF: L1	OBJ: 6.4.1
46.	ANS: valence electrons	DIF: L2	OBJ: 6.4.1
47.	ANS: iron	DIF: L2	OBJ: 6.4.1
48.	ANS: cations	DIF: L1	OBJ: 6.4.1
49.	ANS: copper	DIF: L1	OBJ: 6.4.3
50.	ANS: chromium	DIF: L2	OBJ: 6.4.3

SHORT ANSWER

| 51. | ANS: Group 7A, the halogens | DIF: L1 | OBJ: 6.1.2 |
| 52. | ANS: rubidium | DIF: L1 | OBJ: 6.1.2 |

53. ANS: lithium, Li, and fluorine, F; an ionic compound
DIF: L2   OBJ: 6.1.1

54. ANS: Bromine; it gains electrons rather than losing them.
DIF: L1   OBJ: 6.1.3

55. ANS: iodine, I   DIF: L2   OBJ: 6.1.4

56. ANS: in compounds containing only nonmetals
DIF: L1   OBJ: 6.2.1

57.	ANS: polar	DIF: L1	OBJ: 6.2.3
58.	ANS: substance AB	DIF: L2	OBJ: 6.2.3
59.	ANS: bromine, Br	DIF: L2	OBJ: 6.3.1
60.	ANS: sodium ions	DIF: L1	OBJ: 6.3.1

61. ANS: because the symbol for magnesium, Mg, comes first in the chemical name and formula
DIF: L1   OBJ: 6.3.2

62. ANS: malleability and the ability to conduct an electric current
DIF: L1   OBJ: 6.4.2

63. ANS: Metals contain a shared pool of electrons that are free to move about.
DIF: L2   OBJ: 6.4.2

| 64. | ANS: sodium chloride | DIF: L1 | OBJ: 6.1.5, 6.4.1, 6.4.3 |
| 65. | ANS: an alloy | DIF: L1 | OBJ: 6.4.3 |

ESSAY

66. ANS: The electron configuration of an element determines its reactivity. Fluorine, with seven valence electrons, tends to gain one electron to fill its highest occupied energy level. Neon, with eight valence electrons, has a stable electron configuration. Neon's highest occupied energy level holds the maximum possible number of electrons.
   DIF: L2   OBJ: 6.1.1

67. ANS: An electron dot diagram shows the number of valence electrons. The chemical properties of an element depend on the number of valence electrons in its atoms.
   DIF: L2   OBJ: 6.1.2

68. ANS: Because water molecules are polar, there are strong attractions between water molecules. The molecules on the surface of water drops are pulled toward the center by their attractions to water molecules below the surface.
   DIF: L2   OBJ: 6.2.3

69. ANS: In both lattices, positively charged cations are attracted to negatively charged particles. In an ionic lattice, the negative particles are anions. In a metal lattice, the negative particles are electrons. Because the electrons are mobile, electrons still separate cations when the shape of the metal changes. When an ionic lattice is struck, ions with similar charges are pushed near one another. Repulsions between these ions cause the crystal to shatter.
   DIF: L2   OBJ: 6.1.5, 6.4.1

70. ANS: Possible answer: Metal wires are used to carry electric current. The cables on suspension bridges are made from thin strands of steel.
   DIF: L2   OBJ: 6.4.2

OTHER

71. ANS: The atoms of a metal lose one or more valence electrons and form cations. The atoms of a nonmetal gain one or more electrons and form anions. There is an attraction between the oppositely charged ions.
   DIF: L1   OBJ: 6.1.3

72. ANS: sodium chloride   DIF: L1   OBJ: 6.3.2

73. ANS: covalent   DIF: L1   OBJ: 6.2.1

74. ANS: metallic   DIF: L1   OBJ: 6.4.1

75. ANS: In both metallic and ionic bonds, there are attractions between particles with positive and negative charges, cations and electrons in a metallic bond, and cations and anions in an ionic bond. Ionic bonds are found in compounds. Metallic bonds are found in a single metal or in alloys.
   DIF: L1   OBJ: 6.1.3, 6.4.1

76. ANS: Potassium is a highly reactive metal with one valence electron. Iodine is a highly reactive nonmetal with seven valence electrons. When electrons are transferred from potassium atoms to iodine atoms, there is an attraction between the oppositely charged ions that form. Thus, opposites do attract in an ionic bond.
   DIF: L2   OBJ: 6.1.3

77. ANS: Covalent bonds form between the nonmetals carbon and oxygen. In a covalent bond, atoms share electrons. When potassium and iodine react, electrons are transferred from potassium atoms to iodine atoms. Ionic bonds form between potassium cations and iodide anions. There is no sharing of electrons in an ionic bond.

DIF: L2   OBJ: 6.1.3, 6.2.1

78. ANS: The compounds in rows A and C are both ionic compounds. However, KI is a binary ionic compound, which forms between a metal and a nonmetal. The compound in row C contains a polyatomic hydroxide ion (OH^-). The atoms in a polyatomic ion are joined by covalent bonds.

DIF: L2   OBJ: 6.3.1

79. ANS: The charge on the aluminum ion is 3+. The formula $Al(OH)_3$ indicates that there are three hydroxide ions for each aluminum ion in aluminum hydroxide. Since each hydroxide ion has a 1– charge, each aluminum ion must have a charge of 3+ for the overall charge on the compound to be zero.

DIF: L2   OBJ: 6.1.4, 6.3.1, 6.3.2

80. ANS: K_2S; because sulfur has six valence electrons, its atoms gain two electrons when they form ionic compounds. Potassium atoms donate one valence electron when they form ionic compounds. It takes two potassium atoms to donate two electrons to one sulfur atom.

DIF: L2   OBJ: 6.1.1

Chapter 7 Chemical Reactions

Multiple Choice
Identify the letter of the choice that best completes the statement or answers the question.

_____ 1. The substances that are present before a chemical reaction takes place are called
    a.   reactants.   c.   coefficients.
    b.   products.   d.   elements.

_____ 2. Hydrochloric acid, HCl, is added to solid NaOH. After the reaction is complete, NaCl dissolved in water remains. What are the products of this chemical reaction?
    a.   NaOH and HCl   c.   HCl and NaCl
    b.   NaOH and H_2O d.   NaCl and H_2O

_____ 3. Which of the following does NOT state what the arrow means in a chemical equation?
    a.   forms   c.   conserves
    b.   produces   d.   yields

_____ 4. Which of the following does NOT show the law of conservation of mass?
    a.   24 g of Mg burn in 32 g O_2 to produce 56 g of MgO.
    b.   24 mL of Mg burn in 32 mL O_2 to produce 56 mL of MgO.
    c.   2 atoms of Mg react with 1 molecule of O_2 to produce 2 units of MgO.
    d.   1 atom of Mg reacts with 1 atom of O to produce a unit of MgO that contains 2 atoms.

_____ 5. Which of the following is a chemical equation that accurately represents what happens when sulfur and oxygen react to form sulfur trioxide?
    a.   Sulfur and oxygen react to form sulfur trioxide.
    b.   S and O_2 produce SO_3.
    c. $S + O_2 \rightarrow SO_3$
    d. $2S + 3O_2 \rightarrow 2SO_3$

_____ 6. Which of the following is a balanced chemical equation for the synthesis of NaBr from Na and Br_2?
    a. $Na + Br_2 \rightarrow NaBr$ c. $Na + Br_2 \rightarrow 2NaBr$
    b. $2Na + Br_2 \rightarrow NaBr$ d. $2Na + Br_2 \rightarrow 2NaBr$

_____ 7. Methane, CH_4, burns in oxygen gas to form water and carbon dioxide. What is the correct balanced chemical equation for this reaction?
    a. $CH_4 + O \rightarrow H_2O + CO_2$ c. $CH_4 + O_2 \rightarrow H_2O + CO_2$
    b. $CH_4 + 4O \rightarrow 2H_2O + CO_2$ d. $CH_4 + 2O_2 \rightarrow 2H_2O + CO_2$

_____ 8. How many atoms are present in 2 moles of chromium?
    a. 6.02×10^{23} atoms   c. 1.20×10^{24} atoms
    b. 1.20×10^{23} atoms   d.   52.0 atoms

_____ 9. How many grams of HNO_3 are in 2.6 mol of the compound?
    a.   24.2 g   c.   93.0 g
    b.   63.0 g   d.   163.8 g

_____ 10. How many moles of Cr are in 156 g of the element?
   a. 1.0 mol
   b. 3.0 mol
   c. 6.5 mol
   d. 156 mol

_____ 11. An industrial process makes calcium oxide by decomposing calcium carbonate. Which of the following is NOT needed to calculate the mass of calcium oxide that can be produced from 4.7 kg of calcium carbonate?
   a. the balanced chemical equation
   b. molar masses of the reactants
   c. molar masses of the product
   d. the volume of the unknown mass

_____ 12. The coefficients in a balanced chemical equation always can express the ratio of
   a. moles of reactants and products.
   b. volume of reactants and products.
   c. atoms of reactants and products.
   d. mass of reactants and products.

_____ 13. When magnesium carbonate, $MgCO_2$, reacts with nitric acid, HNO_3, magnesium nitrate and carbonic acid form. Carbonic acid then breaks down into water and carbon dioxide. What two types of reactions take place in this process?
   a. synthesis and decomposition
   b. single-replacement and combustion
   c. double-replacement and decomposition
   d. double-replacement and combustion

_____ 14. Which of the following is NOT always true about a synthesis reaction?
   a. One product is formed.
   b. There is only one reactant.
   c. The general formula is A + B → C.
   d. A reactant might be a compound, or it might be an element.

_____ 15. Which of the following takes place during a redox reaction?
   a. Electrons are gained only.
   b. Electrons are lost only.
   c. Electrons are both gained and lost.
   d. Electrons are neither gained nor lost.

_____ 16. In a chemical reaction, an iron atom became the ion Fe^{2+}. What happened to the iron atom?
   a. It lost electrons and was oxidized.
   b. It lost electrons and was reduced.
   c. It gained electrons and was oxidized.
   d. It gained electrons and was reduced.

_____ 17. In a compound, chemical energy is contained in the
   a. nuclei of the atoms.
   b. unbonded electrons.
   c. bonds.
   d. movement of the electrons.

_____ 18. Which of the following statements is true about what happens during a chemical reaction?
   a. Bonds of the reactants are broken, and bonds of the products are formed.
   b. Bonds of the reactants are formed, and bonds of the products are broken.
   c. The bonds of both the reactants and the products are broken.
   d. The bonds of both the reactants and the products are formed.

_____ 19. In terms of energy, how would you classify the following chemical reaction?
   $$2Cu + O_2 \rightarrow 2CuO + 315 \text{ kJ}$$
   a. endothermic
   b. exothermic
   c. both endothermic and exothermic
   d. neither endothermic nor exothermic

_____ 20. For the chemical reaction $C_2H_6 + 137$ kJ $\rightarrow C_2H_4 + H_2$, the chemical energy of the
   a. reactant is greater than the chemical energy of the products.
   b. products is greater than the chemical energy of the reactant.
   c. reactant and the chemical energy of the products are equal.
   d. reaction is conserved.

_____ 21. The total amount of energy before and after a chemical reaction is the same. Thus, energy is
   a. created.   c. conserved.
   b. destroyed.   d. the same as mass.

_____ 22. For the chemical reaction $H_2 + CO_2 \rightarrow H_2O + CO$, the energy contained in the reactants is 352 kJ, and the energy contained in the products is 394 kJ, assuming 1 mol of each substance is present. Which of the following statements is true?
   a. 42 kJ is released, and the reaction is exothermic.
   b. 42 kJ is released, and the reaction is endothermic.
   c. 42 kJ is absorbed, and the reaction is exothermic.
   d. 42 kJ is absorbed, and the reaction is endothermic.

_____ 23. Reaction rates do NOT tell you how fast
   a. reactants are being consumed.   c. substances are changing state.
   b. products are being formed.   d. energy is being absorbed or released.

_____ 24. In general, if the temperature of a chemical reaction is increased, reaction rate
   a. increases.   c. remains the same.
   b. decreases.   d. cannot be predicted.

_____ 25. A log is burning in a fireplace. If the amount of oxygen reaching the log is decreased, which of the following statements is true?
   a. The reaction rate increases.
   b. The reaction rate decreases.
   c. The reaction rate remains the same.
   d. The reaction rate depends only on the temperature.

_____ 26. When the forward and reverse paths of a change occur at the same rate,
   a. the system is conserved.   c. the change must be physical.
   b. the system is in equilibrium.   d. the change must be chemical.

_____ 27. The equation $2NO_2 \leftrightarrow N_2O_4$ shows a system
   a. in chemical equilibrium.   c. that does not reach equilibrium.
   b. in physical equilibrium.   d. that does not change.

_____ 28. What happens to the reaction $2NO_2 \leftrightarrow N_2O_4 + 57.2$ kJ when the temperature of the reaction is increased?
   a. More reactant is formed.
   b. More product is formed.
   c. No change occurs in the amounts of reactant and product present.
   d. The effect depends on whether or not a catalyst is present.

Name _____ Class _____ Date _____

_____ 29. The reaction $H_2CO_3 + H_2O \leftrightarrow H_3O^+ + HCO_3^-$ takes place in water. What happens to the equilibrium when the pressure is increased?
   a. It favors formation of reactants.   c. It does not change.
   b. It favors formation of products.   d. It is conserved.

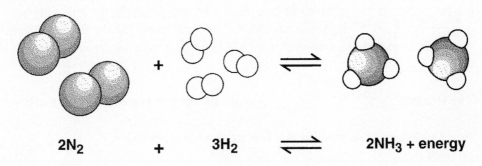

2N₂ + 3H₂ ⇌ 2NH₃ + energy

Figure 7-1

_____ 30. The reaction in Figure 7-1 shows the formation of ammonia from nitrogen and hydrogen in the Haber process. What will be the effect on the equilibrium if the temperature is increased and some of the ammonia is removed from the system?
   a. More ammonia will definitely form.
   b. More reactants will definitely form.
   c. The changes definitely will have no overall effect on the reaction..
   d. Any effect will depend on the amount of change of temperature and concentration.

Completion

Complete each sentence or statement.

31. The statement that in chemical reactions, the total mass of the reactants equals the total mass of the products is the law of _____.

32. In an experiment, 44 g of propane were burned, producing 132 g of carbon dioxide and 72 g of water. The mass of oxygen that was needed for the reaction was _____.

33. A(An) _____ is the number that appears before a formula in a chemical equation.

34. The molar mass of chlorine is _____.

35. A sample of HBr contains 186 g of the compound. The sample contains _____ moles of HBr.

36. Butane burns as shown in the balanced chemical equation $2C_4H_{10} + 13O_2 \rightarrow 10H_2O + 8CO_2$. If 6 mol of butane burn, _____ mol of carbon dioxide are produced.

37. An iron fence is left unpainted, and it reacts with the oxygen in the air, forming rust. The formation of rust is an oxidation-reduction reaction, but it is also an example of a(an) _____ reaction.

38. Single-replacement reactions can take place with nonmetals. In the following equation, assume that A and C are nonmetals and B is a metal. Complete the following general equation for the replacement of a nonmetal in a compound by another nonmetal: $A + BC \rightarrow$ _____.

39. The element _____ is always present in a combustion reaction.

40. In a double-replacement reaction, there are two reactants and _____ product(s).

41. When fluorine reacts with a metal, it forms an F^- ion. The fluorine atom has gained an electron and undergone _____.

42. During a chemical reaction, energy is released during the _____ of chemical bonds.

43. In terms of energy, the general chemical equation $AB + CD + energy \rightarrow AD + CB$ represents a(an) _____ reaction.

44. Cooking requires continuous adding of energy to the chemical reactions that are taking place. The chemical reactions involved in cooking can be described as _____.

45. For a certain chemical reaction, the reactants contain 362 kJ of chemical energy, and the products contain 342 kJ of chemical energy. In order for energy to be conserved, 20 kJ of energy must be _____.

46. Measuring how quickly a reactant disappears is one way to measure the _____ of the reaction.

47. A chunk of limestone, which is calcium carbonate, reacts with acid at a certain rate. If the limestone was crushed, the rate of reaction between the acid and the limestone would _____.

48. A catalyst is used in a catalytic converter in vehicles to help control pollution. For example, the catalytic converter _____ the rate at which carbon monoxide is oxidized to carbon dioxide. ($2CO + O_2 \rightarrow 2CO_2$)

49. The statement that when a change is introduced to a system in equilibrium, the equilibrium shifts in the direction that relieves the stress on the system is known as _____.

50. Many manufacturing processes involve chemical reactions that reach equilibrium. One way to increase the amount of product formed is to decrease the _____ of the product in the system.

Short Answer

51. How does the law of conservation of mass explain why only a bit of ash is left after burning a large sheet of paper?

52. What is the purpose of balancing a chemical equation?

53. A student balanced the chemical equation $Mg + O_2 \rightarrow MgO$ by writing $Mg + O_2 \rightarrow MgO_2$. Was the equation balanced correctly? Explain your answer. If the equation was not balanced correctly, write the correctly balanced equation.

54. How many moles of nitrogen are contained in 1.61×10^{24} atoms of nitrogen?

55. How many grams of Mn are in 4.0 mol of the element?

56. In a decomposition reaction, a compound is broken down into two or more simpler substances. Explain why the term *compound* is used to refer to the reactant and the term *substances* is used to refer to the products.

57. Magnesium will replace silver in a compound. What are the products of a single-replacement reaction between magnesium and silver nitrate?

58. What are the products of the double-replacement reaction between potassium chloride and silver acetate?

59. When most fuels burn, water and carbon dioxide are the two main products. Why can't you say that water and carbon dioxide are products of all combustion reactions?

60. In the reaction between bromine and sodium, a bromine atom gains an electron. What ion is formed? Is the bromine oxidized, or is it reduced?

61. Contrast the forming and breaking of chemical bonds in terms of energy changes.

62. Explain how energy is conserved during chemical reactions.

63. Explain why batteries and film will stay fresh longer if they are kept in a refrigerator or freezer.

64. Explain why ice in liquid water at 0°C is an example of physical equilibrium.

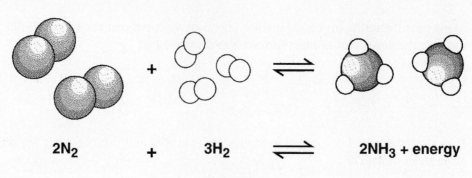

$$2N_2 \quad + \quad 3H_2 \quad \rightleftharpoons \quad 2NH_3 + energy$$

Figure 7-1

65. In Figure 7-1, both the reactants and the product of the reaction are gases. In this equilibrium, the reaction that produces fewer gas molecules is favored. Explain why increasing the pressure on the reaction favors the formation of ammonia rather than the formation of the reactants.

Problem

66. Balance the following chemical equation.
$Cu + HNO_3 \rightarrow Cu(NO_3)_2 + NO_2 + H_2O$

67. When iron metal reacts with oxygen, the reaction can form Fe_2O_3. Write a balanced chemical equation for this reaction, and find the number of moles of oxygen that are needed to form 6 mol of Fe_2O_3.

68. Sodium reacts with chlorine gas to form sodium chloride. Write a balanced chemical equation for the reaction, and find the mass of chlorine gas that will react with 96.6 g of sodium.

Essay
On a separate sheet of paper, write an answer to each of the following questions.

69. Which two types of reactions are also always redox reactions? Explain your answer.

70. Explain the difference between a physical equilibrium and a chemical equilibrium.

Name _____ Class _____ Date _____

USING SCIENCE SKILLS

Unbalanced equation:

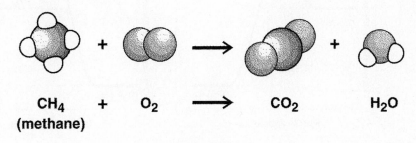

CH_4 + O_2 ⟶ CO_2 H_2O
(methane)

Figure 7-2

71. **Interpreting Graphics** How many of each type of atom are present on each side of the equation in Figure 7-2?

72. **Inferring** If the total number of atoms on the left side of the equation in Figure 7-2 equaled the total number of atoms on the right side of the equation, would this necessarily mean that the equation was balanced? Explain your answer.

73. **Drawing Conclusions** If there are 4 hydrogen atoms on the left side of equation in Figure 7-2, how many hydrogen atoms must there be on the right side in order to balance this reaction?

74. **Problem Solving** How do you balance the number of hydrogen atoms in the equation in Figure 7-2?

75. **Communicating Results** What is the balanced chemical equation for the reaction represented in Figure 7-2?

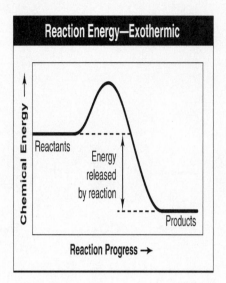
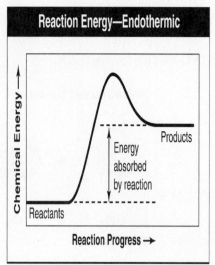

Figure 7-3

76. **Applying Concepts** In an exothermic reaction as seen in Figure 7-3, do the reactants or the products contain more chemical energy?

77. **Inferring** Cooking an egg white involves an endothermic reaction. Which has more chemical energy in its chemical bonds—an uncooked egg white or a cooked egg white? Use Figure 7-3 to explain your answer.

78. **Problem Solving** If the bonds in the reactants of Figure 7-3 contained 432 kJ of chemical energy and the bonds in the products contained 478 kJ of chemical energy, what would be the amount of energy change during the reaction? Would this energy be absorbed or released?

79. **Using Tables and Graphs** What do the peaks on the graphs in Figure 7-3 represent?

80. **Interpreting Graphics** Although the amount of energy involved is small enough that it is not noticed, iron rusts according to the following word equation:

    iron + oxygen → rust + energy

    Which of the energy diagrams in Figure 7-3 could be applied to the formation of rust? Explain your answer.

Chapter 7   Chemical Reactions
Answer Section

MULTIPLE CHOICE

1.	ANS: A	DIF:	L1	OBJ:	7.1.1	
2.	ANS: D	DIF:	L2	OBJ:	7.1.1	
3.	ANS: C	DIF:	L1	OBJ:	7.1.1	
4.	ANS: B	DIF:	L2	OBJ:	7.1.1	
5.	ANS: D	DIF:	L2	OBJ:	7.1.2	
6.	ANS: D	DIF:	L1	OBJ:	7.1.2	
7.	ANS: D	DIF:	L2	OBJ:	7.1.2	
8.	ANS: C	DIF:	L1	OBJ:	7.1.3	
9.	ANS: D	DIF:	L2	OBJ:	7.1.3	
10.	ANS: B	DIF:	L1	OBJ:	7.1.3	
11.	ANS: D	DIF:	L2	OBJ:	7.1.4	
12.	ANS: A	DIF:	L1	OBJ:	7.1.4	
13.	ANS: C	DIF:	L2	OBJ:	7.2.1	
14.	ANS: B	DIF:	L1	OBJ:	7.2.1	
15.	ANS: C	DIF:	L1	OBJ:	7.2.2	
16.	ANS: A	DIF:	L2	OBJ:	7.2.2	
17.	ANS: C	DIF:	L1	OBJ:	7.3.1	
18.	ANS: A	DIF:	L2	OBJ:	7.3.1	
19.	ANS: B	DIF:	L1	OBJ:	7.3.2	
20.	ANS: B	DIF:	L2	OBJ:	7.3.2	
21.	ANS: C	DIF:	L1	OBJ:	7.3.3	
22.	ANS: D	DIF:	L2	OBJ:	7.3.3	
23.	ANS: C	DIF:	L2	OBJ:	7.4.1	
24.	ANS: A	DIF:	L1	OBJ:	7.4.1	
25.	ANS: B	DIF:	L1	OBJ:	7.4.1	
26.	ANS: B	DIF:	L1	OBJ:	7.5.1	
27.	ANS: A	DIF:	L1	OBJ:	7.5.1	
28.	ANS: A	DIF:	L2	OBJ:	7.5.2	
29.	ANS: C	DIF:	L2	OBJ:	7.5.2	
30.	ANS: D	DIF:	L2	OBJ:	7.5.2	

COMPLETION

31.	ANS: conservation of mass	DIF:	L1	OBJ:	7.1.1
32.	ANS: 160 g	DIF:	L2	OBJ:	7.1.1
33.	ANS: coefficient	DIF:	L1	OBJ:	7.1.2
34.	ANS: 35.5 g/mol	DIF:	L1	OBJ:	7.1.3
35.	ANS: 2.3	DIF:	L2	OBJ:	7.1.3
36.	ANS: 24	DIF:	L1	OBJ:	7.1.4

37.	ANS:	synthesis	DIF:	L2	OBJ:	7.2.1
38.	ANS:	C + BA	DIF:	L2	OBJ:	7.2.1
39.	ANS:	oxygen	DIF:	L1	OBJ:	7.2.1
40.	ANS:	two	DIF:	L1	OBJ:	7.2.1
41.	ANS:	reduction	DIF:	L1	OBJ:	7.2.2
42.	ANS:	forming	DIF:	L2	OBJ:	7.3.1
43.	ANS:	endothermic	DIF:	L1	OBJ:	7.3.2
44.	ANS:	endothermic	DIF:	L2	OBJ:	7.3.2
45.	ANS:	released	DIF:	L2	OBJ:	7.3.3
46.	ANS:	rate	DIF:	L1	OBJ:	7.4.1
47.	ANS:	increase	DIF:	L2	OBJ:	7.4.1
48.	ANS:	speeds up	DIF:	L2	OBJ:	7.4.1
49.	ANS:	LeChâtelier's principle	DIF:	L1	OBJ:	7.5.2
50.	ANS:	concentration	DIF:	L2	OBJ:	7.5.2

SHORT ANSWER

51. ANS: In addition to the ash, gases are formed. The total mass of the paper and oxygen equals the total mass of the ash and the gases formed.
DIF: L1   OBJ: 7.1.1

52. ANS: A balanced chemical equation shows that mass is conserved. The number of each type of atom in the reactants must equal the number of each type of atom in the products.
DIF: L1   OBJ: 7.1.2

53. ANS: The equation was not balanced correctly because it was balanced by changing a subscript instead of changing coefficients. The correctly balanced equation is $2Mg + O_2 \rightarrow 2MgO$.
DIF: L2   OBJ: 7.1.2

54. ANS: 2.67 mol   DIF: L2   OBJ: 7.1.3

55. ANS: The molar mass of Mn is 55 g/mol, so 4.0 mol of Mn have a mass of 220 g.
DIF: L1   OBJ: 7.1.3

56. ANS: The reactant must be a compound because it is being broken down; an element cannot be broken down in a chemical reaction. The products can be either compounds or elements, and substances include both compounds and elements.
DIF: L2   OBJ: 7.2.1

57. ANS: magnesium nitrate, $Mg(NO_3)_2$, and silver, Ag
DIF: L1   OBJ: 7.2.1

58. ANS: silver chloride and potassium acetate
DIF: L1   OBJ: 7.2.1

59. ANS: Some other substances, such as hydrogen, also burn. When the fuel does not contain carbon, carbon dioxide does not form.
DIF: L2   OBJ: 7.2.1

60. ANS: The bromide ion, Br^-, forms. The bromine is reduced.
DIF: L1   OBJ: 7.2.2

61. ANS: Forming chemical bonds releases energy. Breaking chemical bonds requires (absorbs) energy.
DIF: L1   OBJ: 7.3.1

62. ANS: The amount of energy contained in the bonds of the reactants plus any energy absorbed by the reactants to break the bonds must equal the amount of energy contained in the bonds of the products plus any energy given off when the products are formed.
   DIF: L1   OBJ: 7.3.3

63. ANS: Lowering the temperature lowers the rate of reaction, so the reactants in the film and batteries are less likely to react before they are used.
   DIF: L2   OBJ: 7.4.1

64. ANS: Equilibrium exists because liquid water is freezing and ice is melting at the same rate. The equilibrium is physical because no new substances form.
   DIF: L1   OBJ: 7.5.1

65. ANS: There are more gas molecules on the reactant side. Increased pressure will thus cause the system to shift in the direction that decreases the pressure of the system (that is, produces fewer gas molecules) and the reaction will shift to form more product.
   DIF: L1   OBJ: 7.5.2

PROBLEM

66. ANS: $Cu + 4HNO_3 \rightarrow Cu(NO_3)_2 + 2NO_2 + 2H_2O$
   DIF: L2   OBJ: 7.1.2

67. ANS: $4Fe + 3O_2 \rightarrow 2Fe_2O_3$; 9 mol O_2 DIF: L2   OBJ: 7.1.4

68. ANS: $2Na + Cl_2 \rightarrow 2NaCl$; 149 g Cl_2 DIF: L2   OBJ: 7.1.4

ESSAY

69. ANS: Single-replacement reactions are redox reactions because one element in the compound is reduced, and the free element is oxidized. Combustion is a redox reaction because oxygen is always reduced, and another element is oxidized.
   DIF: L2   OBJ: 7.2.2

70. ANS: In a physical equilibrium, there is a difference in the form of the substance, but its chemical composition remains the same. In a chemical equilibrium, chemical changes occur, and the reactants are different substances than the products.
   DIF: L2   OBJ: 7.5.1

OTHER

71. ANS: On the left side, there are 1 carbon atom, 4 hydrogen atoms, and 2 oxygen atoms. On the right side, there are 1 carbon atom, 3 oxygen atoms, and 2 hydrogen atoms.
   DIF: L1   OBJ: 7.1.2

72. ANS: No; the total number of atoms can be the same without the number of each type of atoms on both sides being the same.
   DIF: L1   OBJ: 7.1.2

73. ANS: 4 hydrogen atoms   DIF: L1   OBJ: 7.1.2

74. ANS: Place a coefficient of 2 in front of water on the right side. There will then be 4 hydrogen atoms on both sides of the equation.
   DIF: L1   OBJ: 7.1.2

75. ANS: $CH_4 + 2O_2 \rightarrow CO_2 + H_2O$ DIF: L1   OBJ: 7.1.2

76. ANS: the reactants   DIF: L2   OBJ: 7.3.2

77. ANS: The cooked egg white has more chemical energy in its chemical bonds because energy was absorbed during the reaction.
DIF: L2   OBJ: 7.3.2

78. ANS: 46 kJ would be absorbed during the reaction.
DIF: L2   OBJ: 7.3.2

79. ANS: the amount of energy required to break the chemical bonds of the reactants
DIF: L2   OBJ: 7.3.2

80. ANS: The diagram on the left; rusting is an exothermic reaction because it releases energy. This diagram represents the energy changes in an exothermic reaction.
DIF: L2   OBJ: 7.3.2

Name _____ Class _____ Date _____

Multiple Choice
Identify the letter of the choice that best completes the statement or answers the question.

_____   1.   In order for a solution to form,
   a.   one substance must dissolve in another.   c.   the solvent must be water.
   b.   a solid must dissolve in a liquid.   d.   a gas must dissolve in a liquid.

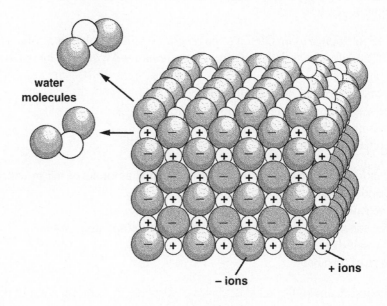

water
molecules

+ ions

− ions

Figure 8-1

_____   2.   Study Figure 8-1. When the ionic compound KI is dissolved in water, the I^- ions are pulled into solution by the attraction between
   a.   the K^+ and I^- ions.
   b.   the K^+ ion and the negative end of a water molecule.
   c.   the I^- ion and the negative end of a water molecule.
   d.   the I^- ion and the positive end of a water molecule.

_____   3.   A salt is dissolved in water, which has a boiling point of 100°C. The boiling point of the solution will be
   a.   greater than 100°C.   c.   exactly equal to 100°C.
   b.   less than 100°C.   d.   exactly equal to 0°C.

_____   4.   The more particles a solute forms in solution, the greater is its effect on the freezing point of the solution. Which of the following will lower the freezing point the most if 1 mol of it is added to 1 L of water?
   a.   the molecular compound propanol, C_2H_5OH
   b.   the ionic compound NaCl
   c.   the ionic compound $MgCl_2$
   d.   the ionic compound $AlCl_3$

_____ 5. During the formation of a solution, energy is
    a. either released or absorbed.   c. released only.
    b. neither released nor absorbed.   d. absorbed only.

_____ 6. The amount of energy required to break the attractions among the solute particles and among the solvent particles is
    a. greater than the energy released as attractions form between solute and solvent particles.
    b. less than the energy released as attractions form between solute and solvent particles.
    c. equal to the energy released as attractions form between solute and solvent particles.
    d. equal to the heat of solution.

_____ 7. All materials that are considered to be insoluble will dissolve in a solvent to a very small extent. The rate of dissolving of a rock in a streambed would be increased by all of the following EXCEPT
    a. breaking the rock into smaller pieces.
    b. moving the rock to a faster-moving current.
    c. moving the rock to warmer water.
    d. reducing the exposure of the rock to the water.

_____ 8. A student dissolved equal amounts of salt in equal amounts of warm water, room-temperature water, and ice water. Which of the following is true?
    a. The salt dissolved most quickly in the warm water.
    b. The salt dissolved most quickly in the room-temperature water.
    c. The salt dissolved most quickly in the ice water.
    d. none of the above

_____ 9. The maximum amount of a solute that will dissolve in a certain amount of solvent at a given temperature is that solute's
    a. solubility.   c. degree of saturation.
    b. concentration.   d. rate of solution.

_____ 10. The solubility of carbon dioxide gas in water can be increased by
    a. increasing the temperature.   c. increasing the pressure.
    b. agitating the mixture.   d. using more solvent.

_____ 11. One way to determine the degree of saturation of a solid-liquid solution is to drop a crystal of the solute into the solution. If the crystal sits at the bottom of the container, the solution is
    a. saturated.   c. supersaturated.
    b. unsaturated.   d. concentrated.

_____ 12. A solution that contains more solute than it would normally hold at that temperature is said to be
    a. saturated.   c. supersaturated.
    b. unsaturated.   d. concentrated.

_____ 13. To calculate the molarity of a solution, you need to know the moles of solute and the
    a. volume of the solvent.   c. mass of the solution.
    b. volume of the solution.   d. volume of the solute.

_____ 14. A 25-g sample of sugar was dissolved in 50 g of water. The concentration of the solution is
   a. 50 percent by mass.   c. 0.5 M.
   b. 33 percent by mass.   d. 50 percent by volume.

_____ 15. Which of the following is NOT a property of an acid?
   a. tastes sour   c. changes the color of an indicator
   b. usually reacts with a metal   d. feels slippery

_____ 16. A girl tasted each of the following foods. Which of the following would NOT taste acidic to her?
   a. lime   c. orange
   b. tomato   d. celery

_____ 17. A base is defined as a compound that produces
   a. hydroxide ions in solution.   c. hydronium ions in solution.
   b. hydrogen ions in solution.   d. sodium ions in solution.

_____ 18. Which of the following is NOT a common property of bases?
   a. feels slippery   c. reacts with metals
   b. tastes bitter   d. changes colors of indicators

_____ 19. The products of the neutralization reaction between hydrochloric acid and magnesium hydroxide are
   a. $MgCl$ and H_2O.   c. HCl and $MgOH$.
   b. $MgCl_2$ and H_2O.   d. HCl and $Mg(OH)_2$.

_____ 20. The salt that is formed during the reaction between potassium hydroxide and hydrochloric acid is
   a. $NaCl$.   c. KCl.
   b. H_2O.   d. K_2Cl.

_____ 21. An acid can be defined as
   a. a proton acceptor.
   b. a proton donor.
   c. neither a proton donor nor a proton acceptor.
   d. both a proton donor and a proton acceptor.

_____ 22. Ammonia, NH_3, can be classified as a base because in a chemical reaction with an acid, ammonia will
   a. produce hydroxide ions in solution.   c. donate a proton and become NH_2^-.
   b. produce hydronium ions in solution.   d. accept a proton and become NH_4^+.

_____ 23. Tomatoes have a hydronium ion concentration of 1×10^{-4} M. What is the pH of a tomato?
   a. 4   c. 10
   b. −4   d. 1×10^{-4}

_____ 24. The hydroxide ion concentration in pure water at 25°C is NOT equal to
    a. the hydronium ion concentration.
    b. 1×10^{-7} M.
    c. the hydroxide concentration in a solution with a pH of 7.
    d. 1×10^7 M.

_____ 25. A compound has a pH of 1 in solution, where it has completely ionized. The compound is a
    a. strong base.   c. strong acid.
    b. weak base.   d. weak acid.

_____ 26. Calcium hydroxide forms very few hydroxide ions in solution, but it is still considered a strong base because
    a. calcium hydroxide is insoluble.
    b. all the calcium hydroxide in solution ionizes.
    c. all the calcium hydroxide in solution dissociates.
    d. very little of the calcium hydroxide in solution ionizes.

_____ 27. Which of the following would NOT form a buffer solution?
    a. $NH_3 + NH_4Cl$ c. $HCl + NaCl$
    b. $HC_2H_3O_2 + NaC_2H_3O_2$ d. $H_2CO_3 + NaHCO_3$

_____ 28. A small amount of acid is added to a buffer solution. The pH of the solution will
    a. increase.   c. stay about the same.
    b. decrease.   d. become neutral.

_____ 29. A substance that ionizes or dissociates into ions when placed in water is always a(an)
    a. conductor.   c. strong acid.
    b. electrolyte.   d. strong base.

_____ 30. Which of the following are examples of strong electrolytes?
    a. strong and weak bases   c. weak acids and weak bases
    b. strong acids and strong bases   d. pure water and buffers

Completion

Complete each sentence or statement.

31. When sugar dissolves in water, water is the _____ and sugar is the _____.

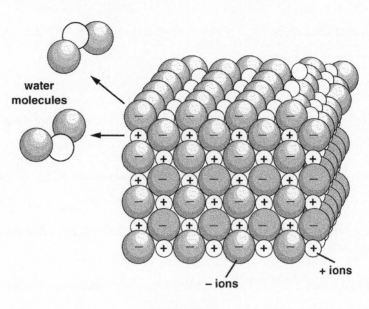

Figure 8-1

32. Study Figure 8-1. When KBr dissolves in water, the K^+ and Br^- ions are pulled into solution in a process known as _____.

33. A substance dissolves in water by breaking up into smaller pieces. These pieces of the same substance spread throughout the water. This process is known as _____.

34. The physical properties of a solution that differ from those of its solute and solvent include freezing point, boiling point, and _____.

35. Antifreeze is added to a radiator because it _____ the boiling point and _____ the freezing point of the solution contained in the radiator.

36. A food packet taken on a camping trip has a warming packet. This packet contains water and a solute that releases heat when it is dissolved. The dissolving process for this solute and solvent can be described as _____.

37. The rate that a solid solute dissolves in a liquid solvent depends on the frequency and energy of the _____ between the particles of the solute and solvent.

38. Stirring increases the rate of solution of a solid in a liquid because solute particles in solution are moved _____ the surface of the solute.

39. Table salt is _____ soluble in cold water than it is in hot water.

40. The statement "203.9 g of table sugar will form a saturated solution in 100 g of water" is not complete because _____ is not mentioned.

41. If a saturated solution of sugar water is heated, the solution will become
    _____.

42. An acid produces _____ when it is dissolved in water.

43. Most acids form ions in solution by _____, and most bases form ions in
    solution by _____.

44. The products of the reaction between potassium hydroxide, KOH, and nitric acid, HNO_3, are
    _____ and _____.

45. When a substance donates a proton during a chemical reaction, that substance can be
    classified as a(an) _____.

46. The pH of a solution is 11. The concentration of hydronium ions in the solution is
    _____.

47. The pH of a solution describes the concentration of _____ in solution.

48. Acids that contain carbon are weak acids, which means that they _____
    only to a small extent in solution.

49. Many foods are acidic. These foods do not hurt you when you eat them because they contain
    _____ acids.

50. Acetic acid is considered a weak _____ because it only partially ionizes.

Short Answer

51. If a liquid dissolves in a gas, in what state will the solution be? Explain your answer.

52. Both ionization and dissociation produce ions of the solute in solution. How do the two
    processes differ?

53. Which will freeze at a higher temperature—a freshwater marsh or a saltwater marsh? Explain
    your answer.

54. Compare and contrast an exothermic chemical reaction and an exothermic solution formation
    by dissociation.

55. A solid solute is added to a liquid solvent. The solution is stirred, but it is also cooled. Can
    you predict whether the solution process will speed up or not? Explain your answer.

56. What is the difference between a saturated solution and an unsaturated solution?

57. If you are reporting the concentration of a solution formed by dissolving a solid in a liquid, would you most likely express the concentration in percent by mass or percent by volume? Explain your answer.

58. You place a drop of a solution on red litmus paper, and no color change occurs. Can you conclude that the solution is neutral because no color change occurred? Explain your answer.

59. A certain material feels slippery. Is the material more likely to be an acid or a base? Explain your answer.

60. What are the products of a neutralization reaction?

61. Explain how water can act as either a proton donor or a proton acceptor, depending on the other reactant. Use examples.

62. If you are told that a material is a base, what does that tell about the pH of the material?

63. Carbonic acid ionizes only partially in solution. What type of acid is acetic acid?

64. What is a buffer solution?

65. What type of electrolyte is a weak acid?

Problem

66. A sample of 54.7 g of HCl gas is dissolved to make 1 L of solution. What is the molarity of the solution?

67. Rubbing alcohol is often a 70 percent solution by volume of alcohol and water. If a bottle of rubbing alcohol contains 0.50 L, what volume of alcohol does it contain?

68. The buffer system in the blood contains HCO_3^- ions and H_2CO_3. Write a balanced chemical equation that shows what happens when a small amount of acid is added to blood and another equation that shows what happens when a small amount of base is added.

Essay
On a separate sheet of paper, write an answer to each of the following questions.

69. Compare and contrast the factors that affect rate of solution and those that affect solubility.

70. Describe how you would prepare 2.00 L of a 1.20-M solution of potassium chloride, KCl, in water.

Other

USING SCIENCE SKILLS

Substance	Solubility (g/100 g H$_2$O, 20˚C)	Substance	Solubility (g/100 g H$_2$O, 20˚C)
Barium hydroxide	3.89	Potassium chloride	34.2
Barium nitrate	9.02	Sodium chloride	35.9
Calcium hydroxide	0.173	Sucrose (table sugar)	203.9

Figure 8-2

71. **Classifying** A 71.8-g sample of NaCl was added to 200.0 g of water at 20°C. Is the solution saturated, unsaturated, or supersaturated? Use Figure 8-2 to answer this question.

72. **Calculating** Potassium chloride was added to 40 g of water at 20°C until the solution was saturated. How much potassium chloride was used? Use Figure 8-2 to answer this question.

73. **Applying Concepts** A boy wanted to make candy from crystalized sugar. He dissolved 300.0 g of sucrose in 75 g of water at 100°C. To the nearest gram, how much sugar crystalized out of the saturated solution when it cooled to 20°C? Use Figure 8-2 to answer this question.

74. **Calculating** A sample of calcium hydroxide is placed into a jar containing water. The mass of the calcium hydroxide sample is 1.34 g. Assume the water is at 20°C and that the resulting calcium hydroxide solution is saturated. What mass of water was present in the jar? Use Figure 8-2 to answer this question.

75. **Using Tables and Graphs** A student was given a sample of either barium hydroxide or barium nitrate. How could she use the solubility information from Figure 8-2 to determine which compound she was given?

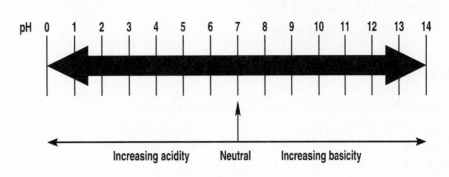

Figure 8-3

76. **Interpreting Graphics** Detergent has a pH of about 10. Is detergent acidic or basic? Use Figure 8-3 to answer this question.

77. **Drawing Conclusions** Oven cleaner has a pH of 14, and household ammonia has a pH of about 11.2. What generalization might you make about whether most cleaners contain acids or bases? Use Figure 8-3 to answer this question.

78. **Applying Concepts** Unpolluted rain has a pH of about 6. Is this rain acidic, basic, or neutral? Why is the term *acid rain* used to refer to rain that has been polluted with oxides of nitrogen and sulfur? This rain frequently has a pH between 4 and 5 and has been found to have a pH as low as 1.8. Use Figure 8-3 to answer these questions.

79. **Problem Solving** Stomach acid has a pH of about 2. What conclusion can you reach about the pH of an antacid solution that is used to neutralize excess stomach acid? Use Figure 8-3 to answer this question.

80. **Inferring** Sea water has a pH of about 8, and pure water has a pH of 7. Would sea water change the color of red litmus paper? Explain your answer. Use Figure 8-3 to answer this question.

Chapter 8   Solutions, Acids, and Bases
Answer Section

MULTIPLE CHOICE

1.	ANS:	A	DIF:	L1	OBJ:	8.1.1
2.	ANS:	D	DIF:	L2	OBJ:	8.1.1
3.	ANS:	A	DIF:	L1	OBJ:	8.1.2
4.	ANS:	D	DIF:	L2	OBJ:	8.1.2
5.	ANS:	A	DIF:	L1	OBJ:	8.1.3
6.	ANS:	A	DIF:	L2	OBJ:	8.1.3
7.	ANS:	D	DIF:	L2	OBJ:	8.1.4
8.	ANS:	A	DIF:	L1	OBJ:	8.1.4
9.	ANS:	A	DIF:	L1	OBJ:	8.2.1
10.	ANS:	C	DIF:	L2	OBJ:	8.2.1
11.	ANS:	A	DIF:	L2	OBJ:	8.2.2
12.	ANS:	C	DIF:	L1	OBJ:	8.2.2
13.	ANS:	B	DIF:	L1	OBJ:	8.2.3
14.	ANS:	B	DIF:	L2	OBJ:	8.2.3
15.	ANS:	D	DIF:	L1	OBJ:	8.3.1
16.	ANS:	D	DIF:	L2	OBJ:	8.3.1
17.	ANS:	A	DIF:	L1	OBJ:	8.3.2
18.	ANS:	C	DIF:	L2	OBJ:	8.3.2
19.	ANS:	B	DIF:	L2	OBJ:	8.3.3
20.	ANS:	C	DIF:	L1	OBJ:	8.3.3
21.	ANS:	B	DIF:	L1	OBJ:	8.3.4
22.	ANS:	D	DIF:	L2	OBJ:	8.3.4
23.	ANS:	A	DIF:	L2	OBJ:	8.4.1
24.	ANS:	D	DIF:	L2	OBJ:	8.4.1
25.	ANS:	C	DIF:	L2	OBJ:	8.4.2
26.	ANS:	C	DIF:	L2	OBJ:	8.4.2
27.	ANS:	C	DIF:	L2	OBJ:	8.4.3
28.	ANS:	C	DIF:	L1	OBJ:	8.4.3
29.	ANS:	B	DIF:	L1	OBJ:	8.4.4
30.	ANS:	B	DIF:	L2	OBJ:	8.4.4

COMPLETION

31.	ANS:	solvent, solute	DIF:	L1	OBJ:	8.1.1
32.	ANS:	dissociation	DIF:	L1	OBJ:	8.1.1
33.	ANS:	dispersion	DIF:	L2	OBJ:	8.1.1
34.	ANS:	conductivity	DIF:	L1	OBJ:	8.1.2

35. ANS:
    raises, lowers
    increases, decreases
    DIF: L2   OBJ: 8.1.2
36. ANS: exothermic   DIF: L1   OBJ: 8.1.3
37. ANS: collisions   DIF: L1   OBJ: 8.1.4
38. ANS: away from   DIF: L2   OBJ: 8.1.4
39. ANS: less   DIF: L1   OBJ: 8.2.1
40. ANS: temperature   DIF: L2   OBJ: 8.2.2
41. ANS: unsaturated   DIF: L1   OBJ: 8.2.2
42. ANS: hydronium ions   DIF: L1   OBJ: 8.3.1
43. ANS: ionizing, dissociating DIF: L2   OBJ: 8.3.2
44. ANS:
    potassium nitrate, water
    KNO_3, H_2O
    DIF: L2   OBJ: 8.3.3
45. ANS: acid   DIF: L1   OBJ: 8.3.4
46. ANS: 1×10^{-11} M   DIF: L2   OBJ: 8.4.1
47. ANS:
    hydronium ions
    H_3O^+
    DIF: L2   OBJ: 8.4.1
48. ANS:
    ionize
    form ions
    DIF: L1   OBJ: 8.4.2
49. ANS: weak   DIF: L2   OBJ: 8.4.2
50. ANS: electrolyte   DIF: L2   OBJ: 8.4.4

SHORT ANSWER

51. ANS: A gas; the state of the solvent determines the state of the solution.
    DIF: L1   OBJ: 8.1.1
52. ANS: Dissociation is a physical change involving solutes that are ionic compounds.
    Ionization is a chemical change involving molecular compounds.
    DIF: L2   OBJ: 8.1.1
53. ANS: A freshwater marsh; in a saltwater marsh, the dissolved salt lowers the freezing point
    of the water.
    DIF: L1   OBJ: 8.1.2
54. ANS: In an exothermic chemical reaction, chemical changes occur, and the reactants and the
    products are not the same substances. In an exothermic solution formation by dissociation, the
    solute undergoes a physical change and does not change identity. Energy is released in both
    processes.
    DIF: L2   OBJ: 8.1.3
55. ANS: No; stirring favors an increased rate, and cooling favors a slower rate.
    DIF: L2   OBJ: 8.1.4

56. ANS: A saturated solution contains all the solute it can hold at that temperature. More solute will dissolve at that temperature in an unsaturated solution.
DIF: L1   OBJ: 8.2.2

57. ANS: Percent by mass; it is more convenient to measure the mass of a solid solute than it is to measure its volume.
DIF: L1   OBJ: 8.2.3

58. ANS: No; both a neutral and an acidic solution would result in the litmus paper remaining red.
DIF: L2   OBJ: 8.3.1

59. ANS: One property of a base is that it feels slippery, so the material is more likely to be a base.
DIF: L1   OBJ: 8.3.2

60. ANS: a salt and water   DIF: L1   OBJ: 8.3.3

61. ANS: Water can accept a proton to become a hydronium ion or donate a proton to become a hydroxide ion. Examples: $HCl + H_2O \rightarrow Cl^- + H_3O^+$; $NH_3 + H_2O \rightarrow NH_4^+ + OH^-$
DIF: L2   OBJ: 8.3.4

62. ANS: The pH of a base is greater than 7.   DIF: L1   OBJ: 8.4.1

63. ANS: a weak acid   DIF: L1   OBJ: 8.4.2

64. ANS: a solution that resists change in its pH when small amounts of acid or base are added to it
DIF: L1   OBJ: 8.4.3

65. ANS: a weak electrolyte   DIF: L1   OBJ: 8.4.4

PROBLEM

66. ANS: 1.50 M   DIF: L2   OBJ: 8.2.3
67. ANS: 0.35 L   DIF: L2   OBJ: 8.2.3
68. ANS: $HCO_3^- + H^+ \rightarrow H_2CO_3$; $H_2CO_3 + OH^- \rightarrow HCO_3^- + H_2O$
DIF: L2   OBJ: 8.4.3

ESSAY

69. ANS: Both are affected by temperature. Rate of solution is also affected by surface area and stirring because both of these factors affect the number of collisions between solute and solvent particles. Solubility is also affected by polarity of the solute and solvent and, if a gas is involved, pressure. The number of collisions does not affect solubility unless a gas is involved.
DIF: L2   OBJ: 8.2.1

70. ANS: One liter of the solution would contain 1.20 mol KCl, so 2.00 L would contain 2.40 mol KCl. The molar mass of KCl is 74.55 g/mol, so you would use 179 g of KCl. Add the KCl to enough distilled water to dissolve it, then add additional water to make 2.00 L of solution.
DIF: L2   OBJ: 8.2.3

OTHER

71. ANS: saturated   DIF: L2   OBJ: 8.2.2

72. ANS: 13.7 g KCl   DIF: L2   OBJ: 8.2.2

73. ANS: 147 g sucrose   DIF: L2   OBJ: 8.2.2

74. ANS: 775 g of water   DIF: L2   OBJ: 8.2.2

75. ANS: She could measure a mass that is between the two solubilities, such as 5 g. If all of the compound dissolves in 100 g of water at 20°C, it is barium nitrate. If the compound forms a saturated solution with some undissolved solute, the compound is barium hydroxide.
    DIF: L2   OBJ: 8.2.2

76. ANS: basic   DIF: L1   OBJ: 8.4.1

77. ANS: Most cleaners contain bases.   DIF: L1   OBJ: 8.4.1

78. ANS: Slightly acidic; other acids also form in rain when oxides of nitrogen and sulfur dissolve in water.
    DIF: L1   OBJ: 8.4.1

79. ANS: The antacid solution must be basic, so its pH is greater than 7.
    DIF: L1   OBJ: 8.4.1

80. ANS: Yes; since sea water has a pH greater than 7, it is a base. Red litmus paper turns blue when it comes into contact with a base.
    DIF: L1   OBJ: 8.4.1

Name _____ Class _____ Date _____

Chapter 9 Carbon Chemistry

Multiple Choice
Identify the letter of the choice that best completes the statement or answers the question.

Two Forms of Carbon

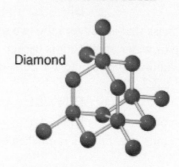

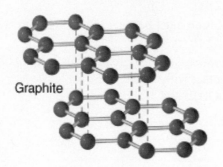

Figure 9-1

_____ 1. Figure 9-1 is a model of graphite. Which of the following statements is true about graphite?
  a.   Within each layer, the atoms form alternating single and double bonds.
  b.   Graphite is an example of a network solid.
  c.   Each carbon atom in graphite is bonded to four other carbon atoms.
  d.   The bonds between graphite layers are weaker than the bonds within graphite layers.

_____ 2. In buckminsterfullerene, carbon atoms are
  a.   bonded in a network solid.
  b.   bonded to three other carbon atoms in a widely spaced layer.
  c.   bonded in alternating hexagons and pentagons on the surface of a hollow sphere.
  d.   not bonded to each other.

_____ 3. Which of the following statements helps explain why there are millions of carbon compounds?
  a.   Carbon has four valence electrons.
  b.   Carbon atoms form bonds with other carbon atoms.
  c.   Carbon atoms can form single, double, and triple bonds.
  d.   all of the above

_____ 4. Which of the following statements is true?
   a. Organic compounds always contain carbon and hydrogen.
   b. Organic compounds contain only carbon and hydrogen.
   c. Organic compounds are produced only in organisms.
   d. About 10 percent of all known compounds are organic compounds.

_____ 5. The carbon atoms in a hydrocarbon CANNOT be arranged in
   a. straight chains.   c. rings.
   b. branched chains   d. a network solid.

_____ 6. Butane has the formula C_4H_{10}. Which of the following is the formula of cyclobutane?
   a. C_4H_4 c. C_4H_8
   b. C_4H_6 d. C_4H_{10}

_____ 7. Which of the following is another name for a saturated hydrocarbon?
   a. alkane   c. alkyne
   b. alkene   d. alkali

_____ 8. Which of the following is a saturated hydrocarbon?
   a. isopropane   c. pentyne
   b. butene   d. benzene

_____ 9. The prefix *dec-* means "ten." Which of the following best describes the structure of decene?
   a. It contains ten carbon atoms and only single bonds.
   b. It contains ten carbon atoms and at least one double bond.
   c. It contains ten carbon atoms and at least one triple bond.
   d. It contains a total of ten atoms.

_____ 10. Which of the following compounds is most reactive?
   a. ethane   c. ethyne
   b. ethene   d. They are all equally reactive.

_____ 11. Which of the following is NOT an example of a fossil fuel?
   a. coal   c. natural gas
   b. petroleum   d. methanol

_____ 12. Burning coal usually produces more soot than burning natural gas or petroleum products because coal
   a. formed in ancient swamps.
   b. is formed from the remains of marine organisms.
   c. contains aromatic hydrocarbons with high molar masses.
   d. contains a mixture of hydrocarbons.

_____ 13. What are the main products of the incomplete combustion of fossil fuels?
   a. water and carbon dioxide   c. water and carbon monoxide
   b. oxygen and hydrocarbons   d. carbon dioxide and hydrocarbons

_____ 14. One of the gases released after gasoline burns in a car's engine is carbon monoxide. Which of the following statements explains why there is carbon monoxide in this mixture of gases?
   a. Not enough oxygen is present when gasoline is burned in the engine.
   b. Gasoline contains carbon monoxide.
   c. The combustion of gasoline in the engine is complete.
   d. Carbon monoxide is produced during the complete combustion of a fossil fuel.

_____ 15. Which of the following is NOT a result of the complete combustion of fossil fuels?
   a. The amount of carbon dioxide in the atmosphere increases.
   b. The amount of carbon monoxide in the atmosphere increases.
   c. Nitrogen oxides are released into the atmosphere.
   d. Sulfur dioxide is released into the atmosphere.

_____ 16. Which of the following statements explains why inhaling carbon monoxide is dangerous?
   a. Carbon monoxide reacts with oxygen to produce carbon dioxide.
   b. Carbon monoxide keeps hemoglobin in the blood from carrying oxygen to cells.
   c. Carbon monoxide is a colorless, odorless gas.
   d. all of the above

_____ 17. In the compound CH_3F, the fluorine atom is a(an)
   a. functional group.   c. hydroxyl group.
   b. substituted hydrocarbon.   d. amino group.

_____ 18. The functional group in butanoic acid, which is an organic acid, is the
   a. amino group.   c. carboxyl group.
   b. hydroxyl group.   d. butane group.

_____ 19. Propanoic acid and ethyl alcohol can react. The products of this reaction are water and an
   a. organic base.   c. organic acid.
   b. ester.   d. amine.

_____ 20. The smell of rotten fish is caused by the presence of an
   a. amine.   c. ester.
   b. alcohol.   d. organic acid.

_____ 21. When monomers link together, they usually form
   a. a polymer.   c. ionic bonds.
   b. another monomer.   d. alkanes.

_____ 22. In a polymer, monomers are linked by
   a. ionic bonds.   c. metallic bonds.
   b. covalent bonds.   d. polyatomic ions.

_____ 23. Which of the following exists as both a natural and a synthetic polymer?
   a. cellulose   c. polyethylene
   b. nylon   d. rubber

_____ 24. Which of the following statements is true regarding natural rubber and synthetic rubber?
   a. Both types of rubber contain different monomers.
   b. Both types of rubber have an unlimited supply.
   c. Both types of rubber are made from petroleum.
   d. Both types of rubber have the same properties.

_____ 25. Natural polymers are produced
   a. only in plant cells.
   b. only in animal cells.
   c. in both plant and animal cells.
   d. in neither plant nor animal cells.

_____ 26. The monomers from which proteins are made are
   a. sugars.
   b. amino acids.
   c. nucleic acids.
   d. starches.

_____ 27. Plants convert energy from sunlight into chemical energy during
   a. cellular respiration.
   b. photosynthesis.
   c. vaporization.
   d. depolymerization.

_____ 28. Which of the following statements is true?
   a. Photosynthesis occurs only in plants, and cellular respiration occurs only in animals.
   b. Photosynthesis occurs only in animals, and cellular respiration occurs only in plants.
   c. Both photosynthesis and cellular respiration occur in plants.
   d. Both photosynthesis and cellular respiration occur in animals.

_____ 29. Proteins that act as catalysts for chemical reactions that occur in cells are
   a. vitamins.
   b. enzymes.
   c. carbohydrates.
   d. amino acids.

_____ 30. Which of the following statements is true about an enzyme?
   a. An enzyme allows a reaction to occur that would never occur without the enzyme.
   b. An enzyme allows a reaction to proceed at temperatures near 37°C.
   c. An enzyme cannot be produced within cells.
   d. An enzyme can control all the reactions in a cell.

Completion
Complete each sentence or statement.

31. Diamond is an example of a(an) _____ in which all the carbon atoms are linked by covalent bonds.

32. More than 90 percent of all known compounds are organic compounds, mainly because carbon contains _____ valence electrons and can form multiple carbon-to-carbon bonds.

33. Straight-chain hydrocarbons that contain one to three carbon atoms are likely to be _____ at room temperature.

Name _____ Class _____ Date _____

34. Compounds with the same molecular formula but different structural formulas are
    _____.

35. In a saturated hydrocarbon, all the bonds are _____ bonds.

36. Suppose a saturated and unsaturated hydrocarbon both contain the same number of carbon
    atoms. The saturated hydrocarbon contains more of the element _____ than
    the unsaturated hydrocarbon does.

37. $H_2C=CH_2$ is the formula for the hydrocarbon _____.

38. Both kerosene and gasoline are separated from petroleum during fractional distillation.
    Kerosene has a higher boiling point than gasoline does. Of kerosene and gasoline,
    _____ will be removed first from the petroleum vapors during fractional
    distillation.

39. The primary products of the complete combustion of fossil fuels are
    _____ and _____.

40. Some products of the combustion of fossil fuels cause the _____ of rain to
    increase.

41. The two functional groups in amino acids are the _____ group and the
    _____ group.

42. The manufacture of chlorofluorocarbons has been restricted because they deplete Earth's
    _____ layer.

43. The compound polypropylene is used to make many common products, such as beverage
    containers. The monomer used to make polypropylene is _____.

44. High-density polyethylene (HDPE) is much harder than low-density polyethylene (LDPE).
    You can conclude that there are more carbon atoms in a chain of
    _____.

45. Glucose is the monomer in the natural polymers _____ and
    _____.

46. The strands of DNA are held together in the double helix by
    _____ between hydrogen atoms on one strand and nitrogen or
    oxygen atoms on the other strand.

47. The energy that your body needs is released by the process of _____.

48. During photosynthesis, _____ energy is converted to
    _____ energy in the bonds of the products.

Name _____ Class _____ Date _____

49. Vitamins B and C are examples of vitamins that can dissolve in _____.

50. Some enzymes require a(an) _____, which is often a metal ion or a water-soluble _____, to function.

Short Answer

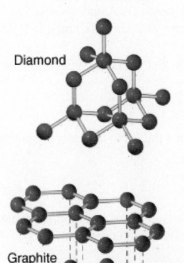

Figure 9-1

51. Based on the structure of graphite shown in Figure 9-1, explain why graphite is a good lubricant.

52. What elements do organic compounds always contain?

53. How can butane and isobutane both have the formula C_4H_{10}?

54. Compare the bonding in alkenes and alkynes.

55. Classify the compounds ethyne, heptane, and benzene.

56. What fossil fuel formed from the remains of buried plants in ancient swamps?

57. What is the functional group in the compound ethanol?

58. What two products are formed from the reaction of a halocarbon and a base?

59. What type of compound is often found in flowers and fruit flavorings?

60. What polymer contains at least 100 amino acid monomers?

61. What synthetic fiber was produced when researchers were trying to make synthetic silk?

62. One important difference between DNA and RNA is that RNA contains the base uracil instead of thymine. What base will pair with uracil in RNA—adenine, guanine, or cytosine?

63. Which polymer formed from glucose monomers cannot be digested by humans?

64. Why can't people survive without plants?

65. Why might it be harmful for a person to take large quantities of many vitamins each day?

Problem

66. Write a balanced chemical equation for the complete combustion of methane, CH_4, and one for the incomplete combustion of methane.

67. Write a balanced chemical equation for the formation of carbonic acid from carbon dioxide and water.

Essay
On a separate sheet of paper, write an answer to each of the following questions.

68. In terms of their structures, explain why diamond is so much harder than graphite.

69. Suppose a gas furnace is producing a large amount of carbon monoxide. What process is causing carbon monoxide to be produced, and how can the amount that is produced be reduced?

70. Describe the structure of the nucleotides in DNA, and explain how two strands join to form the double helix.

Other

USING SCIENCE SKILLS

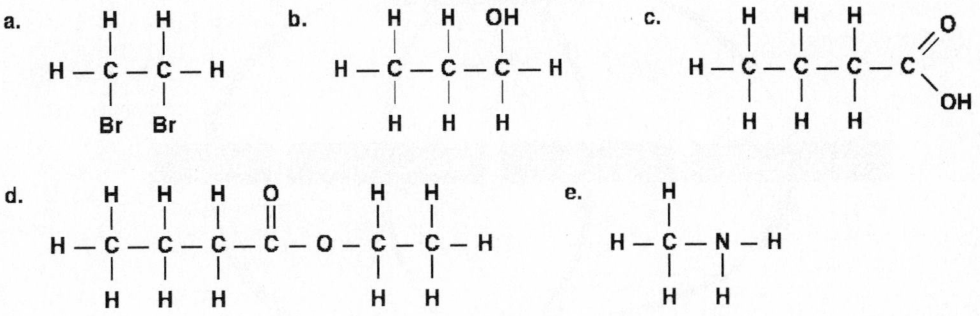

a.
$$H - \overset{\overset{\displaystyle H}{|}}{\underset{\underset{\displaystyle Br}{|}}{C}} - \overset{\overset{\displaystyle H}{|}}{\underset{\underset{\displaystyle Br}{|}}{C}} - H$$

b.
$$H - \overset{\overset{\displaystyle H}{|}}{\underset{\underset{\displaystyle H}{|}}{C}} - \overset{\overset{\displaystyle H}{|}}{\underset{\underset{\displaystyle H}{|}}{C}} - \overset{\overset{\displaystyle OH}{|}}{\underset{\underset{\displaystyle H}{|}}{C}} - H$$

c.
$$H - \overset{\overset{\displaystyle H}{|}}{\underset{\underset{\displaystyle H}{|}}{C}} - \overset{\overset{\displaystyle H}{|}}{\underset{\underset{\displaystyle H}{|}}{C}} - \overset{\overset{\displaystyle H}{|}}{\underset{\underset{\displaystyle H}{|}}{C}} - C \overset{O}{\underset{OH}{}}$$

d.
$$H - \overset{\overset{\displaystyle H}{|}}{\underset{\underset{\displaystyle H}{|}}{C}} - \overset{\overset{\displaystyle H}{|}}{\underset{\underset{\displaystyle H}{|}}{C}} - \overset{\overset{\displaystyle H}{|}}{\underset{\underset{\displaystyle H}{|}}{C}} - \overset{\overset{\displaystyle O}{||}}{C} - O - \overset{\overset{\displaystyle H}{|}}{\underset{\underset{\displaystyle H}{|}}{C}} - \overset{\overset{\displaystyle H}{|}}{\underset{\underset{\displaystyle H}{|}}{C}} - H$$

e.
$$H - \overset{\overset{\displaystyle H}{|}}{\underset{\underset{\displaystyle H}{|}}{C}} - \overset{\overset{\displaystyle }{}}{\underset{\underset{\displaystyle H}{|}}{N}} - H$$

Figure 9-2

71. **Inferring** The ester ethyl butanoate provides the taste and smell to pineapple. Identify the structural formula in Figure 9-2 for ethyl butanoate.

72. **Interpreting Graphics** Amines are formed during the breakdown of proteins in animal cells. Identify the structural formula in Figure 9-2 for an amine, and name the functional group.

73. **Interpreting Graphics** Which of the structures in Figure 9-2 is the formula for propanol? What is the functional group in this compound?

74. **Applying Concepts** Which diagram in Figure 9-2 shows the structural formula of a halocarbon? Why is the prefix *halo-* used?

75. **Using Models** Butanoic acid is found in rancid butter. Which of the structural formulas in Figure 9-2 is butanoic acid? What is the functional group in an organic acid?

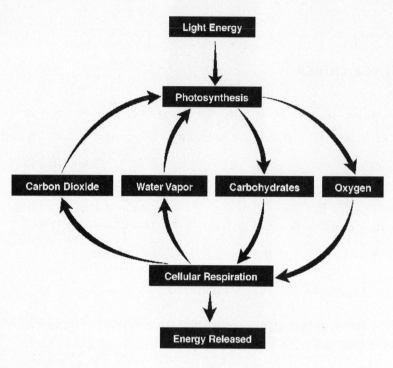

Figure 9-3

76. **Interpreting Graphics** Water is a product of which process described in Figure 9-3? In which process is water a reactant?

77. **Interpreting Graphics** Which process described in Figure 9-3 produces carbohydrates? In which process are carbohydrates reactants?

78. **Inferring** What role does energy play in the cycle of photosynthesis and cellular respiration? Use Figure 9-3 to answer this question.

79. **Predicting** Predict how reducing the number of plants grown worldwide might affect the composition of the atmosphere. Use Figure 9-3 to answer this question.

80. **Drawing Conclusions** What elements are cycled through the processes of photosynthesis and cellular respiration? Use Figure 9-3 to answer this question.

Chapter 9   Carbon Chemistry
Answer Section

MULTIPLE CHOICE

1.	ANS: D	DIF:	L1	OBJ:	9.1.1
2.	ANS: C	DIF:	L2	OBJ:	9.1.1
3.	ANS: D	DIF:	L1	OBJ:	9.1.2
4.	ANS: A	DIF:	L2	OBJ:	9.1.2
5.	ANS: D	DIF:	L1	OBJ:	9.1.3
6.	ANS: C	DIF:	L2	OBJ:	9.1.3
7.	ANS: A	DIF:	L1	OBJ:	9.1.4
8.	ANS: A	DIF:	L2	OBJ:	9.1.4
9.	ANS: B	DIF:	L2	OBJ:	9.1.5
10.	ANS: C	DIF:	L1	OBJ:	9.1.5
11.	ANS: D	DIF:	L1	OBJ:	9.1.6
12.	ANS: C	DIF:	L2	OBJ:	9.1.6
13.	ANS: C	DIF:	L1	OBJ:	9.1.7
14.	ANS: A	DIF:	L2	OBJ:	9.1.7
15.	ANS: B	DIF:	L1	OBJ:	9.1.8
16.	ANS: B	DIF:	L2	OBJ:	9.1.8
17.	ANS: A	DIF:	L1	OBJ:	9.2.1
18.	ANS: C	DIF:	L2	OBJ:	9.2.1
19.	ANS: B	DIF:	L2	OBJ:	9.2.2
20.	ANS: A	DIF:	L1	OBJ:	9.2.2
21.	ANS: A	DIF:	L1	OBJ:	9.3.1
22.	ANS: B	DIF:	L2	OBJ:	9.3.1
23.	ANS: D	DIF:	L1	OBJ:	9.3.2
24.	ANS: A	DIF:	L2	OBJ:	9.3.2
25.	ANS: C	DIF:	L1	OBJ:	9.3.3
26.	ANS: B	DIF:	L2	OBJ:	9.3.3
27.	ANS: B	DIF:	L1	OBJ:	9.4.1
28.	ANS: C	DIF:	L2	OBJ:	9.4.1
29.	ANS: B	DIF:	L2	OBJ:	9.4.2
30.	ANS: B	DIF:	L2	OBJ:	9.4.2

COMPLETION

31.	ANS: network solid	DIF:	L1	OBJ:	9.1.1
32.	ANS: four	DIF:	L2	OBJ:	9.1.2
33.	ANS: gases	DIF:	L2	OBJ:	9.1.3
34.	ANS: isomers	DIF:	L1	OBJ:	9.1.3
35.	ANS: single	DIF:	L1	OBJ:	9.1.4
36.	ANS: hydrogen	DIF:	L2	OBJ:	9.1.4

37.	ANS: ethene	DIF: L2	OBJ: 9.1.5
38.	ANS: kerosene	DIF: L2	OBJ: 9.1.6
39.	ANS: carbon dioxide, water	DIF: L1	OBJ: 9.1.7
40.	ANS: acidity	DIF: L1	OBJ: 9.1.8
41.	ANS: amino, carboxyl	DIF: L2	OBJ: 9.2.1
42.	ANS: ozone	DIF: L1	OBJ: 9.2.2

43. ANS:
propylene
propene
DIF: L2   OBJ: 9.3.1

44. ANS:
high-density polyethylene
HDPE
DIF: L2   OBJ: 9.3.2

45.	ANS: starch, cellulose	DIF: L1	OBJ: 9.3.3
46.	ANS: intermolecular attractions	DIF: L1	OBJ: 9.3.3
47.	ANS: cellular respiration	DIF: L1	OBJ: 9.4.1
48.	ANS: light, chemical	DIF: L2	OBJ: 9.4.1
49.	ANS: water	DIF: L1	OBJ: 9.4.2
50.	ANS: co-enzyme, vitamin	DIF: L2	OBJ: 9.4.2

SHORT ANSWER

51. ANS: Each carbon atom in graphite forms strong covalent bonds to three other atoms within a layer. However, the bonds between the graphite layers are weak, allowing the layers to slide easily past one another.
DIF: L2   OBJ: 9.1.1

52. ANS: carbon and hydrogen   DIF: L1   OBJ: 9.1.2

53. ANS: The compounds are isomers. Butane is a straight-chain alkane. Isobutane is a branched-chain alkane.
DIF: L2   OBJ: 9.1.3

54. ANS: Alkenes are hydrocarbons that contain at least one carbon-carbon double bond. Alkynes are hydrocarbons that contain at least one carbon-carbon triple bond.
DIF: L2   OBJ: 9.1.4

55. ANS: Ethyne is an alkyne, heptane is an alkane, and benzene is an aromatic hydrocarbon.
DIF: L1   OBJ: 9.1.5

56.	ANS: coal	DIF: L1	OBJ: 9.1.6
57.	ANS: the hydroxyl group, –OH	DIF: L1	OBJ: 9.2.1
58.	ANS: an alcohol and a salt	DIF: L2	OBJ: 9.2.2
59.	ANS: esters	DIF: L1	OBJ: 9.2.2
60.	ANS: a protein	DIF: L1	OBJ: 9.3.1
61.	ANS: nylon	DIF: L1	OBJ: 9.3.2
62.	ANS: adenine	DIF: L2	OBJ: 9.3.3
63.	ANS: cellulose	DIF: L1	OBJ: 9.3.3

64. ANS: People need the energy stored in plants and the oxygen produced during photosynthesis.
DIF: L1   OBJ: 9.4.1
65. ANS: Vitamins that are soluble in fat can build up in body tissues over time.
DIF: L1   OBJ: 9.4.2

PROBLEM

66. ANS:
Complete combustion: $CH_4 + 2O_2 \rightarrow CO_2 + 2H_2O$
Incomplete combustion: $2CH_4 + 3O_2 \rightarrow 2CO + 4H_2O$
DIF: L2   OBJ: 9.1.7
67. ANS: $CO_2 + H_2O \rightarrow H_2CO_3$ DIF: L1   OBJ: 9.1.8

ESSAY

68. ANS: Diamond is a network solid in which all the atoms are linked by covalent bonds. The structure is rigid, compact, and strong. In graphite, carbon atoms are arranged in widely spaced layers. Because the attractions between layers are weak, the layers can slide easily past one another. Therefore, graphite is soft and slippery.
DIF: L2   OBJ: 9.1.1
69. ANS: Carbon monoxide is produced during incomplete combustion of a fossil fuel. The amount of oxygen available for combustion needs to be increased.
DIF: L2   OBJ: 9.1.7
70. ANS: A nucleotide in DNA contains a phosphate group, a sugar (deoxyribose), and one of four organic bases. When the strands line up, pairs of bases (adenine and thymine, cytosine and guanine) are arranged like rungs on a ladder. Strong intermolecular attractions hold the strands together as they twist around one another.
DIF: L2   OBJ: 9.3.3

OTHER

71. ANS: D   DIF: L2   OBJ: 9.2.1
72. ANS: E; the amino group, $-NH_2$ DIF: L2   OBJ: 9.2.1
73. ANS: B; the hydroxyl group, $-OH$ DIF: L2   OBJ: 9.2.1
74. ANS: A; the functional group is a halogen.
DIF: L2   OBJ: 9.2.1
75. ANS: C; the carboxyl group, $-COOH$ DIF: L2   OBJ: 9.2.1
76. ANS: cellular respiration; photosynthesis
DIF: L1   OBJ: 9.4.1
77. ANS: photosynthesis; cellular respiration
DIF: L1   OBJ: 9.4.1

78. ANS: Light energy is absorbed during photosynthesis. This energy is stored as chemical energy in the covalent bonds of molecules. During cellular respiration, this energy stored in the products of photosynthesis is released as heat.

   DIF: L1   OBJ: 9.4.1

79. ANS: The amount of carbon dioxide removed from the atmosphere and the amount of oxygen released into the atmosphere would be reduced.

   DIF: L1   OBJ: 9.4.1

80. ANS: carbon, hydrogen, and oxygen   DIF: L1   OBJ: 9.4.1

Name _____ Class _____ Date _____

Chapter 10   Nuclear Chemistry

Multiple Choice
Identify the letter of the choice that best completes the statement or answers the question.

_____ 1. What is the process in which an unstable atomic nucleus emits charged particles or energy or both?
   a. radioactivity
   b. oxidation
   c. decomposition
   d. none of the above

_____ 2. Uranium-238 undergoes nuclear decay. Therefore, uranium-238 will
   a. remain stable.
   b. change into a different element altogether.
   c. emit neutral particles and no energy.
   d. none of the above

_____ 3. What type of nuclear decay produces energy instead of a particle?
   a. alpha decay
   b. beta decay
   c. gamma decay
   d. electron decay

_____ 4. When radium-226 decays to form radon-222, the radium nucleus emits a(an)
   a. alpha particle.
   b. beta particle.
   c. gamma ray.
   d. electron.

_____ 5. What type of radiation is emitted when polonium-212 forms lead-208?
   a. an alpha particle
   b. a beta particle
   c. gamma radiation
   d. all of the above

_____ 6. Carbon-14 forms nitrogen-14 by
   a. alpha decay.
   b. beta decay.
   c. gamma decay.
   d. none of the above

_____ 7. Which of the following statements is NOT true?
   a. You are exposed to nuclear radiation every day.
   b. Most of the nuclear radiation you are exposed to occurs naturally in the environment.
   c. Naturally occurring nuclear radiation is called background radiation.
   d. All natural radiation is at a level low enough to be safe.

_____ 8. Alpha-emitting substances, such as radon gas, can be a serious health hazard only if
   a. they are inhaled or eaten.
   b. their radiation strikes the skin.
   c. exposure to them is external.
   d. none of the above

_____ 9. Which of the following is NOT a step in the operation of a Geiger counter?
   a. Nuclear radiation ionizes gas in a tube.
   b. Ionized gas produces an electric current.
   c. Magnets cause the ions to conduct electricity.
   d. The electric current is detected and measured.

_____ 10. Many people work near a source of nuclear radiation. To detect the amount of exposure they have to radiation, they most likely will use a
   a. Geiger counter.   c. radon kit.
   b. film badge.   d. lead shield.

_____ 11. The half-life of tritium, or hydrogen-3, is 12.32 years. After about 37 years, how much of a sample of tritium will be left?
   a. $\dfrac{1}{8}$ c. $\dfrac{1}{3}$

   b. $\dfrac{1}{4}$ d. $\dfrac{1}{2}$

_____ 12. The half-life of a radioisotope is the amount of time it takes for
   a. half the sample to decay.
   b. all the sample to decay.
   c. the age of an artifact to be calculated.
   d. detectable radiation to be absorbed by a sample.

_____ 13. Which of the following statements is true?
   a. Chemical reaction rates vary with the conditions of the change, but nuclear decay rates do not.
   b. Nuclear decay rates vary with the conditions of the change, but chemical reaction rates do not.
   c. Both chemical reaction rates and nuclear decay rates vary with the conditions of the change.
   d. Neither chemical reaction rates nor nuclear decay rates vary with the conditions of the change.

_____ 14. In a water solution, HCl and NaOH react to form H_2O and NaCl. Radium-226 undergoes alpha decay to form radon-222. The temperature of both of these reactions is increased. Which of the following statements is true?
   a. The rate of the chemical reaction will increase, but the rate of the nuclear reaction remains the same.
   b. The rate of the nuclear reaction will increase, but the rate of the chemical reaction remains the same.
   c. The rates of both reactions will increase.
   d. The rates of both reactions will remain the same.

_____ 15. Which of the following is a radioisotope used to date rock formations?
   a. carbon-14   c. cobalt-60
   b. potassium-40   d. carbon-12

_____ 16. Carbon-14 has a half-life of 5730 years. If the age of an object older than 50,000 years cannot be determined by radiocarbon dating, then
   a. carbon-14 levels in a sample are undetectable after approximately ten half-lives.
   b. carbon-14 levels in a sample are undetectable after approximately nine half-lives.
   c. the half-life of carbon-14 is too long to accurately date the object.
   d. a radioisotope with a shorter half-life should be used to date the object.

____ 17. Transmutation involves
   a. nuclear change.
   b. chemical change.
   c. both a nuclear change and a chemical change.
   d. neither a nuclear nor chemical change.

____ 18. Which of the following is NOT an example of a transmutation?
   a. Uranium-238 emits an alpha particle and forms thorium-234.
   b. Uranium-238 is bombarded with a neutron to produce uranium-239.
   c. Potassium-38 emits a beta particle and forms argon-38.
   d. Plutonium-239 is bombarded with two neutrons to produce americium-241 and a beta particle.

____ 19. Which of the following is an example of a transuranium element?
   a. samarium, Sm   c. curium, Cm
   b. uranium, U   d. thorium, Th

____ 20. When curium-242 is bombarded with an alpha particle, two products are formed, one of which is a neutron. What is the other product?
   a. californium-246   c. californium-247
   b. californium-245   d. plutonium-239

____ 21. Which of the following particles is smaller than the rest?
   a. electron   c. neutron
   b. proton   d. quark

____ 22. The main purpose of a particle accelerator is to
   a. magnetize small particles.
   b. speed up small particles.
   c. slow down reaction products.
   d. reproduce reaction conditions found in nature.

____ 23. In general, the nucleus of a small atom is stable. Therefore, over very short distances, such as those in a small nucleus,
   a. the strong nuclear force is much greater than the electric force.
   b. the electric force is much greater than the strong nuclear force.
   c. the strong nuclear force equals the electric force.
   d. the strong nuclear force and the electric force are both attractive.

Name _____ Class _____ Date _____

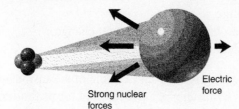

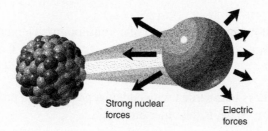

Figure 10-1

_____ 24. Study Figure 10-1. The strong nuclear force felt by a single proton in a large nucleus
   a.   is much greater than that felt by a single proton in a small nucleus.
   b.   is much less than that felt by a single proton in a small nucleus.
   c.   is about the same as that felt by a single proton in a small nucleus.
   d.   is about the same as the electric force felt by a single proton in a small nucleus.

_____ 25. During nuclear fission, great amounts of energy are produced from
   a.   very small amounts of mass.   c.   a series of chemical reactions.
   b.   tremendous amounts of mass.   d.   particle accelerators.

_____ 26. Suppose three neutrons are released when an atom in a sample of fissionable nuclei undergoes
   fission. Each of these neutrons has enough energy to cause another fission reaction in another
   nucleus of the material. If the reaction is not controlled, how many atoms will have undergone
   fission after a series of five additional nuclear fissions?
   a.   15   c.   243
   b.   18   d.   729

_____ 27. Which of the following is an advantage of using nuclear power plants to produce electricity?
   a.   Nuclear power plants do not pollute the air.
   b.   Nuclear power plants produce wastes that are easy to dispose.
   c.   Nuclear power plants produce more stable wastes compared to fossil fuel combustion.
   d.   all of the above

_____ 28. Which of the following is NOT a way that water is used in a nuclear power station?
   a. Water cools the steam in the turbine chamber.
   b. Water is changed to steam by heat released by the reactor core.
   c. Steam makes the turbines rotate.
   d. Running water cools the rotating turbines.

_____ 29. In what state must matter exist for fusion reactions to take place?
   a. solid   c. gas
   b. liquid   d. plasma

_____ 30. Which of the following is NOT an advantage of using a fusion reaction instead of a fission reaction to produce energy?
   a. Workers are not in as much danger from radiation.
   b. Hydrogen is used, and hydrogen is easily obtained from water.
   c. No harmful waste products are produced.
   d. Fusion reactors require less energy than fission reactors do.

Completion
Complete each sentence or statement.

31. Francium has 36 isotopes, but only francium-223 occurs in nature. Francium-223 spontaneously emits particles and energy, so francium-223 is a(an) _____ of francium.

32. An alpha particle is the same as a(an) _____ nucleus.

33. In the symbol $^4_2$He, the superscript *4* is the _____ for helium, and the subscript *2* is the _____ for helium.

34. You want to be shielded from all three types of nuclear radiation. If you find shielding that blocks _____ radiation, then it will most likely also block the other two types.

35. A less common type of radioactive particle emitted is the positron. If potassium-38 forms argon-38 by positron emission, the mass number of a positron is _____, and the charge is _____.

36. When a human body is exposed to external nuclear radiation, the amount of tissue damage depends on the _____ power of the radiation.

37. When nuclear radiation enters the tube of a Geiger counter, it _____ the atoms of the gas contained in the tube.

38. A sample of a radioisotope had a mass of 100.0 g. After exactly 24 days, 6.25 g of the sample remained. The half-life of the isotope is _____ days.

39. A rock containing a radioisotope is broken down into a powder, greatly increasing its surface area. At the same time, the temperature of the sample was lowered 25°C. The half-life of the radioisotope will _____.

40. In radiocarbon dating, the carbon-14 levels in the object being dated is compared to the carbon-14 levels in the _____.

41. In the first artificial transmutation, a nitrogen-14 atom reacted with an alpha particle to produce _____ and a proton.

42. Scientists can synthesize a transuranium element by the artificial _____ of a lighter element.

43. The particle that makes up protons and neutrons and is thought to be a basic unit of matter is a(an) _____.

44. One purpose of collision experiments is to study _____ structure.

45. In nuclear reactions, _____ is converted into energy.

46. Strong nuclear forces act on both _____ and _____; electric forces in the nucleus act only among _____.

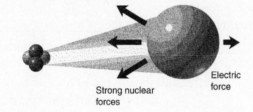

A Nuclear Forces Acting on a Proton of a Small Nucleus

Strong nuclear forces

Electric force

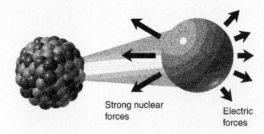

B Nuclear Forces Acting on a Proton of a Large Nucleus

Strong nuclear forces

Electric forces

Figure 10-1

47. Study Figure 10-1. As the size of the nucleus increases, the number of _____ forces acting on each proton remains about the same, but the number of _____ forces acting on each proton increases.

48. In a(an) _____, neutrons released during a fission reaction cause a series of other fission reactions.

49. The fission reaction within a nuclear reactor is kept under control by the use of _____ that absorb extra _____.

50. Although the fusion of hydrogen to produce helium is the most common fusion reaction occurring in the sun, several other fusion reactions occur. In one of these, two helium-4 nuclei fuse to form one unstable _____ nucleus.

Short Answer

51. How did the physicist Becquerel first observe the effects of nuclear decay?

52. How is an electron in a stable atom similar to a beta particle?

53. What particle will balance the following nuclear equation?
$$^{234}_{91}\text{Pa} \rightarrow \,^{234}_{92}\text{U} + ?$$

54. What is one common source of background radiation?

55. Radiation treatments are commonly used to treat cancerous tumors. Explain why the radiation for these treatments comes in many different beams from many different directions toward the body instead of just one beam aimed toward the tumor.

56. Describe the structure of a film badge that detects radiation.

57. A sample of uranium-238 is heated from room temperature to 55°C. How will increasing the temperature of the sample affect the half-life of the radioisotope?

58. In general terms, how do scientists perform artificial transmutations?

59. Americium-241 is used in smoke detectors. What two particles are used to bombard an atom of plutonium-239 to create an atom of americium-241 if a beta particle is also produced?
$$\frac{239}{94}Pu + 2? \rightarrow \frac{241}{95}Am + \frac{0}{-1}e$$

60. In terms of electrical attraction, why is it necessary to accelerate an alpha particle in order for it to effectively bombard a nucleus of a large atom?

61. In terms of forces, when does a nucleus become radioactive?

62. Use the equation $E = mc^2$ to explain why large amounts of energy are produced by very small amounts of mass during nuclear fission.

63. What happens during a meltdown in a nuclear reactor?

64. What radioisotope is used as the fuel for a nuclear reactor?

65. What two problems must be overcome before fusion can be used to produce energy?

Problem

66. Astatine-218 has a half-life of 1.6 s. Suppose you have a 1.2-g sample of astatine-218. How much of the sample remains unchanged after 6.4 seconds?

67. A sample of phosphorus-32 has a half-life of 14.28 days. If 25 g of this radioisotope remain unchanged after approximately 57 days, what was the mass of the original sample?

68. After 15 minutes, 30 g of a sample of polonium-218 remain unchanged. If the original sample had a mass of 960 g, what is the half-life of polonium-218?

Essay

On a separate sheet of paper, write an answer to each of the following questions.

69. Compare and contrast the processes of fission and fusion.

70. Explain the path followed by carbon-14 atoms from when they form in the atmosphere until they are found in compounds in the human body.

Other

USING SCIENCE SKILLS

Nuclear Radiation			
Radiation Type	**Symbol**	**Charge**	**Mass (amu)**
Alpha particle	α, ^4_2He	2+	4
Beta particle	β, $^0_{-1}\text{He}$	1−	$\dfrac{1}{1836}$
Gamma ray	γ	0	0

Figure 10-2

71. **Drawing Conclusions** A beta particle does have mass, so why is zero the mass number for a beta particle? Use Figure 10-2 to answer this question.

72. **Calculating** Study Figure 10-2. What type of nuclear radiation completes the following decay equation?

$$^{218}_{84}\text{Po} \rightarrow ^{214}_{82}\text{Pb} + \text{?}$$

73. **Calculating** Study Figure 10-2. What type of nuclear radiation completes the following decay equation?

$$^{210}_{83}\text{Bi} \rightarrow ^{210}_{84}\text{Po} + \text{?}$$

74. **Using Tables and Graphs** Why doesn't emission of gamma radiation change either the mass number or the atomic number of the nucleus? Use Figure 10-2 to answer this question.

75. **Drawing Conclusions** Study Figure 10-2. Explain how the mass and atomic numbers of an alpha particle can be used to determine the number of neutrons in the particle.

Half-lives and Radiation of Selected Radioisotopes		
Isotope	**Half-life**	**Nuclear Radiation Emitted**
Radon-222	3.82 days	α
Iodine-131	8.07 days	β
Thorium-234	24.1 days	β, γ
Carbon-14	5730 years	β
Uranium-235	7.04×10^8 years	α, γ

Figure 10-3

76. **Applying Concepts** What product isotope is formed by the decay of radon-222? Use Figure 10-3 to answer this question.

77. **Calculating** Assume you have a 100-g sample of iodine-131. What product isotope is formed by the decay of this radioisotope? How much iodine-131 will remain unchanged after 24.21 days?

78. **Calculating** Study Figure 10-3. How much nitrogen-14 will be produced from a 200-g sample of carbon-14 after 17,190 years?

79. **Applying Concepts** A rock sample contains one-fourth as much radium-226 as the relatively newly formed rock around it contains. How old is the rock sample? Use Figure 10-3 to answer this question.

80. **Using Tables and Graphs** What product isotope is produced by the decay of thorium-234? If an initial sample contains 48 g of thorium-234, how much of this product isotope will be present after 72.3 days?

Chapter 10   Nuclear Chemistry
Answer Section

MULTIPLE CHOICE

1.	ANS: A	DIF:	L1	OBJ:	10.1.1
2.	ANS: B	DIF:	L2	OBJ:	10.1.1
3.	ANS: C	DIF:	L1	OBJ:	10.1.2
4.	ANS: A	DIF:	L2	OBJ:	10.1.2
5.	ANS: A	DIF:	L1	OBJ:	10.1.3
6.	ANS: B	DIF:	L2	OBJ:	10.1.3
7.	ANS: D	DIF:	L1	OBJ:	10.1.4
8.	ANS: A	DIF:	L2	OBJ:	10.1.4
9.	ANS: C	DIF:	L2	OBJ:	10.1.5
10.	ANS: B	DIF:	L1	OBJ:	10.1.5
11.	ANS: A	DIF:	L2	OBJ:	10.2.1
12.	ANS: A	DIF:	L1	OBJ:	10.2.1
13.	ANS: A	DIF:	L1	OBJ:	10.2.2
14.	ANS: A	DIF:	L2	OBJ:	10.2.2
15.	ANS: B	DIF:	L1	OBJ:	10.2.3
16.	ANS: B	DIF:	L2	OBJ:	10.2.3
17.	ANS: A	DIF:	L1	OBJ:	10.3.1
18.	ANS: B	DIF:	L2	OBJ:	10.3.1
19.	ANS: C	DIF:	L1	OBJ:	10.3.2
20.	ANS: B	DIF:	L2	OBJ:	10.3.2
21.	ANS: D	DIF:	L1	OBJ:	10.3.3
22.	ANS: B	DIF:	L2	OBJ:	10.3.3
23.	ANS: A	DIF:	L2	OBJ:	10.4.1
24.	ANS: C	DIF:	L1	OBJ:	10.4.1
25.	ANS: A	DIF:	L1	OBJ:	10.4.2
26.	ANS: C	DIF:	L2	OBJ:	10.4.2
27.	ANS: A	DIF:	L1	OBJ:	10.4.3
28.	ANS: D	DIF:	L2	OBJ:	10.4.3
29.	ANS: D	DIF:	L1	OBJ:	10.4.4
30.	ANS: D	DIF:	L2	OBJ:	10.4.4

COMPLETION

31.	ANS: radioisotope	DIF:	L2	OBJ:	10.1.1
32.	ANS: helium	DIF:	L1	OBJ:	10.1.2
33.	ANS: mass number, atomic number	DIF:	L1	OBJ:	10.1.2
34.	ANS: gamma	DIF:	L2	OBJ:	10.1.2
35.	ANS: 0, +1	DIF:	L2	OBJ:	10.1.3
36.	ANS: penetrating	DIF:	L1	OBJ:	10.1.4

37.	ANS:	ionizes	DIF:	L2	OBJ:	10.1.5
38.	ANS:	6	DIF:	L1	OBJ:	10.2.1
39.	ANS:	remain the same	DIF:	L2	OBJ:	10.2.2
40.	ANS:	atmosphere	DIF:	L1	OBJ:	10.2.3
41.	ANS:	oxygen-17	DIF:	L2	OBJ:	10.3.1
42.	ANS:	transmutation	DIF:	L1	OBJ:	10.3.2
43.	ANS:	quark	DIF:	L1	OBJ:	10.3.3
44.	ANS:	atomic	DIF:	L1	OBJ:	10.3.3
45.	ANS:	mass	DIF:	L1	OBJ:	10.4.1
46.	ANS:	protons, neutrons, protons	DIF:	L2	OBJ:	10.4.1
47.	ANS:	strong nuclear, electric	DIF:	L2	OBJ:	10.4.1
48.	ANS:	chain reaction	DIF:	L1	OBJ:	10.4.2
49.	ANS:	control rods, neutrons	DIF:	L2	OBJ:	10.4.3
50.	ANS:	beryllium-8	DIF:	L2	OBJ:	10.4.4

SHORT ANSWER

51. ANS: Uranium salts wrapped in paper left a pattern on unexposed photographic film. He concluded that the salts emitted rays that exposed the film.
DIF: L1   OBJ: 10.1.1

52. ANS: Both particles are identical in mass and charge.
DIF: L2   OBJ: 10.1.2

53. ANS: a beta particle   DIF: L1   OBJ: 10.1.3

54. ANS: Accept any of the following: collisions between cosmic rays and particles in the atmosphere; radioisotopes in air, water, rocks, plants, and animals.
DIF: L1   OBJ: 10.1.4

55. ANS: Focusing the beam from many different directions keeps healthy tissue from being exposed to too much radiation. The only tissue that receives a large amount of radiation is the tumor.
DIF: L2   OBJ: 10.1.4

56. ANS: Photographic film is wrapped in paper so that the film is exposed by nuclear radiation only, not by light.
DIF: L1   OBJ: 10.1.5

57. ANS: Temperature change does not affect the speed of a nuclear reaction, so it does not affect the half-life.
DIF: L1   OBJ: 10.2.2

58. ANS: Scientists bombard atomic nuclei with high-energy particles such as protons, neutrons, or alpha particles.
DIF: L1   OBJ: 10.3.1

59. ANS: neutrons   DIF: L2   OBJ: 10.3.2

60. ANS: Both the nucleus and the alpha particle are positively charged. The alpha particles must be accelerated enough to overcome the repulsion of two positively charged particles.
DIF: L2   OBJ: 10.3.3

61. ANS: when the strong nuclear force can no longer overcome the repulsive electric forces among protons
DIF: L1   OBJ: 10.4.1

62. ANS: The amount of energy produced equals the amount of mass times the speed of light squared. Because the speed of light is such a large number, a very small amount of mass multiplied by this large number produces a large amount of energy.
    DIF: L2   OBJ: 10.4.2
63. ANS: The core of the reactor melts and radioactive material might be released.
    DIF: L1   OBJ: 10.4.3
64. ANS: uranium-235   DIF: L1   OBJ: 10.4.3
65. ANS: containment of the plasma and attainment of extremely high temperatures
    DIF: L1   OBJ: 10.4.4

PROBLEM

66. ANS: 0.075 g   DIF: L2   OBJ: 10.2.1
67. ANS: 400 g   DIF: L2   OBJ: 10.2.1
68. ANS: 3 min   DIF: L2   OBJ: 10.2.1

ESSAY

69. ANS: Possible answer: During fission, a larger nucleus is broken down into two smaller nuclei. During fusion, a larger nucleus is formed from smaller nuclei. Fission produces potentially harmful products, but fusion does not. Fission is currently used as a power source, but fusion requires too much energy and is too difficult to contain.
    DIF: L2   OBJ: 10.4.4
70. ANS: Carbon-14 is produced in the atmosphere when neutrons produced by cosmic rays collide with nitrogen-14 atoms. Carbon-14 reacts with oxygen in the atmosphere, forming carbon dioxide. Plants take in the carbon dioxide during photosynthesis. When humans eat plants, the carbon-14 atoms in the plants are incorporated into compounds in the human body.
    DIF: L2   OBJ: 10.2.3

OTHER

71. ANS: The mass of the beta particle is so small ($\frac{1}{1836}$ amu) that it is not significant compared to the mass of a proton or neutron (1 amu).
    DIF: L1   OBJ: 10.1.3
72. ANS: an alpha particle   DIF: L1   OBJ: 10.1.3
73. ANS: a beta particle   DIF: L1   OBJ: 10.1.3
74. ANS: Gamma radiation is not a particle. It is a ray of energy that has neither charge nor mass.
    DIF: L1   OBJ: 10.1.3
75. ANS: The atomic number tells the number of protons. The mass number tells the total number of protons and neutrons. The mass number (4) minus the atomic number (2) tells you that there are 2 neutrons in an alpha particle.
    DIF: L1   OBJ: 10.1.3
76. ANS: polonium-218   DIF: L2   OBJ: 10.2.3

77.	ANS: xenon-131; 12.5 g	DIF: L2	OBJ: 10.2.3
78.	ANS: 175 g	DIF: L2	OBJ: 10.2.3
79.	ANS: 3240 years old	DIF: L2	OBJ: 10.2.3
80.	ANS: protactinium-234; 42 g	DIF: L2	OBJ: 10.2.3

Name _____ Class _____ Date _____

Chapter 11 Motion

Multiple Choice
Identify the letter of the choice that best completes the statement or answers the question.

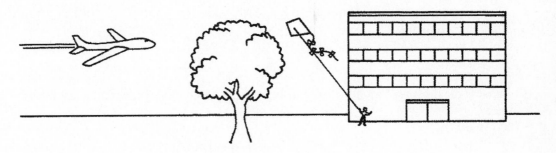

Figure 11-1

_____ 1. Examine Figure 11-1. If you were standing under the tree, which object would appear to be moving?
   a. the tree
   b. the airplane
   c. the boy
   d. the building

_____ 2. A passenger in the rear seat of a car moving at a steady speed is at rest relative to
   a. the side of the road.
   b. a pedestrian on the corner ahead.
   c. the front seat of the car.
   d. the wheels of the car.

_____ 3. Which distance can be most accurately measured with a ruler?
   a. the length of a river
   b. the width of a book
   c. the distance between two cities
   d. the size of an object under a microscope

_____ 4. One kilometer equals 1000 meters. What does the prefix *kilo-* mean?
   a. 1
   b. 10
   c. 100
   d. 1000

_____ 5. A person walks 1 mile every day for exercise, leaving her front porch at 9:00 A.M. and returning to her front porch at 9:25 A.M. What is the total displacement of her daily walk?
   a. 1 mile
   b. 0
   c. 25 minutes
   d. none of the above

_____ 6. A person drives north 3 blocks, then turns east and drives 3 blocks. The driver then turns south and drives 3 blocks. How could the driver have made the distance shorter while maintaining the same displacement?
   a. by driving east 3 blocks from the starting point
   b. by driving north 1 block and east 4 blocks
   c. by driving west 3 blocks from the starting point
   d. by driving back to the starting point by the same route

Name _____ Class _____ Date _____

____ 7. A ball is rolled uphill a distance of 3 meters before it slows, stops, and begins to roll back. The ball rolls downhill 6 meters before coming to rest against a tree. What is the magnitude of the ball's displacement?
a. 3 meters   c. 9 meters
b. 6 meters   d. 18 meters

____ 8. Displacement vectors of 1 km south, 3 km north, 6 km south, and 2 km north combine to a total displacement of
a. 12 km.   c. 4 km.
b. 6 km.   d. 2 km.

____ 9. What is the most appropriate SI unit to express the speed of a cyclist in the last leg of a 10-km race?
a. km/s   c. m/s
b. km/h   d. cm/h

____ 10. Speed is the ratio of the distance an object moves to
a. the amount of time needed to travel the distance.
b. the direction the object moves.
c. the displacement of the object.
d. the motion of the object.

____ 11. Instantaneous speed is measured
a. at the starting point.   c. at a particular instant.
b. when the object reaches its destination.   d. over the duration of the trip.

____ 12. A car traveled 88 km in 1 hour, 90 km in the next 2 hours, and then 76 km in 1 hour before reaching its destination. What was the car's average speed?
a. 254 km/h   c. 209 km/h
b. 63.5 km/h   d. 74.5 km/h

____ 13. The slope of a line on a distance-time graph is
a. distance.   c. speed.
b. time.   d. displacement.

____ 14. A horizontal line on a distance-time graph means the object is
a. moving at a constant speed.   c. slowing down.
b. moving faster.   d. at rest.

____ 15. What is the speed of a bobsled whose distance-time graph indicates that it traveled 100 m in 25 s?
a. 4 m/s   c. 0.25 mph
b. 250 m/s   d. 100 m/s

____ 16. A distance-time graph indicates that an object moves 100 m in 4 s and then remains at rest for 1 s. What is the average speed of the object?
a. 50 m/s   c. 20 m/s
b. 25 m/s   d. 100 m/s

Name _____ Class _____ Date _____

____ 17. A river current has a velocity of 5 km/h relative to the shore, and a boat moves in the same direction as the current at 5 km/h relative to the river. How can the velocity of the boat relative to the shore be calculated?
  a. by subtracting the river current vector from the boat's velocity vector
  b. by dividing the river current vector by the boat's velocity vector
  c. by multiplying the vectors
  d. by adding the vectors

____ 18. Vector addition is used when motion involves
  a. more than one direction.   c. more than one speed.
  b. more than one velocity.   d. all of the above

____ 19. The rate at which velocity changes is called
  a. speed.   c. acceleration.
  b. vectors.   d. motion.

____ 20. Which example identifies a change in motion that produces acceleration?
  a. a speed skater moving at a constant speed on a straight track
  b. a ball moving at a constant speed around a circular track
  c. a particle moving in a vacuum at constant velocity
  d. a vehicle moving down the street at a steady speed

____ 21. Objects in free fall near the surface of the Earth experience
  a. constant speed.   c. constant acceleration.
  b. constant velocity.   d. constant distance.

____ 22. Which example describes constant acceleration due ONLY to a change in direction?
  a. increasing speed while traveling around a curve
  b. an object at rest
  c. traveling around a circular track
  d. an object in free fall

____ 23. Suppose you increase your walking speed from 1 m/s to 3 m/s in a period of 2 s. What is your acceleration?
  a. 1 m/s^2 c. 4 m/s^2
  b. 2 m/s^2 d. 6 m/s^2

____ 24. An object moving at 30 m/s takes 5 s to come to a stop. What is the object's acceleration?
  a. 30 m/s^2 c. −6 m/s^2
  b. −30 m/s^2 d. 6 m/s^2

____ 25. The slope of a speed-time graph indicates
  a. direction.   c. velocity.
  b. acceleration.   d. speed.

____ 26. A speed-time graph shows that a car moves at 10 m/s for 10 s. The car's speed then steadily decreases until it comes to a stop at 30 s. Which of the following describes the slope of the speed-time graph from 10 s to 30 s?
  a. linear, horizontal   c. linear, sloping downward
  b. curved, upward   d. linear, sloping upward

____ 27. An object that is accelerating may be
    a. slowing down.   c. changing direction.
    b. gaining speed.   d. all of the above

____ 28. A train approaching a crossing changes speed from 25 m/s to 10 m/s in 240 s. How can the train's acceleration be described?
    a. The train's acceleration is positive.   c. The train will come to rest in 6 minutes.
    b. The train is not accelerating.   d. The train's acceleration is negative.

____ 29. What is instantaneous acceleration?
    a. how fast a speed is changing at a specific instant
    b. how fast a velocity is changing at a specific instant
    c. how fast a direction is changing at a specific instant
    d. all of the above

____ 30. Which of the following statements is true?
    a. An object that is accelerating is always changing direction.
    b. An object has an instantaneous acceleration, even if the acceleration vector is zero.
    c. An object at rest has an instantaneous acceleration of zero.
    d. Instantaneous acceleration is always changing.

Completion
Complete each sentence or statement.

31. The motion of an object looks different to observers in different

    _____.

32. The SI unit for measuring _____ is the meter.

33. The direction and length of a straight line from the starting point to the ending point of an object's motion is _____.

34. Displacement and velocity are examples of _____ because they have both magnitude and direction.

35. The sum of two or more vectors is called the _____.

36. Speed is measured in units of _____.

37. A car's speedometer measures _____.

38. $\bar{v} = \dfrac{d}{t}$ is the equation that defines _____.

39. A constant slope on a distance-time graph indicates _____ speed.

Name ______________________ Class ____________________ Date ________

40. The difference between speed and velocity is that velocity indicates the ____________________ of motion and speed does not.

41. A distance-time graph indicates an object moves 20 km in 2 h. The average speed of the object is ____________________ km/h.

42. Because its ____________________ is always changing, an object moving in a circular path experiences a constant change in velocity.

43. Two or more velocities add by ____________________.

44. A moving object does not ____________________ if its velocity remains constant.

45. Freely falling objects accelerate at 9.8 m/s^2 because the force of ____________________ acts on them.

46. The velocity of an object moving in a straight line changes at a constant rate when the object is experiencing constant ____________________.

47. The acceleration of a moving object is calculated by dividing the change in ____________________ by the time over which the change occurs.

48. Accelerated motion is represented by a(an) ____________________ line on a distance-time graph.

49. A car that increases its speed from 20 km/h to 100 km/h undergoes ____________________ acceleration.

50. ______________________________ is how fast a velocity is changing at a specific instant.

Short Answer

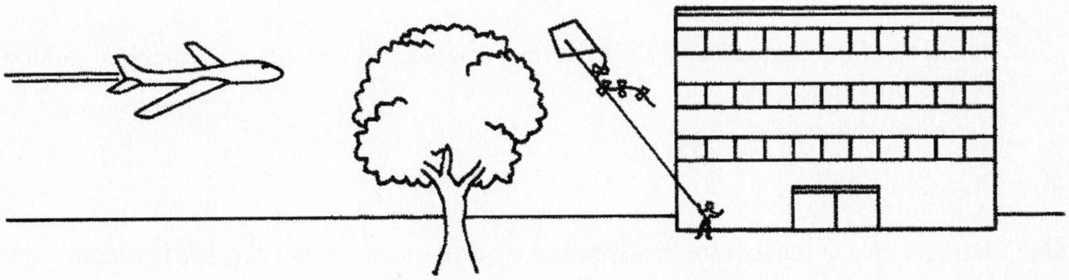

Figure 11-1

51. From which frame of reference in Figure 11-1 does the tree appear to be in motion?

52. What is the SI unit best suited for measuring the height of a building?

53. Distance is a measure of length. What information does displacement give in addition to distance?

54. A child rolls a ball 4 m across a room. The ball hits the wall and rolls halfway back toward the child. Using vector addition, calculate the ball's displacement.

55. Which is the most suitable SI unit for expressing the speed of a race car?

56. What are two types of speed that can be used to describe the motion of a car driving on the highway?

57. Bus A travels 300 m in 12 s. Bus B travels 200 m in 12 s. Both vehicles travel at constant speed. How do the distance-time graphs for these two speeds differ?

58. What is the significance of the slope in a distance-time graph?

59. Vector addition allows you to add what two quantities for any number of vectors?

60. What types of changes in motion cause acceleration?

61. How is motion described when the velocity of an object changes by the same amount each second?

62. $a = \dfrac{v_f - v_i}{t}$ is the equation for calculating the acceleration of an object. Write out the relationship shown in the equation, using words.

63. In the equation for acceleration, $a = \dfrac{v_f - v_i}{t}$, how can you describe acceleration if the numerator is negative?

64. What information does the slope of a speed-time graph provide?

65. The slope of the curve at a single point on a distance-time graph of accelerated motion gives what information?

Problem

66. During a race, a runner runs at a speed of 6 m/s. Four seconds later, she is running at a speed of 10 m/s. What is the runner's acceleration? Show your work.

67. If you ride your bike at an average speed of 2 km/h and need to travel a total distance of 20 km, how long will it take you to reach your destination? Show your work.

Name _____ Class _____ Date _____

Essay

On a separate sheet of paper, write an answer to each of the following questions.

68. Explain how velocity is different from speed.

69. Picture a ball traveling at a constant speed around the inside of a circular structure. Is the ball accelerating? Explain your answer.

70. A girl walks from her home to a friend's home 3 blocks north. She then walks east 2 blocks to the post office, 1 block north to the library, and 1 block east to the park. From the park, she walks 2 blocks west to the movie theater. After the movie, she walks 4 blocks south to the pet store. What is the girl's displacement from her starting point to the pet store? Where is the location of the pet store in relation to her home? Calculate the distance she walked in blocks.

Other

USING SCIENCE SKILLS

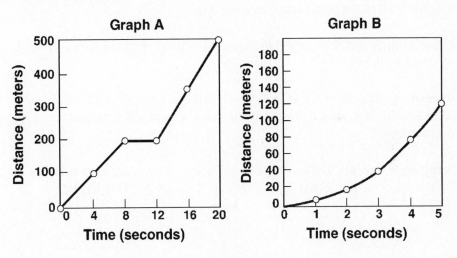

Figure 11-2

71. **Using Tables and Graphs** Which graph in Figure 11-2 shows periods of constant speed? Explain your answer.

72. **Interpreting Graphics** Look at Figure 11-2. Describe the motion of the object in Graph A.

73. **Using Models** Which graph in Figure 11-2 shows acceleration? How do you know?

74. **Calculating** Using Graph A in Figure 11-2, calculate the average speed of the object in motion from 12 s to 20 s. Explain your calculation.

75. **Comparing and Contrasting** Compare Graphs A and B in Figure 11-2. At a time of 2 seconds, which graph shows a greater velocity? How do you know?

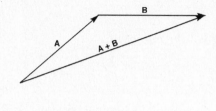

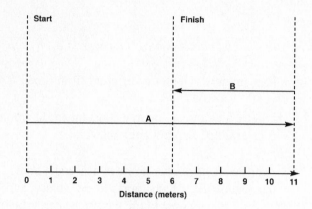

Figure 11-3A   **Figure 11-3B**

76. **Interpreting Graphics** Figure 11-3B illustrates the displacement of an object moving in a plane. Explain what information is provided by arrows A and B.

77. **Calculating** Using vector addition, calculate the distance traveled by the object and the displacement of the object represented by Figure 11-3B.

78. **Using Models** Arrows A and B in Figure 11-3A represent velocities. Describe the motion modeled by the vectors.

79. **Predicting** Suppose vector B in Figure 11-3B had a length of 12 m (instead of 5 m). What would be the distance the object moved? What would be the magnitude of the object's displacement?

80. **Applying Concepts** Vectors A and B in Figure 11-3A represent the path walked by a student from home to school. What does the resultant vector A + B represent?

Chapter 11   Motion
Answer Section

MULTIPLE CHOICE

1.	ANS: B	DIF:	L1	OBJ:	11.1.1
2.	ANS: C	DIF:	L2	OBJ:	11.1.1
3.	ANS: B	DIF:	L2	OBJ:	11.1.2
4.	ANS: D	DIF:	L1	OBJ:	11.1.2
5.	ANS: B	DIF:	L1	OBJ:	11.1.3
6.	ANS: A	DIF:	L2	OBJ:	11.1.3
7.	ANS: A	DIF:	L1	OBJ:	11.1.4
8.	ANS: D	DIF:	L2	OBJ:	11.1.4
9.	ANS: B	DIF:	L1	OBJ:	11.2.1
10.	ANS: A	DIF:	L2	OBJ:	11.2.1
11.	ANS: C	DIF:	L1	OBJ:	11.2.2
12.	ANS: B	DIF:	L2	OBJ:	11.2.2
13.	ANS: C	DIF:	L1	OBJ:	11.2.3
14.	ANS: D	DIF:	L2	OBJ:	11.2.3
15.	ANS: A	DIF:	L1	OBJ:	11.2.4
16.	ANS: C	DIF:	L2	OBJ:	11.2.4
17.	ANS: D	DIF:	L1	OBJ:	11.2.5
18.	ANS: D	DIF:	L2	OBJ:	11.2.5
19.	ANS: C	DIF:	L1	OBJ:	11.3.1
20.	ANS: B	DIF:	L2	OBJ:	11.3.1
21.	ANS: C	DIF:	L1	OBJ:	11.3.2
22.	ANS: C	DIF:	L2	OBJ:	11.3.2
23.	ANS: A	DIF:	L1	OBJ:	11.3.3
24.	ANS: C	DIF:	L2	OBJ:	11.3.3
25.	ANS: B	DIF:	L1	OBJ:	11.3.4
26.	ANS: C	DIF:	L2	OBJ:	11.3.4
27.	ANS: D	DIF:	L1	OBJ:	11.3.5
28.	ANS: D	DIF:	L2	OBJ:	11.3.5
29.	ANS: B	DIF:	L1	OBJ:	11.3.6
30.	ANS: C	DIF:	L2	OBJ:	11.3.6

COMPLETION

31. ANS: frames of reference   DIF: L1   OBJ: 11.1.1
32. ANS:
    distance
    length
    DIF: L1   OBJ: 11.1.2
33. ANS: displacement   DIF: L1   OBJ: 11.1.3

34. ANS: vectors   DIF: L2   OBJ: 11.1.3
35. ANS: resultant vector   DIF: L1   OBJ: 11.1.4
36. ANS: meters per second   DIF: L1   OBJ: 11.2.1
37. ANS: instantaneous speed   DIF: L1   OBJ: 11.2.2
38. ANS: average speed   DIF: L2   OBJ: 11.2.2
39. ANS: constant   DIF: L2   OBJ: 11.2.3
40. ANS: direction   DIF: L1   OBJ: 11.2.3
41. ANS: 10   DIF: L2   OBJ: 11.2.4
42. ANS: direction   DIF: L1   OBJ: 11.2.5
43. ANS: vector addition   DIF: L2   OBJ: 11.2.5
44. ANS: accelerate   DIF: L1   OBJ: 11.3.1
45. ANS: gravity   DIF: L1   OBJ: 11.3.2
46. ANS: acceleration   DIF: L2   OBJ: 11.3.2
47. ANS:
     speed
     velocity
     DIF: L1   OBJ: 11.3.3
48. ANS: curved   DIF: L2   OBJ: 11.3.4
49. ANS: positive   DIF: L2   OBJ: 11.3.5
50. ANS: Instantaneous acceleration   DIF: L2   OBJ: 11.3.6

SHORT ANSWER

51. ANS: the airplane   DIF: L2   OBJ: 11.1.1
52. ANS: the meter   DIF: L2   OBJ: 11.1.2
53. ANS: direction   DIF: L1   OBJ: 11.1.3
54. ANS: 4 m + (–2 m) = 2 m   DIF: L2   OBJ: 11.1.4
55. ANS: km/h   DIF: L2   OBJ: 11.2.1
56. ANS: average speed and instantaneous speed
     DIF: L1   OBJ: 11.2.2
57. ANS: The slope of the line representing Bus A is steeper than the slope of the line
     representing Bus B.
     DIF: L2   OBJ: 11.2.3
58. ANS: The slope is the change in distance divided by the change in time, which gives speed.
     DIF: L1   OBJ: 11.2.4
59. ANS: magnitude and direction   DIF: L1   OBJ: 11.2.5
60. ANS: changes in speed, direction, or both
     DIF: L2   OBJ: 11.3.1
61. ANS: constant acceleration   DIF: L1   OBJ: 11.3.2
62. ANS: Acceleration equals the final velocity minus the initial velocity divided by the time.
     DIF: L1   OBJ: 11.3.3
63. ANS: The acceleration is negative.   DIF: L1   OBJ: 11.3.5
64. ANS: acceleration   DIF: L1   OBJ: 11.3.4
65. ANS: instantaneous acceleration   DIF: L1   OBJ: 11.3.6

PROBLEM

66. ANS: $a = \dfrac{v_f - v_i}{t}$ $\dfrac{10\,m/s - 6\,m/s}{4s} = \dfrac{4\,m/s}{4s} = 1\,m/s^2$

 DIF: L2   OBJ: 11.3.3

67. ANS: $\overline{v} = \dfrac{d}{t}$ $t\overline{v} = d$ $t = d/\overline{v}$ $t = 20\,km/2\,km/h = 10$

 DIF: L2   OBJ: 11.2.2

ESSAY

68. ANS: Speed is equal to the distance traveled divided by the time required to cover the distance. Velocity describes both speed and the direction of motion.
 DIF: L2   OBJ: 11.2.5

69. ANS: Acceleration can be described as changes in speed, direction, or both. The ball is moving at a constant speed, but its direction is changing constantly. Because its direction is changing, the ball is experiencing constant acceleration.
 DIF: L2   OBJ: 11.3.2

70. ANS: The girl's displacement from home is 1 block east. The pet store is located 1 block east of her home. The girl walked a total distance of 13 blocks.
 DIF: L2   OBJ: 11.1.4

OTHER

71. ANS: Graph A shows periods of constant speed (0–8 s, 8–12 s, 12–20 s).
 DIF: L1   OBJ: 11.2.2

72. ANS: The object moves at constant speed for 8 seconds, is at rest for the next 4 seconds, and then moves at constant speed for the next 8 seconds.
 DIF: L1   OBJ: 11.3.4

73. ANS: Graph B shows acceleration. The upward slope of the line indicates that an increasing distance is covered each second.
 DIF: L1   OBJ: 11.3.5

74. ANS: The object moved a distance of 300 m in 8 s. The object's average speed is 37.5 m/s.
 $\overline{v} = 300\,m/8\,s = 37.5\,m/s$
 DIF: L2   OBJ: 11.2.4

75. ANS: Graph A; the slope is steeper.   DIF: L2   OBJ: 11.2.3

76. ANS: Arrows A and B are vectors with magnitude (distance) and direction.
 DIF: L2   OBJ: 11.1.3

77. ANS: The object moved a total distance of 11 m + 5 m = 16 m. The object's displacement is 11 m – 5 m = 6 m to the right.
 DIF: L2   OBJ: 11.1.4

78. ANS: Figure 11-3A models an object subject to two relative velocities. Vector A + B represents velocity of the object.
 DIF: L2   OBJ: 11.2.5

79. ANS: The distance would be 11 m + 12 m = 23 m. The displacement magnitude would be 11 m + (−12 m) = −1 m, or 1 m to the left.
   DIF: L2   OBJ: 11.1.4
80. ANS: the displacement   DIF: L2   OBJ: 11.2.5

Chapter 12   Forces and Motion

Multiple Choice
Identify the letter of the choice that best completes the statement or answers the question.

____ 1. The SI unit of force is the
    a. joule.
    b. kilogram.
    c. meter.
    d. newton.

____ 2. Which of the following relationships is correct?
    a. $1 N = 1 kg$
    b. $1 N = 1 kg \cdot m$
    c. $1 N = 1 kg \cdot m/s$
    d. $1 N = 1 kg \cdot m/s^2$

____ 3. When an unbalanced force acts on an object,
    a. the object's motion does not change.
    b. the object accelerates.
    c. the weight of the object decreases.
    d. the inertia of the object increases.

____ 4. When a pair of balanced forces acts on an object, the net force that results is
    a. greater in size than both forces combined.
    b. greater in size than one of the forces.
    c. equal in size to one of the forces.
    d. equal to zero.

____ 5. What kind of friction occurs as a fish swims through water?
    a. fluid
    b. rolling
    c. sliding
    d. static

____ 6. As you push a cereal box across a tabletop, the sliding friction acting on the cereal box
    a. acts in the direction of motion.
    b. equals the weight of the box.
    c. is usually greater than static friction.
    d. acts in the direction opposite of motion.

____ 7. The forces acting on a falling leaf are
    a. air resistance and fluid friction.
    b. gravity and air resistance.
    c. gravity and static friction.
    d. weight and rolling friction.

____ 8. An open parachute increases air resistance of a falling sky diver by
    a. decreasing the weight of the diver.
    b. increasing surface area.
    c. increasing the terminal velocity.
    d. reducing fluid friction.

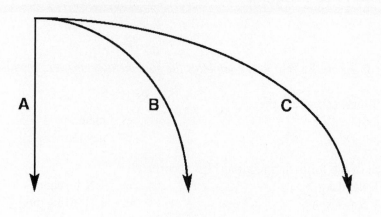

Figure 12-1

_____ 9. Figure 12-1 shows the motion of three balls. The curved paths followed by balls B and C are examples of
a. centripetal motion.
b. constant motion.
c. linear motion.
d. projectile motion.

_____ 10. Projectile motion is caused by
a. the downward force of gravity.
b. an initial forward velocity.
c. a final vertical velocity.
d. the downward force of gravity and an initial forward velocity.

_____ 11. The property of matter that resists changes in motion is called
a. friction.
b. gravity.
c. inertia.
d. weight.

_____ 12. An orange might roll off your cafeteria tray when you stop suddenly because of
a. the balanced forces acting on the orange.   c. the friction forces acting on the orange.
b. the centripetal force acting on the orange.   d. the orange's inertia.

_____ 13. According to Newton's second law of motion, the acceleration of an object equals the net force acting on the object divided by the object's
a. mass.
b. momentum.
c. velocity.
d. weight.

_____ 14. If a force of 10 N is applied to an object with a mass of 1 kg, the object will accelerate at
a. 0.1 m/s^2.
b. 9 m/s^2.
c. 10 m/s^2.
d. 11 m/s^2.

_____ 15. Your weight equals your
a. mass.
b. mass divided by the net force acting on you.
c. mass times the acceleration due to gravity.
d. mass times your speed.

Name _____ Class _____ Date _____

____ 16. The acceleration due to gravity on the surface of Mars is about one-third the acceleration due to gravity on Earth's surface. The weight of a space probe on the surface of Mars is about
  a. nine times greater than its weight on Earth's surface.
  b. three times greater than its weight on Earth's surface.
  c. one-third its weight on Earth's surface.
  d. the same as its weight on Earth's surface.

____ 17. Newton's third law of motion describes
  a. action and reaction forces.   c. centripetal forces.
  b. balanced forces.   d. net force.

____ 18. In which of the following are action and reaction forces involved?
  a. when a tennis racket strikes a tennis ball   c. when rowing a boat
  b. when stepping from a curb   d. all of the above

____ 19. The product of an object's mass and velocity is its
  a. centripetal force.   c. net force.
  b. momentum.   d. weight.

____ 20. What is conserved when two objects collide in a closed system?
  a. acceleration   c. speed
  b. momentum   d. velocity

____ 21. What is the momentum of a 50-kilogram ice skater gliding across the ice at a speed of 2 m/s?
  a. $25\dfrac{kg}{m/s}$ c. 50 kg
  b. 48 kg·m/s   d. 100 kg·m/s

____ 22. What force is responsible for the repulsion between two positively-charged particles?
  a. centripetal   c. gravitational
  b. electric   d. nuclear

____ 23. When opposite poles of two magnets are brought together, the poles
  a. attract each other.   c. cancel each other.
  b. repel each other.   d. cause a net force of zero.

____ 24. Which universal force acts only on the protons and neutrons in a nucleus?
  a. electric   c. magnetic
  b. gravitational   d. strong nuclear

____ 25. With which of the following is the weak nuclear force associated?
  a. lightning   c. ocean tides
  b. nuclear decay   d. static cling

____ 26. Which of the following universal forces is the most effective over long distances?
  a. electric   c. magnetic
  b. gravitational   d. strong nuclear

_____ 27. As an astronaut travels far away from Earth, her weight
   a. decreases because gravity decreases.
   b. decreases because her mass decreases.
   c. increases because gravity increases.
   d. remains the same because her mass remains the same.

_____ 28. The gravitational force between two objects increases as mass
   a. decreases or distance decreases.   c. increases or distance decreases.
   b. decreases or distance increases.   d. increases or distance increases.

_____ 29. The force that keeps an object moving in a circle is called
   a. centripetal force.   c. inertia.
   b. fluid friction.   d. momentum.

_____ 30. The centripetal force acting on a satellite in orbit
   a. acts as an unbalanced force on the satellite.
   b. changes the direction of the satellite.
   c. is a center-directed force.
   d. all of the above

Completion
Complete each sentence or statement.

31. A push or pull is an example of a(an) _____.

32. The type of force measured by a grocery store spring scale is _____.

33. The sum of all the forces acting on an object is called the _____.

34. If the forces acting on an object produce a net force of zero, the forces are called _____.

35. The force that opposes the motion of objects that touch as they move pass each other is called _____.

36. It usually takes more force to start an object sliding than it does to keep an object sliding because static friction is usually _____ than sliding friction.

37. The two forces acting on a falling object are gravity and _____.

38. When a falling object reaches terminal velocity, the net force acting on it is _____.

39. The drag force acting on an falling sky diver is also known as _____.

40. The path of motion of a thrown javelin is an example of _____ motion.

41. The tendency of an object to resist any change in its motion is called

_____.

42. During a head-on auto collision, _____ causes a passenger in the front seat to continue moving _____.

43. The acceleration of an object is equal to the net _____ acting on the object divided by the object's _____.

44. The force of gravity acting on an object is the object's _____.

45. If a golf ball and bowling ball are rolling at the same speed, the _____ ball has greater momentum.

46. When you push on a wall, the _____ pushes back on you.

47. In a closed system, the loss of momentum of one object _____ the gain in momentum of another object.

48. The observation that a charged object can attract or repel other charged objects led scientists to conclude that there are _____ types of charges.

49. The universal force that is most effective over the longest distances is

_____.

50. The centripetal force acting on the moon continuously changes the _____ of the moon's motion.

Short Answer

51. How can an arrow be used to represent the size and direction of a force?

52. What happens to the magnitude of the fluid friction acting on a submarine as the submarine's speed increases?

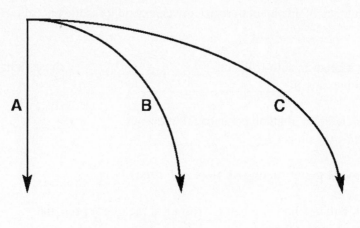

Figure 12-1

53. Figure 12-1 shows the paths followed by three balls. Each ball started moving at the same time. Ball A was dropped and balls B and C were thrown sideways. Compare the times for each ball to reach the ground.

54. What is the direction of the net force on a falling sky diver before she reaches terminal velocity? After she is falling at terminal velocity?

55. How can you double the acceleration of an object if you cannot alter the object's mass?

56. During a collision, a seat belt slows the speed of a crash-test dummy. What is the direction of the net force exerted by the seat belt compared to the direction of the dummy's motion?

57. How are the size and direction of action-reaction forces are related?

58. Why don't action-reaction forces cancel each other?

59. What law states that if no net force acts on a system, then the total momentum of the system does not change?

60. A billiard ball with a momentum of 20 kg·m/s strikes a second ball at rest and comes to a complete stop. What is the change in momentum of the second ball?

61. Compare the speed of a moving golf ball with the speed of a moving bowling ball if both balls have the same amount of momentum.

62. Electric force and magnetic force are the only forces that can both do what?

63. One end of a bar magnet attracts one end of a second bar magnet. What will happen if the second bar magnet is reversed?

64. Which of the universal forces acts only on protons and neutrons in the nucleus of an atom?

65. What is the primary cause of Earth's ocean tides?

Problem

66. A crane exerts a net force of 900 N upward on a 750-kilogram car as the crane starts to lift the car from the deck of a cargo ship. What is the acceleration of the car during this time? Show your work.

67. The mass of a newborn baby is 4.2 kilograms. What is the baby's weight? (The acceleration due to gravity at Earth's surface is 9.8 m/s^2.) Show your work.

68. A small 32-kilogram canoe broke free of its dock and is now floating downriver at a speed of 2.5 m/s. What is the canoe's momentum? Show your work.

69. A small engine causes a 0.20-kg model airplane to accelerate at a rate of 12 m/s^2. What is the net force on the model airplane? Show your work.

Essay
On a separate sheet of paper, write an answer to each of the following questions.

70. Why does a biker have to pedal harder to travel at a constant speed into the wind on a windy day compared to traveling on the same road at the same speed on a calm day?

Other

USING SCIENCE SKILLS

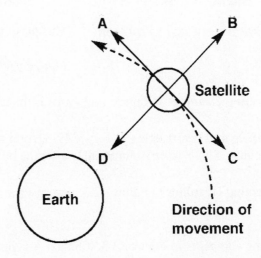

Figure 12-2

71. **Interpreting Graphics** In Figure 12-2, what is the direction of the centripetal force acting on the satellite at this location in its orbit?

72. **Predicting** What happens to the size of the centripetal force due to gravity acting on the satellite in Figure 12-2 if the satellite moves farther from Earth?

73. **Applying Concepts** The centripetal force acting on the satellite in Figure 12-2 is one of a pair of action-reaction forces. On what object is the other force in the pair acting?

74. **Interpreting Graphics** In Figure 12-2, what property of the satellite tends to keep it moving along through its orbit?

75. **Inferring** As shown in Figure 12-2, what is the direction of the fluid friction acting on the satellite as it moves through the outer layer of Earth's atmosphere?

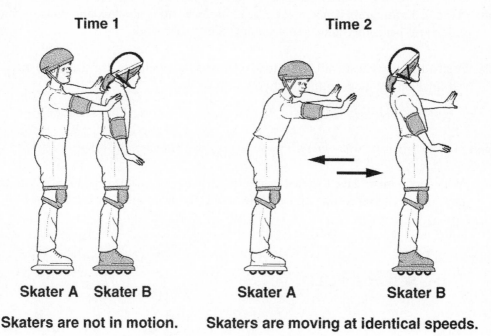

Figure 12-3

76. **Interpreting Graphics** In Figure 12-3, what is the momentum of each skater at Time 1?

77. **Comparing and Contrasting** In Figure 12-3, compare the size and direction of the momentums of both skaters immediately after the push shown at Time 2.

78. **Interpreting Graphics** In Figure 12-3, describe the motion of Skater B after Skater A pushes her.

79. **Applying Concepts** In Figure 12-3, if Skater A is pushing Skater B, why does Skater A move?

80. **Applying Concepts** Suppose that the skaters repeat the demonstration in Figure 12-3 again. This time Skater B is holding a 10-kilogram mass. If Skater A pushes exactly as he did the first time, will Skater A's motion be different this time? Explain your answer.

Chapter 12   Forces and Motion
Answer Section

MULTIPLE CHOICE

1.	ANS: D	DIF: L1	OBJ: 12.1.1
2.	ANS: D	DIF: L2	OBJ: 12.1.1
3.	ANS: B	DIF: L1	OBJ: 12.1.2
4.	ANS: D	DIF: L2	OBJ: 12.1.2
5.	ANS: A	DIF: L1	OBJ: 12.1.3
6.	ANS: D	DIF: L2	OBJ: 12.1.3
7.	ANS: B	DIF: L1	OBJ: 12.1.4
8.	ANS: B	DIF: L2	OBJ: 12.1.4
9.	ANS: D	DIF: L1	OBJ: 12.1.5
10.	ANS: D	DIF: L2	OBJ: 12.1.5
11.	ANS: C	DIF: L1	OBJ: 12.2.1
12.	ANS: D	DIF: L2	OBJ: 12.2.1
13.	ANS: A	DIF: L1	OBJ: 12.2.2
14.	ANS: C	DIF: L2	OBJ: 12.2.2
15.	ANS: C	DIF: L1	OBJ: 12.2.3
16.	ANS: C	DIF: L2	OBJ: 12.2.3
17.	ANS: A	DIF: L1	OBJ: 12.3.1
18.	ANS: D	DIF: L2	OBJ: 12.3.1
19.	ANS: B	DIF: L1	OBJ: 12.3.2
20.	ANS: B	DIF: L1	OBJ: 12.3.2
21.	ANS: D	DIF: L2	OBJ: 12.3.2
22.	ANS: B	DIF: L1	OBJ: 12.4.1
23.	ANS: A	DIF: L2	OBJ: 12.4.1
24.	ANS: D	DIF: L1	OBJ: 12.4.2
25.	ANS: B	DIF: L2	OBJ: 12.4.2
26.	ANS: B	DIF: L1	OBJ: 12.4.3
27.	ANS: A	DIF: L1	OBJ: 12.4.3
28.	ANS: C	DIF: L2	OBJ: 12.4.3
29.	ANS: A	DIF: L1	OBJ: 12.4.4
30.	ANS: D	DIF: L2	OBJ: 12.4.4

COMPLETION

31.	ANS: force	DIF: L1	OBJ: 12.1.1
32.	ANS: weight	DIF: L2	OBJ: 12.1.1
33.	ANS: net force	DIF: L1	OBJ: 12.1.2

34. ANS:
    balanced forces
    balanced
    DIF: L2   OBJ: 12.1.2
35. ANS: friction   DIF: L1   OBJ: 12.1.3
36. ANS:
    greater
    larger
    DIF: L2   OBJ: 12.1.3
37. ANS:
    air resistance
    drag
    DIF: L1   OBJ: 12.1.4
38. ANS: zero   DIF: L2   OBJ: 12.1.4
39. ANS: air resistance   DIF: L2   OBJ: 12.1.4
40. ANS: projectile   DIF: L1   OBJ: 12.1.5
41. ANS: inertia   DIF: L1   OBJ: 12.2.1
42. ANS: inertia, forward   DIF: L2   OBJ: 12.2.1
43. ANS: force, mass   DIF: L1   OBJ: 12.2.2
44. ANS: weight   DIF: L1   OBJ: 12.2.3
45. ANS: bowling   DIF: L1   OBJ: 12.3.1
46. ANS: wall   DIF: L2   OBJ: 12.3.1
47. ANS: equals   DIF: L1   OBJ: 12.3.2
48. ANS: two   DIF: L2   OBJ: 12.4.1
49. ANS: gravity   DIF: L2   OBJ: 12.4.3
50. ANS: direction   DIF: L2   OBJ: 12.4.4

SHORT ANSWER

51. ANS: The length of the arrow represents the size of the force, and the direction of the arrow
    represents the direction of the force.
    DIF: L2   OBJ: 12.1.1
52. ANS: It increases.   DIF: L1   OBJ: 12.1.3
53. ANS: Each ball will reach the ground in the same amount of time.
    DIF: L2   OBJ: 12.1.5
54. ANS: Down; there is no net force on the sky diver.
    DIF: L1   OBJ: 12.2.2
55. ANS: Double the net force acting on the object.
    DIF: L1   OBJ: 12.2.2
56. ANS: The direction of the net force is opposite the direction of the dummy's motion.
    DIF: L2   OBJ: 12.2.2
57. ANS: equal in size, opposite in direction   DIF: L1   OBJ: 12.3.1
58. ANS: The action force and the reaction force act on different objects. For forces to cancel,
    they must act on the same object.
    DIF: L1   OBJ: 12.3.1
59. ANS: law of conservation of momentum   DIF: L1   OBJ: 12.3.2

60. ANS: 20 kg·m/s   DIF: L2   OBJ: 12.3.2
61. ANS: The speed of the golf ball is much greater than the speed of the bowling ball.
    DIF: L2   OBJ: 12.3.2
62. ANS: attract and repel   DIF: L1   OBJ: 12.4.1
63. ANS: The ends of the bar magnets will now repel each other.
    DIF: L1   OBJ: 12.4.1
64. ANS: strong nuclear force   DIF: L1   OBJ: 12.4.2
65. ANS: the gravitational pull of the moon   DIF: L1   OBJ: 12.4.3

PROBLEM

66. ANS: $\text{Acceleration} = \dfrac{\text{Net force}}{\text{Mass}}$, $a = \dfrac{F}{m}$

    $$a = \frac{900\,\text{N}}{750\,\text{kg}} = \frac{1.2\,\text{N}}{\text{kg}} = \frac{1.2\,\frac{\text{kg}\cdot\text{m}}{\text{s}^2}}{\text{kg}} = 1.2\,\text{m/s}^2$$

    $a = 1.2\,\text{m/s}^2$, upward

    DIF: L2   OBJ: 12.2.2

67. ANS: $\text{Weight} = \text{Mass} \times \text{Acceleration due to gravity}$

    $$W = mg$$

    $$W = 4.2\,\text{kg} \times 9.8\,\text{m/s}^2$$

    $$W = 41\,\text{kg}\cdot\text{m/s}^2 = 41\,\text{N}$$

    DIF: L2   OBJ: 12.2.3

68. ANS: $\text{Momentum} = \text{Mass} \times \text{Velocity}$

    $\text{Momentum} = 32\,\text{kg} \times 2.5\,\text{m/s} = 80\,\text{kg}\cdot\text{m/s}$, downriver

    DIF: L2   OBJ: 12.3.2

69. ANS: $a = \dfrac{F}{m}$

    $$F = ma = 0.20\,\text{kg} \times 12\,\text{m/s}^2 = 2.4\,\text{kg}\cdot\text{m/s}^2 = 2.4\,\text{N}$$

    DIF: L2   OBJ: 12.2.2

ESSAY

70. ANS: On both the calm and windy days, the net force on the biker is zero because the biker is traveling at constant speed. On a calm day, the biker must pedal so that the forward-directed force applied to the bike balances the forces of friction opposing the forward motion. The friction forces primarily take the form rolling friction and fluid friction. On a windy day, the fluid friction force is much greater, so the rider must pedal harder to maintain the same constant speed.
    DIF: L2   OBJ: 12.1.2, 12.2.2

71. ANS: D   DIF: L1   OBJ: 12.4.4

72. ANS: The centripetal force will become less.
     DIF: L1   OBJ: 12.4.3

73. ANS: Earth   DIF: L1   OBJ: 12.3.1

74. ANS: inertia   DIF: L1   OBJ: 12.2.1

75. ANS: C   DIF: L1   OBJ: 12.1.3

76. ANS: 0 kg·m/s   DIF: L2   OBJ: 12.3.2

77. ANS: The momentums of both skaters are equal in size but opposite in direction.
     DIF: L2   OBJ: 12.3.2

78. ANS: The push on Skater B by Skater A accelerates Skater B forward.
     DIF: L2   OBJ: 12.2.1

79. ANS: According to Newton's third law of motion, as Skater A pushes on Skater B, an equal
     and opposite force pushes back on Skater A. The unbalanced force causes Skater B to
     accelerate backward.
     DIF: L2   OBJ: 12.1.2, 12.3.1

80. ANS: No; Skater A is exerting the same force on Skater B as before and so Skater B is
     exerting the same force on Skater A as before. The result is that Skater's A motion will be the
     same.
     DIF: L2   OBJ: 12.3.1

Chapter 13   Forces in Fluids

Multiple Choice

Identify the letter of the choice that best completes the statement or answers the question.

_____ 1. In order to calculate pressure exerted on a surface, what quantity is divided by the surface area?
a. altitude   c. mass
b. force   d. volume

_____ 2. If the air inside a balloon exerts a force of 1 N on an area of 0.5 m^2, what is the pressure inside the balloon?
a. 0.5 N/m^2 c. 1.5 N/m^2
b. 1 N/m^2 d. 2 N/m^2

_____ 3. What is the SI unit of pressure?
a. g/cm^3 c. a newton
b. m/s^2 d. a pascal

_____ 4. A pressure of 10 N/m^2 equals
a. 1 Pa.   c. 100 Pa.
b. 10 Pa.   d. 1000 Pa.

_____ 5. Where is fluid pressure greatest?
a. 30 centimeters below the surface of a swimming pool
b. 1 meter below the surface of a swimming pool
c. 2 meters below the surface of a swimming pool
d. The pressure is the same in all parts of a swimming pool.

_____ 6. Which of the following materials is NOT a fluid?
a. air   c. gasoline
b. cork   d. water

_____ 7. Which of the following is NOT possible?
a. compressing 10 liters of oxygen gas into a 1 liter volume
b. compressing 2 liters of water into a 1 liter volume
c. filling a balloon using helium gas from a pressurized tank
d. allowing 5 liters of compressed air to expand to a volume of 100 liters

_____ 8. The pressure of a fluid at a specific depth
a. depends only on the type of fluid.   c. varies with the total volume of the fluid.
b. is exerted only in the downward   d. all of the above.
direction.

_____ 9. Two identical test tubes are filled with equal volumes of water and mercury. Which of the following statements is true?
   a.   The weight of each liquid is the same.
   b.   The bottom area of each test tube is the same.
   c.   The pressure at the bottom of each test tube is the same.
   d.   all of the above.

_____ 10. Atmospheric pressure is caused by
   a.   air currents.
   b.   the weight of the atmosphere above a particular location.
   c.   clouds.
   d.   the altitude above sea level.

_____ 11. The pressure of air at sea level is approximately
   a.   0 kPa.   c.   101 kPa.
   b.   10 kPa.   d.   1000 kPa.

_____ 12. Which principle states that a change in the pressure at any point in a fluid in a closed container is transmitted equally and unchanged in all directions throughout the fluid?
   a.   Archimedes' principle   c.   Newton's principle
   b.   Bernoulli's principle   d.   Pascal's principle

_____ 13. The operation of a hydraulic lift system is explained by
   a.   Archimedes' principle.   c.   Newton's principle.
   b.   Bernoulli's principle.   d.   Pascal's principle.

_____ 14. Where will the greatest increase in pressure occur if you squeeze the middle of an upright, closed soft-drink bottle?
   a.   The greatest increase in pressure will occur at the top of the bottle.
   b.   The greatest increase in pressure will occur in the middle of the bottle.
   c.   The greatest increase in pressure will occur on the bottom of the bottle.
   d.   The pressure will increase equally everywhere within the bottle.

_____ 15. The hydraulic system of a dump truck is designed to multiply
   a.   distance.   c.   pressure.
   b.   force.   d.   speed.

Name _____ Class _____ Date _____

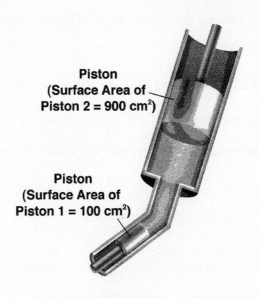

Figure 13-1

_____ 16. In Figure 13-1, Piston 1 exerts a pressure of 10 Pa on the fluid in the hydraulic lift. What is the fluid pressure on Piston 2?
  a. 1 Pa
  b. 5 Pa
  c. 30 Pa
  d. 90 Pa

_____ 17. Which of the following states Bernoulli's principle?
  a. As the speed of a fluid decreases, the pressure within the fluid decreases.
  b. As the speed of a fluid increases, the pressure within the fluid decreases.
  c. As the speed of a fluid changes, the pressure of the fluid remains constant.
  d. none of the above

_____ 18. The upward force acting on the wing of an airplane in flight is called
  a. drag.
  b. lift.
  c. thrust.
  d. weight.

_____ 19. Which of the following statements is true about an airplane wing during flight?
  a. Air above the wing travels faster than air below the wing.
  b. Air below the wing travels faster than air above the wing.
  c. The wing exerts pressure equally in all directions.
  d. The lift acting on the wing reduces the weight of the wing.

_____ 20. The upward force acting on an object submerged in a fluid is called
  a. buoyant force.
  b. drag.
  c. pressure.
  d. weight.

_____ 21. A brick weighs 21 N. Measured underwater, it weighs 12 N. What is the size of the buoyant force exerted by the water on the brick?
  a. 33 N
  b. 21 N
  c. 12 N
  d. 9 N

_____ 22. The strength of the buoyant force acting on an object in a fluid depends on the object's
     a. mass.   c. volume.
     b. surface area.   d. weight.

_____ 23. The buoyant force on an object in a fluid is equal to the weight of the
     a. fluid.   c. fluid displaced by the object.
     b. fluid surrounding the object.   d. object.

_____ 24. The relationship between buoyant force and weight of a displaced fluid was first stated by
     a. Archimedes.   c. Newton.
     b. Bernoulli.   d. Pascal.

_____ 25. A ball is floating partially submerged in a liquid. The buoyant force acting on the ball equals the
     a. volume of the ball below the surface.   c. mass of the ball.
     b. volume of the ball above the surface.   d. weight of the ball.

_____ 26. Which of the following substances will float in corn syrup? (The density of corn syrup is 1.38 g/cm^3.)
     a. aluminum ($2.7 \ g/cm^3$)   c. mercury ($13.6 \ g/cm^3$)
     b. magnesium ($1.75 \ g/cm^3$)   d. rubber ($1.23 \ g/cm^3$)

_____ 27. Which of the following materials will sink in water? (The density of water $1.00 \ g/cm^3$.)
     a. balsa wood ($0.12 \ g/cm^3$)   c. ethanol ($0.798 \ g/cm^3$)
     b. cooking oil ($0.82 \ g/cm^3$)   d. steel ($7.18 \ g/cm^3$)

_____ 28. A cork is floating in salty water. As more salt is added to the water to increase its density, the cork will
     a. float at a higher level in the water.   c. sink.
     b. float at a lower level in the water.   d. float at the same level in the water.

_____ 29. Two identical corks float in separate beakers. One beaker contains water. The other contains very salty water. Which of the following statements is true?
     a. The corks both float at the same level in the liquid.
     b. The cork in the very salty water floats at a lower level than the other cork.
     c. The corks will eventually sink.
     d. Both corks are subject to the same buoyant force.

_____ 30. Why does a hot-air balloon float?
     a. The shape of the balloon provides lift.
     b. The volume of the air displaced by the balloon is less than the volume of the balloon.
     c. The weight of the air displaced is less than the volume of the balloon.
     d. The weight of the balloon is less than the weight of the air displaced by the balloon.

Completion
Complete each sentence or statement.

31. Pressure is the result of force distributed over a(an) _____.

32. The formula, $\dfrac{\text{Force}}{\text{Area}}$, is used to calculate _____.

33. The SI unit of pressure is the _____.

34. A pascal, the SI unit of pressure, is equal to 1 newton per _____.

35. A substance that flows and assumes the shape of its container is a(an)
_____.

36. As a liquid is added to a beaker, the pressure exerted by the liquid on the bottom of the beaker
_____.

37. The pressure exerted by a fluid at any given depth is exerted _____ in all
directions.

38. As your altitude increases, air pressure _____.

39. A hydraulic jack is an application of _____ principle.

40. A device that uses pressurized fluids acting on pistons of different sizes to change a force is
called a(an) _____.

41. As the speed of a fluid increases, the _____ within the fluid decreases.

42. In a hydraulic lift system, the fluid pressure exerted throughout the system is
_____.

43. The downward force produced when air flows over the winglike spoiler on a race car is an
example of _____ principle.

44. The apparent loss of weight of an object in a fluid is called _____.

45. The direction of the buoyant force on an object placed in a fluid is _____.

46. Even a rock at the bottom of a lake has a(an) _____ force acting upward on
it.

47. The unit g/cm^3 is often used to express _____.

48. As you climb a high mountain, the buoyant force exerted on you by the atmosphere
_____.

49. A submerged submarine alters its _____ to rise or fall in the water.

50. The weight of an object that sinks in a fluid is _____ than the buoyant force acting on it.

Short Answer

51. Which exerts greater pressure on the floor—standing flat-footed or standing on tiptoes?

52. If you know the air pressure exerted on a tabletop, how can you calculate the force exerted on the tabletop?

53. Rank the following measurements in order of increasing pressure:
2 kPa, 10 N/m^2, 300 N/m^2, 0.1 Pa

54. For a fluid that is not moving, what are the two factors that determine the pressure that the fluid exerts?

55. How do the particles of a liquid exert pressure on a container?

56. Why aren't organisms that live on the seafloor crushed by water pressure?

57. Why does a partially inflated weather balloon expand as it rises?

58. On what principle are hydraulic systems based?

59. A ball of clay sinks when placed in water. The same piece of clay floats if it is made into the shape of a boat. Compare the volume of water displaced by the ball with the volume displaced by the boat shape.

60. Compare the size and direction of the lift on a plane with its weight as it flies at a constant speed and altitude.

61. When you weigh yourself on a bathroom scale, what buoyant force affects the weight reading?

62. How is the weight of water displaced by a floating cork related to the buoyant force?

63. How are density and buoyancy related?

64. If you use a spring scale to measure the weight of a submerged object that has neutral buoyancy, what will the scale read?

65. Compare the weight of an object to the buoyant force acting on it if the object sinks in the fluid.

Problem

66. The dimensions of a brick that weighs 21 N are 0.19 m × 0.090 m × 0.055 m. What pressure does the brick exert on the ground if it is resting on its largest face? Show your work.

67. Express a pressure of 2500 N/m² in kilopascals.

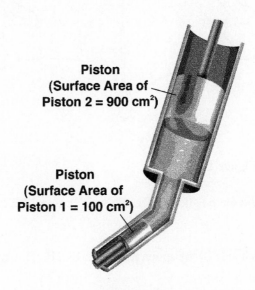

**Piston
(Surface Area of
Piston 2 = 900 cm²)**

**Piston
(Surface Area of
Piston 1 = 100 cm²)**

Figure 13-1

68. In Figure 13-1, a force of 1000 N is exerted on Piston 1 of the hydraulic lift shown. What force will be exerted on Piston 2? Show your work.

Essay
On a separate sheet of paper, write an answer to each of the following questions.

69. To prevent a window from exploding outward during a strong windstorm, it is left slightly open. Explain why a slightly open window might not blow out.

70. A cube of wood displaces half its volume when floating in water. When a 0.5-N washer is added to the cube, it floats just at the point where it is completely submerged in the water. What is the buoyant force acting on the cube when the washer is removed?

Name _____ Class _____ Date _____

Other

USING SCIENCE SKILLS

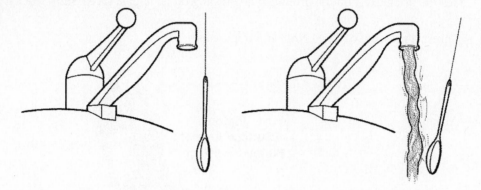

Figure 13-2A   **Figure 13-2B**

71. **Observing** How did the position of the spoon in Figure 13-2 change after the faucet was turned on?

72. **Inferring** On which side of the spoon in Figure 13-2B is the pressure of the air greater?

73. **Applying Concepts** According to Bernoulli's principle, is the spoon shown in Figure 13-2B pulled toward the stream of water or pushed toward the stream of water? Explain your answer.

74. **Drawing Conclusion** In Figure 13-2B, what effect does the stream of water have on the motion of the air around it?

75. **Predicting** What will happen to the spoon in Figure 13-2B if the water from the faucet is allowed to flow at a faster rate?

Name _____ Class _____ Date _____

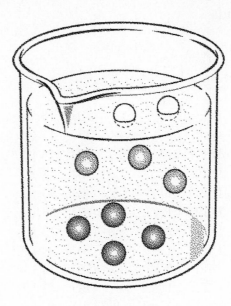

Figure 13-3

76. **Comparing and Contrasting** How does the fluid pressure exerted on the black spheres shown in Figure 13-3 compare with the pressure exerted on the gray spheres.

77. **Inferring** In Figure 13-3, spheres of which color have the greatest density?

78. **Applying Concepts** In Figure 13-3, on how many spheres is the buoyant force less than the weight of the sphere?

79. **Applying Concepts** In Figure 13-3, on how many spheres is the buoyant force equal to the weight of the sphere?

80. **Applying Concepts** In Figure 13-3, how many spheres have neutral buoyancy?

Chapter 13   Forces in Fluids
Answer Section

MULTIPLE CHOICE

1.	ANS:	B	DIF:	L1	OBJ:	13.1.1
2.	ANS:	D	DIF:	L2	OBJ:	13.1.1
3.	ANS:	D	DIF:	L1	OBJ:	13.1.2
4.	ANS:	B	DIF:	L2	OBJ:	13.1.2
5.	ANS:	C	DIF:	L1	OBJ:	13.1.3
6.	ANS:	B	DIF:	L1	OBJ:	13.1.3
7.	ANS:	B	DIF:	L2	OBJ:	13.1.3
8.	ANS:	A	DIF:	L1	OBJ:	13.1.4
9.	ANS:	B	DIF:	L2	OBJ:	13.1.4
10.	ANS:	B	DIF:	L1	OBJ:	13.1.5
11.	ANS:	C	DIF:	L2	OBJ:	13.1.5
12.	ANS:	D	DIF:	L1	OBJ:	13.2.1
13.	ANS:	D	DIF:	L1	OBJ:	13.2.1
14.	ANS:	D	DIF:	L2	OBJ:	13.2.1
15.	ANS:	B	DIF:	L1	OBJ:	13.2.2
16.	ANS:	C	DIF:	L2	OBJ:	13.2.2
17.	ANS:	B	DIF:	L2	OBJ:	13.2.3
18.	ANS:	B	DIF:	L1	OBJ:	13.2.3
19.	ANS:	A	DIF:	L2	OBJ:	13.2.3
20.	ANS:	A	DIF:	L1	OBJ:	13.3.1
21.	ANS:	D	DIF:	L2	OBJ:	13.3.1
22.	ANS:	C	DIF:	L2	OBJ:	13.3.2
23.	ANS:	C	DIF:	L2	OBJ:	13.3.2
24.	ANS:	A	DIF:	L1	OBJ:	13.3.2
25.	ANS:	D	DIF:	L2	OBJ:	13.3.2
26.	ANS:	D	DIF:	L1	OBJ:	13.3.3
27.	ANS:	D	DIF:	L1	OBJ:	13.3.3
28.	ANS:	A	DIF:	L2	OBJ:	13.3.3
29.	ANS:	D	DIF:	L2	OBJ:	13.3.4
30.	ANS:	D	DIF:	L1	OBJ:	13.3.4

COMPLETION

31.	ANS:	area	DIF:	L1	OBJ:	13.1.1
32.	ANS:	pressure	DIF:	L1	OBJ:	13.1.1
33.	ANS:	pascal	DIF:	L1	OBJ:	13.1.2

34. ANS:
    square meter
    m^2
    DIF: L2   OBJ: 13.1.2
35. ANS: fluid   DIF: L1   OBJ: 13.1.3
36. ANS: increases   DIF: L2   OBJ: 13.1.3
37. ANS: equally   DIF: L2   OBJ: 13.1.4
38. ANS: decreases   DIF: L2   OBJ: 13.1.5
39. ANS: Pascal's   DIF: L2   OBJ: 13.2.1
40. ANS: hydraulic system   DIF: L1   OBJ: 13.2.2
41. ANS: pressure   DIF: L1   OBJ: 13.2.3
42. ANS: constant   DIF: L1   OBJ: 13.2.3
43. ANS: Bernoulli's   DIF: L2   OBJ: 13.2.3
44. ANS: buoyancy   DIF: L1   OBJ: 13.3.1
45. ANS: upward   DIF: L1   OBJ: 13.3.1
46. ANS: buoyant   DIF: L2   OBJ: 13.3.1
47. ANS: density   DIF: L2   OBJ: 13.3.2
48. ANS:
    decreases
    becomes smaller
    DIF: L2   OBJ: 13.3.3
49. ANS: density   DIF: L1   OBJ: 13.3.4
50. ANS:
    greater
    more
    DIF: L2   OBJ: 13.3.4

SHORT ANSWER

51. ANS: standing on tiptoes   DIF: L1   OBJ: 13.1.1
52. ANS: Multiply the air pressure by the area of the tabletop.
    DIF: L2   OBJ: 13.1.1
53. ANS: 0.1 Pa, 10 N/m^2, 300 N/m^2, 2 kPa   DIF: L2   OBJ: 13.1.2
54. ANS: depth and type of fluid   DIF: L1   OBJ: 13.1.3
55. ANS: by coming into contact with the container
    DIF: L1   OBJ: 13.1.3
56. ANS: The pressure within the organisms' bodies balances water pressure. As a result, the net
    force on their bodies is zero.
    DIF: L2   OBJ: 13.1.4
57. ANS: Air pressure that is pushing in on the balloon decreases as the balloon rises.
    DIF: L2   OBJ: 13.1.5
58. ANS: Pascal's principle   DIF: L1   OBJ: 13.2.1
59. ANS: The boat shape displaced a greater volume of water.
    DIF: L2   OBJ: 13.2.2

60. ANS: The lift is the same size as the weight of the plane but acts upward, opposite the direction of the plane's weight.
    DIF: L1   OBJ: 13.2.3

61. ANS: the buoyant force of the atmosphere
    DIF: L1   OBJ: 13.3.1

62. ANS: They are equal.   DIF: L1   OBJ: 13.3.2

63. ANS: When an object is less dense than the fluid it is in, the object will float in the fluid. When an object is more dense than the fluid it is in, the object will sink in the fluid.
    DIF: L2   OBJ: 13.3.3

64. ANS: 0 N or zero   DIF: L2   OBJ: 13.3.4

65. ANS: The buoyant force is less than the weight.
    DIF: L1   OBJ: 13.3.4

PROBLEM

66. ANS: $\text{Pressure} = \dfrac{\text{Force}}{\text{Area}} = \dfrac{\text{Force}}{\text{Length} \times \text{Width}} = \dfrac{21\,\text{N}}{0.19\,\text{m} \times 0.090\,\text{m}}$

    $\text{Pressure} = \dfrac{21\,\text{N}}{0.017\,\text{m}^2} = 1200\,\text{N/m}^2$

    DIF: L2   OBJ: 13.1.1

67. ANS: $2500\,\text{N/m}^2 = 2500\,\text{Pa} \times \dfrac{1\,\text{kPa}}{1000\,\text{Pa}} = 2.5\,\text{kPa}$

    DIF: L2   OBJ: 13.1.2

68. ANS:
    A hydraulic lift multiples force by the a factor equal to the area of the large piston divided by the small piston.

    $\dfrac{\text{Surface area of Piston 2}}{\text{Surface area of Piston 1}} = \dfrac{900\,\text{cm}^2}{100\,\text{cm}^2} = 9$

    The hydraulic lift will multiply the force by a factor of 9.

    $100\,\text{N} \times 9 = 900\,\text{N}$

    The force exerted on Piston 2 is 900 N.
    DIF: L2   OBJ: 13.2.2

ESSAY

69. ANS: A window may explode outward during a windstorm because the outside pressure is much less than the pressure inside the house. By opening the window, the difference in pressures is reduced.
    DIF: L2   OBJ: 13.2.3

70. ANS: 0.5 N; because the 0.5-N washer and the cube floating on its own both displace the same volume, the 0.5-N force equals the buoyant force acting on the cube.
    DIF: L2   OBJ: 13.3.2

OTHER

71. ANS: The spoon moved toward the stream of running water.
    DIF: L2   OBJ: 13.1.1
72. ANS: on the side opposite the stream of water
    DIF: L2   OBJ: 13.1.1
73. ANS: The spoon is pushed toward the stream of water; the pressure of the air on the side of the spoon opposite the stream of water is greater than the pressure of the air on the side of the spoon next to the stream of water.
    DIF: L2   OBJ: 13.2.3
74. ANS: The stream of water causes the nearby air to move.
    DIF: L2   OBJ: 13.2.3
75. ANS: The spoon would move closer to the stream of water.
    DIF: L2   OBJ: 13.2.3
76. ANS: The fluid pressure exerted on the black spheres is greater (about twice as great).
    DIF: L1   OBJ: 13.1.3
77. ANS: black   DIF: L1   OBJ: 13.3.3
78. ANS: four spheres   DIF: L1   OBJ: 13.3.4
79. ANS: five spheres   DIF: L1   OBJ: 13.3.4
80. ANS: three spheres   DIF: L1   OBJ: 13.3.3

Chapter 14 Work, Power, and Machines

Multiple Choice
Identify the letter of the choice that best completes the statement or answers the question.

_____ 1. In which of the following is no work done?
   a. climbing stairs
   b. lifting a book
   c. pushing a shopping cart
   d. none of the above

_____ 2. A force acting on an object does no work if
   a. a machine is used to move the object.
   b. the force is not in the direction of the object's motion.
   c. the force is greater than the force of friction.
   d. the object accelerates.

_____ 3. What is the unit of work?
   a. joule
   b. newton/meter
   c. watt
   d. all of the above

_____ 4. If you exert a force of 10.0 N to lift a box a distance of 0.75 m, how much work do you do?
   a. 0.075 J
   b. 7.5 J
   c. 10.75 J
   d. 75 J

_____ 5. If you perform 30 joules of work lifting a 20-N box from the floor to a shelf, how high is the shelf?
   a. 0.5 m
   b. 0.6 m
   c. 1.5 m
   d. 2 m

_____ 6. The SI unit of power is the
   a. joule.
   b. newton.
   c. newton-meter.
   d. watt.

_____ 7. The power of a machine measures
   a. its rate of doing work.
   b. its strength.
   c. the force it produces.
   d. the work it does.

_____ 8. If you exert a force of 500 N to walk 4 m up a flight of stairs in 4 s, how much power do you use?
   a. 31 W
   b. 500 W
   c. 2000 W
   d. 8000 W

_____ 9. Which of the following statements is true?
   a. To increase power, you can decrease the amount of work you do in a given amount of time, or you can do a given amount of work in less time.
   b. To increase power, you can decrease the amount of work you do in a given amount of time, or you can do a given amount of work in more time.
   c. To increase power, you can increase the amount of work you do in a given amount of time, or you can do a given amount of work in less time.
   d. To increase power, you can increase the amount of work you do in a given amount of time, or you can do a given amount of work in more time.

_____ 10. A 750-W motor might also be rated as a
   a. 0.5-horsepower motor.
   b. 1-horsepower motor.
   c. 2-horsepower motor.
   d. 10-horsepower motor.

_____ 11. About 746 watts equals how many horsepower?
   a. one
   b. two
   c. four
   d. six

_____ 12. A machine is a device that can multiply
   a. force.
   b. power.
   c. work.
   d. all of the above

_____ 13. When a machine does work, it can do all of the following EXCEPT
   a. change the direction of a force.
   b. increase a force and change the distance a force moves.
   c. increase the distance a force moves and change the direction of a force.
   d. increase a force and increase the distance a force moves.

_____ 14. How can a machine make work easier for you?
   a. by decreasing the amount of work you do
   b. by changing the direction of your force
   c. by increasing the work done by the machine
   d. none of the above

_____ 15. How can you make the work output of a machine greater than the work input?
   a. by decreasing friction
   b. by increasing the input force
   c. by increasing the output distance
   d. none of the above

_____ 16. The actual mechanical advantage of a machine
   a. cannot be less than 1.
   b. decreases as the input distance increases.
   c. increases with greater friction.
   d. is less than the ideal mechanical advantage of the machine.

_____ 17. If you know the input distance and output distance of a machine, which of the following can you calculate?
   a. work
   b. actual mechanical advantage
   c. efficiency
   d. ideal mechanical advantage

_____ 18. If you have to apply 30 N of force on a crowbar to lift an rock that weights 330 N, what is the actual mechanical advantage of the crowbar?
   a. 0.09   c. 300
   b. 11   d. 9900

_____ 19. A 100-m long ski lift carries skiers from a station at the foot of a slope to a second station 40 m above. What is the IMA of the lift?
   a. 0.4   c. 40
   b. 2.5   d. 140

_____ 20. Reducing friction in a machine
   a. decreases its actual mechanical advantage.
   b. decreases the work output.
   c. increases its efficiency.
   d. increases its ideal mechanical advantage.

_____ 21. The efficiency of a machine is always less than 100 percent because
   a. a machine cannot have an IMA greater than 1.
   b. some work input is lost to friction.
   c. the work input is too small.
   d. the work output is too great.

_____ 22. A mechanical device requires 400 J of work to do 340 J of work in lifting a crate. What is the efficiency of the device?
   a. 0.9%   c. 85%
   b. 60%   d. 118%

_____ 23. A motor with an efficiency rating of 80 percent must supply 300 J of useful work. What amount of work must be supplied to the motor?
   a. 80 J   c. 375 J
   b. 240 J   d. 540 J

_____ 24. An inclined plane reduces the effort force by
   a. increasing the distance through which the force is applied.
   b. increasing the work.
   c. reducing the effort distance.
   d. reducing the work.

_____ 25. An ax is an example of a(an)
   a. inclined plane.   c. wedge.
   b. lever.   d. wheel and axle.

_____ 26. Which of the following is an example of a wheel and axle?
   a. a doorknob   c. a jar lid
   b. an automobile steering wheel   d. a pencil

_____ 27. The ideal mechanical advantage of a pulley system is equal to the
   a. distance the load has to move.
   b. length of the rope.
   c. number of rope segments supporting the load.
   d. weight of the object being lifted.

_____ 28. The ideal mechanical advantage of a wheel and axle is found by
   a. multiplying the circumference of the wheel by the radius of the axle.
   b. dividing the radius of the wheel by the radius of the axle.
   c. dividing the radius of the axle by the radius of the wheel.
   d. multiplying the radius of the wheel by the radius of the axle.

_____ 29. An example of a compound machine is a
   a. crowbar.   c. ramp.
   b. bicycle.   d. seesaw.

_____ 30. A machine is classified as a compound machine if it
   a. has moving parts.
   b. has an IMA greater than 1.
   c. is made up of two or more simple machines that operate together.
   d. is very efficient.

Completion
Complete each sentence or statement.

31. For work to be done on an object, the object has to _____.

32. Any part of a force that does not act in the direction of an object's motion does no _____ on an object.

33. The SI unit of work is the _____.

34. You calculate work by multiplying the force acting in the direction of _____ by the distance the object moves.

35. The rate at which work is done is called _____.

36. The SI unit of power is the _____.

37. The watt and the horsepower are both units of _____.

38. A machine is a device that changes a(an) _____.

39. A device that changes the size or direction of force used to do work is called a(an) _____.

40. The force that is exerted on a machine is called the _____ force.

41. Besides a reduction in friction, the only way to increase the amount of work output of a machine is to _____ the work input.

42. The _____ of a machine is the number of times that the machine increases the input force.

43. The mechanical efficiency of any machine is always _____ than 100 percent.

44. A(An) _____ can be described as an inclined plane wrapped around a cylinder.

45. The fulcrum is always between the effort force and the resistance force in a(an) _____-class lever.

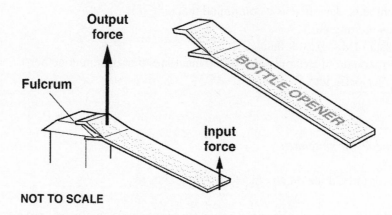

Figure 14-1

46. The bottle opener shown in Figure 14-1 is a(an) _____-class lever.

47. The ideal mechanical advantage of a third-class lever is always _____ than 1.

48. As the thickness of a wedge of given length increases, its IMA _____.

49. Two or more simple machines working together make up a(an) _____ machine.

50. A watch consists of a complex systems of gears. Each gear acts as a continuous _____.

Short Answer

51. How is work done when you lift a book?

Name _____ Class _____ Date _____

52. Why don't you do work as you hold a book motionless over your head?

53. If two swimmers compete in race, does the faster swimmer develop more power?

54. If a simple machine provides an increased output force, what happens to the output distance?

55. Why is the work output of a machine never equal to the work input?

56. If you grease a ramp to make a box slide more easily, what happens to the ramp's mechanical advantage? Explain your answer.

57. If a simple machine could be frictionless, how would its IMA and AMA compare?

58. How does friction affect the calculation of the IMA of a simple machine? Explain your answer.

59. How will a lubricant affect the efficiency of a simple machine such as a pulley?

60. What is the equation for calculating a machine's efficiency?

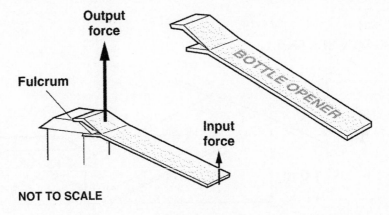

Figure 14-1

61. Compare the size and direction of the input and output forces shown in Figure 14-1.

62. Which has the greater IMA—a screw with closely spaced threads or a screw with threads spaced farther apart?

63. Compare the effects of a fixed pulley and a movable pulley on the size and direction of the input force.

64. How is a pair of scissors a compound machine? Explain your answer.

65. In a compound machine made up of two simple machines, how is the work output of the first simple machine related to the work input of the second simple machine?

Problem

66. A worker uses a cart to move a load of bricks weighing 680 N a distance of 10 m across a parking lot. If he pushes the cart with a constant force of 220 N, what amount of work does he do? Show your work.

67. A girl lifts a 100-N load a height of 2.0 m in a time of 0.5 s. What power does the girl produce? Show your work.

68. The input force of a pulley system must move 6.0 m to lift a 3000-N engine a distance of 0.50 m. What is the IMA of the system? Show your work.

69. A 16-N force applied to the handle of a door produces a 30-N output force. What is the AMA of the handle? Show your work.

70. A force of 12 N is applied to the handle of a screwdriver being used to pry off the lid of a paint can. As the force moves through a distance 0.3 m, the screwdriver does 32 J of work on the lid. What is the efficiency of the screwdriver? Show your work.

Other

USING SCIENCE SKILLS

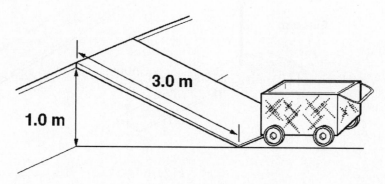

Figure 14-2

71. **Calculating** What is the IMA of the ramp in Figure 14-2? Show your work.

72. **Applying Concepts** If the ramp shown in Figure 14-2 was coated with a smoother surface, how would the AMA of the ramp change?

73. **Applying Concepts** If the ramp shown in Figure 14-2 was coated with a smoother surface, how would the ramp's efficiency change? Explain your answer.

74. **Classifying** What type of simple machine is the ramp shown in Figure 14-2?

75. **Comparing and Contrasting** In a post office, a 3-m long ramp is used to move carts onto a dock that is higher than 1 m. How does the IMA of this ramp compare with the IMA of the ramp shown in Figure 14-2?

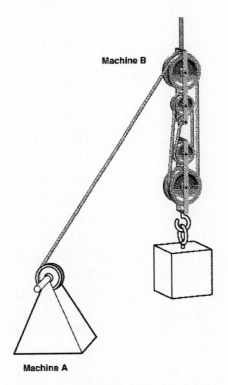

Machine B

Machine A

Figure 14-3

76. **Applying Concepts** Look at Figure 14-3. If Machine A moves through an input distance of 4.0 m, what is the output distance of Machine B?

77. **Classifying** What type of simple machine is Machine A in Figure 14-3?

78. **Interpreting Graphics** What is the IMA of Machine B in Figure 14-3?

79. **Interpreting Graphics** As shown in Figure 14-3, Machines A and B operate together as what type of machine?

80. **Comparing and Contrasting** In Figure 14-3, how does the work input of Machine B compare with the work output of Machine A?

Chapter 14   Work, Power, and Machines
Answer Section

MULTIPLE CHOICE

1.	ANS:	D	DIF:	L1	OBJ:	14.1.1
2.	ANS:	B	DIF:	L2	OBJ:	14.1.1
3.	ANS:	A	DIF:	L1	OBJ:	14.1.2
4.	ANS:	B	DIF:	L2	OBJ:	14.1.2
5.	ANS:	C	DIF:	L2	OBJ:	14.1.2
6.	ANS:	A	DIF:	L1	OBJ:	14.1.3
7.	ANS:	A	DIF:	L1	OBJ:	14.1.3
8.	ANS:	B	DIF:	L2	OBJ:	14.1.3
9.	ANS:	C	DIF:	L2	OBJ:	14.1.3
10.	ANS:	B	DIF:	L2	OBJ:	14.1.4
11.	ANS:	A	DIF:	L1	OBJ:	14.1.4
12.	ANS:	A	DIF:	L1	OBJ:	14.2.1
13.	ANS:	D	DIF:	L2	OBJ:	14.2.1
14.	ANS:	B	DIF:	L1	OBJ:	14.2.2
15.	ANS:	D	DIF:	L2	OBJ:	14.2.2
16.	ANS:	D	DIF:	L1	OBJ:	14.3.1
17.	ANS:	D	DIF:	L2	OBJ:	14.3.1
18.	ANS:	B	DIF:	L1	OBJ:	14.3.2
19.	ANS:	B	DIF:	L2	OBJ:	14.3.2
20.	ANS:	C	DIF:	L1	OBJ:	14.3.3
21.	ANS:	B	DIF:	L2	OBJ:	14.3.3
22.	ANS:	C	DIF:	L1	OBJ:	14.3.4
23.	ANS:	C	DIF:	L2	OBJ:	14.3.4
24.	ANS:	A	DIF:	L1	OBJ:	14.4.1
25.	ANS:	C	DIF:	L1	OBJ:	14.4.1
26.	ANS:	B	DIF:	L2	OBJ:	14.4.1
27.	ANS:	C	DIF:	L1	OBJ:	14.4.2
28.	ANS:	B	DIF:	L1	OBJ:	14.4.2
29.	ANS:	B	DIF:	L1	OBJ:	14.4.3
30.	ANS:	C	DIF:	L2	OBJ:	14.4.3

COMPLETION

31.	ANS:	move	DIF:	L1	OBJ:	14.1.1
32.	ANS:	work	DIF:	L2	OBJ:	14.1.1
33.	ANS:	joule	DIF:	L1	OBJ:	14.1.2
34.	ANS:	motion	DIF:	L2	OBJ:	14.1.2
35.	ANS:	power	DIF:	L1	OBJ:	14.1.3
36.	ANS:	watt	DIF:	L1	OBJ:	14.1.3

37.	ANS: power	DIF: L2	OBJ: 14.1.4
38.	ANS: force	DIF: L1	OBJ: 14.2.1
39.	ANS: machine	DIF: L2	OBJ: 14.2.1
40.	ANS: input	DIF: L1	OBJ: 14.2.2
41.	ANS: increase	DIF: L2	OBJ: 14.2.2
42.	ANS: mechanical advantage	DIF: L1	OBJ: 14.3.1
43.	ANS: less	DIF: L2	OBJ: 14.3.3
44.	ANS: screw	DIF: L1	OBJ: 14.4.1
45.	ANS: first	DIF: L2	OBJ: 14.4.1
46.	ANS: second	DIF: L2	OBJ: 14.4.1
47.	ANS: less	DIF: L1	OBJ: 14.4.2
48.	ANS: decreases	DIF: L2	OBJ: 14.4.2
49.	ANS: compound	DIF: L1	OBJ: 14.4.3
50.	ANS: lever	DIF: L2	OBJ: 14.4.3

SHORT ANSWER

51. ANS: Work is done because a force is applied in the direction in which the book moves.
DIF: L1   OBJ: 14.1.1

52. ANS: There is no movement, so no work is done.
DIF: L1   OBJ: 14.1.1

53. ANS: The swimmer that swims faster develops more power only if both swimmers do the same amount of work.
DIF: L2   OBJ: 14.1.3

54. ANS: The simple machine reduces the output distance.
DIF: L1   OBJ: 14.2.1

55. ANS: Some of work input is used to overcome friction.
DIF: L2   OBJ: 14.2.2

56. ANS: It increases; friction has been reduced.
DIF: L1   OBJ: 14.2.2

57. ANS: They would be equal.   DIF: L2   OBJ: 14.3.1

58. ANS: Friction has no effect; an ideal machine has no friction.
DIF: L1   OBJ: 14.3.2

59. ANS: A lubricant will increase a simple machine's efficiency by decreasing friction.
DIF: L1   OBJ: 14.3.3

60. ANS: $\text{Efficiency} = \dfrac{\text{Work output}}{\text{Work input}} \times 100\%$ DIF: L1   OBJ: 14.3.4

61. ANS: The forces are both upward. The output force is larger than the input force.
DIF: L1   OBJ: 14.4.1

62. ANS: the screw with closely spaced threads
DIF: L1   OBJ: 14.4.2

63. ANS: A fixed pulley changes only the direction of the input force. A movable pulley changes both the direction of the input force and its size.
DIF: L2   OBJ: 14.4.2

64. ANS: A pair of scissors contains two simple machines working together. Each arm is a first-class lever with a wedge, which is the blade, at one end.
    DIF: L1   OBJ: 14.4.3

65. ANS: The work output of the first simple machine is the work input of the second simple machine.
    DIF: L2   OBJ: 14.4.3

PROBLEM

66. ANS: Work = Force × Distance = 220 N × 10 m = 2200 N·m = 2200 J

    Work = 2200 J
    DIF: L2   OBJ: 14.1.2

67. ANS: $\text{Power} = \dfrac{\text{Work}}{\text{Time}} = \dfrac{\text{Force} \times \text{Distance}}{\text{Time}} = \dfrac{100\,\text{N} \times 2.0\,\text{m}}{1\,\text{s}} = 200\,\dfrac{\text{N}\cdot\text{m}}{\text{s}} = 200\,\dfrac{\text{J}}{\text{s}} = 200\,\text{W}$

    Power = 200 W
    DIF: L2   OBJ: 14.1.3

68. ANS: $\text{IMA} = \dfrac{\text{Input distance}}{\text{Output distance}} = \dfrac{6.0\,\text{m}}{0.50\,\text{m}} = 12$

    IMA = 12
    DIF: L2   OBJ: 14.3.2

69. ANS: $\text{AMA} = \dfrac{\text{Output force}}{\text{Input force}} = \dfrac{30\,\text{N}}{16\,\text{N}} = 1.9$

    AMA = 1.9
    DIF: L2   OBJ: 14.3.2

70. ANS: $\text{Efficiency} = \dfrac{\text{Work output}}{\text{Work input}} \times 100\% = \dfrac{\text{Work output}}{\text{Input force} \times \text{Input distance}} \times 100\%$

    $\text{Efficiency} = \dfrac{32\,\text{J}}{12\,\text{N} \times 0.3\,\text{m}} \times 100\% = \dfrac{32\,\text{J}}{36\,\text{N}\cdot\text{m}} \times 100\% = \dfrac{32\,\text{J}}{36\,\text{J}} \times 100\% = 89\%$

    Efficiency = 89%
    DIF: L2   OBJ: 14.4.2

OTHER

71. ANS: $\text{Ideal mechanical advantage} = \dfrac{\text{Input distance}}{\text{Output distance}} = \dfrac{3\,\text{m}}{1\,\text{m}} = 3$

    DIF: L1   OBJ: 14.3.2

72. ANS: The ramp's AMA would increase.   DIF: L1   OBJ: 14.3.1

73. ANS: Its efficiency would increase; friction would decrease.
    DIF: L1   OBJ: 14.3.3

74. ANS: an inclined plane   DIF: L1   OBJ: 14.4.1

75. ANS: It is less.   DIF: L1   OBJ: 14.4.2
76. ANS: 1.0 m   DIF: L2   OBJ: 14.3.2
77. ANS: wheel and axle   DIF: L2   OBJ: 14.4.1
78. ANS: 4   DIF: L2   OBJ: 14.4.2
79. ANS: a compound machine   DIF: L2   OBJ: 14.4.3
80. ANS: The work out of Machine B equals the work output of Machine A.
    DIF: L2   OBJ: 14.4.3

Chapter 15   Energy

Multiple Choice
Identify the letter of the choice that best completes the statement or answers the question.

_____ 1. Work is a transfer of
    a. energy.
    b. force.
    c. mass.
    d. motion.

_____ 2. What is transferred by a force moving an object through a distance?
    a. force
    b. mass
    c. motion
    d. energy

_____ 3. The energy of motion is called
    a. kinetic energy.
    b. potential energy.
    c. thermal energy.
    d. work.

_____ 4. A small 30-kilogram canoe is floating downriver at a speed of 2 m/s. What is the canoe's kinetic energy?
    a. 32 J
    b. 60 J
    c. 120 J
    d. 900 J

_____ 5. A 12-kg sled is moving at a speed of 3.0 m/s. At which of the following speeds will the sled have twice as much kinetic energy?
    a. 1.5 m/s
    b. 4.2 m/s
    c. 6.0 m/s
    d. 9.0 m/s

_____ 6. An object's gravitational potential energy is directly related to all of the following EXCEPT
    a. its height relative to a reference level.
    b. its mass.
    c. its speed.
    d. the acceleration due to gravity.

_____ 7. Which of the following is an example of an object with elastic potential energy?
    a. a wind-up toy that has been wound up
    b. a compressed basketball
    c. a stretched rubber band
    d. all of the above

_____ 8. Why is the gravitational potential energy of an object 1 meter above the moon's surface less than its potential energy 1 meter above Earth's surface?
    a. The object's mass is less on the moon.
    b. The object's weight is more on the moon.
    c. The moon's acceleration due to gravity is less.
    d. both a and c

_____ 9. A 4-kilogram cat is resting on top of a bookshelf that is 2 meters high. What is the cat's gravitational potential energy relative to the floor if the acceleration due to gravity is 9.8 m/s²?
    a. 6 J
    b. 8 J
    c. 20 J
    d. 78 J

Name _____ Class _____ Date _____

____ 10. The gravitational potential energy of an object is always measured relative to the
   a. location where the object's kinetic energy is zero.
   b. position of maximum mechanical energy.
   c. reference level from which the height is measured.
   d. surface of Earth.

____ 11. Which of the following increases when an object becomes warmer?
   a. chemical energy
   b. elastic potential energy
   c. nuclear energy
   d. thermal energy

____ 12. The energy stored in gasoline is
   a. chemical energy.
   b. electromagnetic energy.
   c. mechanical energy.
   d. nuclear energy.

____ 13. The total potential and kinetic energy of all the microscopic particles in an object make up its
   a. chemical energy.
   b. electric energy.
   c. nuclear energy.
   d. thermal energy.

____ 14. Walking converts what type of energy into mechanical energy?
   a. chemical
   b. electromagnetic
   c. nuclear
   d. thermal

____ 15. Nuclear power plants are designed to convert nuclear energy into what type of energy?
   a. chemical
   b. electrical
   c. geothermal
   d. mechanical

____ 16. Solar cells convert what type of energy into electrical energy?
   a. chemical
   b. electromagnetic
   c. nuclear
   d. thermal

____ 17. Which of the following statements is true according to the law of conservation of energy?
   a. Energy cannot be created.
   b. Energy cannot be destroyed.
   c. Energy can be converted from one form to another.
   d. all of the above

____ 18. If no friction acts on a diver during a dive, then which of the following statements is true?
   a. The total mechanical energy of the system increases.
   b. Potential energy can be converted into kinetic energy but not vice versa.
   c. $(KE + PE)_{beginning} = (KE + PE)_{end}$
   d. all of the above

____ 19. The mechanical energy of an object equals its
   a. chemical energy plus its nuclear energy.
   b. kinetic energy plus its potential energy.
   c. nuclear energy.
   d. thermal energy.

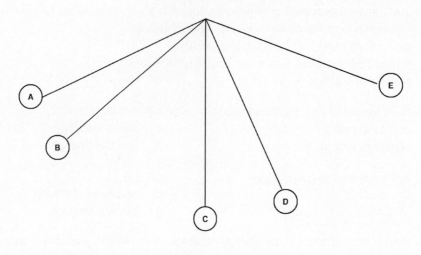

Figure 15-1

____ 20. The kinetic energy of the pendulum bob in Figure 15-1 increases the most between locations
   a. A and B.   c. B and D.
   b. A and C.   d. C and D.

____ 21. The equation $E = mc^2$ relates energy and
   a. force.   c. mass.
   b. gravity.   d. work.

____ 22. In which of the following does Einstein's famous equation apply?
   a. chemical reactions   c. electromagnetic energy conversions
   b. collisions between objects   d. nuclear fission and fusion reactions

____ 23. Which of the following statements is a consequence of the equation $E = mc^2$?
   a. Energy is released when matter is destroyed.
   b. Mass and energy are equivalent.
   c. The law of conservation of energy must be modified to state that mass and energy are
      conserved in any process.
   d. all of the above

____ 24. What is biomass energy?
   a. the chemical energy stored in living things
   b. the electromagnetic energy stored in living things
   c. the nuclear energy stored in living things
   d. the thermal energy stored in living things

____ 25. Nonrenewable energy resources include all of the following EXCEPT
   a. coal.   c. oil.
   b. hydrogen fuel cells.   d. uranium.

_____ 26. Fossil fuels currently account for the majority of the world's energy use because they are
   a. distributed evenly throughout the world.
   b. nonpolluting.
   c. relatively inexpensive and readily available.
   d. renewable energy resources.

_____ 27. A drawback of solar energy is that it
   a. cannot be converted directly into electrical energy.
   b. depends on the climate.
   c. produces water pollution.
   d. is not a renewable resource.

_____ 28. A benefit of a hydrogen fuel cell is that its byproduct is
   a. carbon dioxide.   c. water.
   b. oxygen.   d. uranium.

_____ 29. Which of the following types of transportation is NOT mass transportation?
   a. bus   c. streetcar
   b. car   d. train

_____ 30. Based on your knowledge of energy conservation, which of the following statements is true?
   a. Manufacturers can increase a light bulb's energy efficiency by using technology that
      increases the amount of electromagnetic energy the bulb converts from a given amount
      of electrical energy.
   b. Energy can be conserved by turning off lights when they are not in use.
   c. both a and b
   d. neither a nor b

Completion
Complete each sentence or statement.

31. Energy of an object increases when _____ is done on the object.

32. Energy and work are measured in the SI unit called the _____.

33. If the _____ of an object doubles, its kinetic energy doubles.

34. The kinetic energy of an object is proportional to the square of its _____.

35. Energy that is stored due to position or shape is called _____ energy.

36. When a pole-vaulter flexes the pole, the pole-vaulter increases the pole's
    _____ potential energy.

37. You can calculate an object's gravitational potential energy by using the equation
    _____.

38. Mechanical energy does not include kinetic energy or _____ energy.

39. The sum of the kinetic energy and potential energy of an object is called its _____ energy.

40. All energy can be considered as kinetic energy, _____ energy, or the energy in fields.

41. Wind turbines convert _____ energy into electrical energy.

42. The process of changing energy from one form to another is called energy _____.

43. "Energy cannot be created or destroyed" is a statement of the law of _____.

44. When an apple falls from a tree to the ground, the apple's beginning kinetic energy and ending gravitational potential energy are both equal to _____.

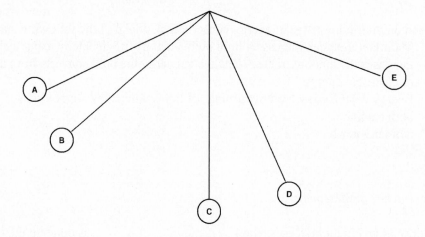

Figure 15-1

45. In Figure 15-1, the kinetic energy of the pendulum bob decreases between locations B and _____.

46. In the equation $E = mc^2$, c is the speed of _____.

47. Energy resources that exist in limited amounts and, once used, cannot be replaced except over the course of millions of years are called _____ energy resources.

48. Flat collector plates through which water flows are found in _____ solar energy systems.

49. Geothermal energy, in addition to being renewable, offers the benefit of being _____.

50. Turning off unused lights or appliances is an example of energy _____.

Short Answer

51. What evidence is there that energy is transferred as a golf club does work on a golf ball?

52. Show that the unit "kg·m^2/s^2," calculated from the kinetic energy equation, is equivalent to a joule.

53. What are the two general types of energy that can be used to classify many forms of energy?

54. Sled A (with its riders) has twice the mass of Sled B (with its riders). If both sleds have the same kinetic energy, which sled is moving faster? Explain your answer.

55. In what two ways can you increase the elastic potential energy of a spring?

56. What is the most familiar form of electromagnetic energy?

57. Why can you model the thermal energy of an object as the "mechanical energy" of the particles that make it up?

58. Describe one energy conversion that takes place in a hydroelectric power plant.

59. What energy conversion takes place as an arrow is shot from a bow?

60. Identify two types of nuclear reactions in which the equation $E = mc^2$ applies.

61. What are two examples of nonrenewable energy resources?

62. What are two examples of renewable energy resources?

63. What is a characteristic of a renewable energy resource?

64. Explain how biomass energy depends on the sun.

65. Why might a consumer buy a more energy-efficient refrigerator even though it may cost more than a conventional refrigerator?

Problem

66. What is the kinetic energy of a 74.0-kg sky diver falling at a terminal velocity of 52.0 m/s? Show your work.

67. A 0.49-kg squirrel jumps from a tree branch that is 3.6 m high to the top of a bird feeder that is 1.5 m high. What is the change in gravitational potential energy of the squirrel? (The acceleration due to gravity is 9.8 m/s^2.) Show your work.

68. A small dog is trained to jump straight up a distance of 1.1 m. How much kinetic energy does the 7.7-kg dog need to jump this high? (The acceleration due to gravity is 9.8 m/s^2.) Show your work.

69. In a nuclear reaction, an amount of matter having a mass of 1.0×10^{-14} kg is converted into energy, which is released. How much energy is released? (The speed of light is 3.0×10^8 m/s.) Show your work.

Essay

On a separate sheet of paper, write an answer to each of the following questions.

70. Compare and contrast biomass energy with the energy from fossil fuels.

Other

USING SCIENCE SKILLS

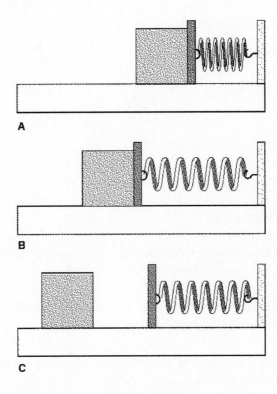

Figure 15-2

71. **Applying Concepts** In Figure 15-2, the block in C has 5 J of kinetic energy. How much work did the compressed spring do on the block? Explain your answer.

72. **Classifying** What form of energy does the compressed spring have in Figure 15-2?

73. **Inferring** In Figure 15-2, what has happened to the stored energy of the spring between A and B?

74. **Applying Concepts** In Figure 15-2, how would the kinetic energy of the block in C be different if the tabletop was not frictionless? Explain your answer.

75. **Interpreting Graphics** In Figure 15-2, how has the kinetic energy of the block changed between A and B?

Name _____ Class _____ Date _____

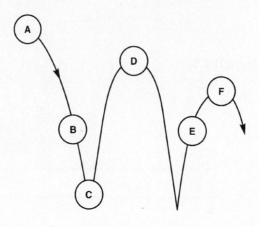

Figure 15-3

76. **Interpreting Graphics** At what location in Figure 15-3 does the ball have the least gravitational potential energy?

77. **Comparing and Contrasting** Compare the gravitational potential energy of the ball at locations B and E shown in Figure 15-3. Explain your answer.

78. **Applying Concepts** In Figure 15-3, does the total mechanical energy of the ball between locations A and F ever equal zero? Explain your answer.

79. **Inferring** In Figure 15-3, is the total mechanical energy of the ball conserved as the ball bounces? Explain your answer.

80. **Applying Concepts** Compare the kinetic energy of the ball in Figure 15-3 as it strikes the floor just before the second bounce with the first bounce (location C).

Chapter 15   Energy
Answer Section

MULTIPLE CHOICE

1.	ANS: A	DIF:	L1	OBJ:	15.1.1
2.	ANS: D	DIF:	L2	OBJ:	15.1.1
3.	ANS: A	DIF:	L1	OBJ:	15.1.2
4.	ANS: B	DIF:	L2	OBJ:	15.1.2
5.	ANS: B	DIF:	L2	OBJ:	15.1.2
6.	ANS: C	DIF:	L1	OBJ:	15.1.3
7.	ANS: D	DIF:	L1	OBJ:	15.1.3
8.	ANS: C	DIF:	L2	OBJ:	15.1.3
9.	ANS: D	DIF:	L1	OBJ:	15.1.4
10.	ANS: C	DIF:	L2	OBJ:	15.1.4
11.	ANS: D	DIF:	L1	OBJ:	15.1.5
12.	ANS: A	DIF:	L1	OBJ:	15.1.5
13.	ANS: D	DIF:	L2	OBJ:	15.1.5
14.	ANS: A	DIF:	L2	OBJ:	15.2.1
15.	ANS: B	DIF:	L1	OBJ:	15.2.1
16.	ANS: B	DIF:	L2	OBJ:	15.2.1
17.	ANS: D	DIF:	L1	OBJ:	15.2.2
18.	ANS: C	DIF:	L2	OBJ:	15.2.2
19.	ANS: B	DIF:	L1	OBJ:	15.2.3
20.	ANS: C	DIF:	L2	OBJ:	15.2.3
21.	ANS: C	DIF:	L1	OBJ:	15.2.4
22.	ANS: D	DIF:	L1	OBJ:	15.2.4
23.	ANS: D	DIF:	L2	OBJ:	15.2.4
24.	ANS: A	DIF:	L1	OBJ:	15.3.1
25.	ANS: B	DIF:	L2	OBJ:	15.3.1
26.	ANS: C	DIF:	L2	OBJ:	15.3.1
27.	ANS: B	DIF:	L1	OBJ:	15.3.1, 15.3.2
28.	ANS: C	DIF:	L2	OBJ:	15.3.2
29.	ANS: B	DIF:	L1	OBJ:	15.3.3
30.	ANS: C	DIF:	L2	OBJ:	15.3.3

COMPLETION

31.	ANS: work	DIF:	L1	OBJ:	15.1.1
32.	ANS: joule	DIF:	L2	OBJ:	15.1.1
33.	ANS: mass	DIF:	L1	OBJ:	15.1.2
34.	ANS: speed	DIF:	L2	OBJ:	15.1.2
35.	ANS: potential	DIF:	L1	OBJ:	15.1.3
36.	ANS: elastic	DIF:	L2	OBJ:	15.1.3

37. ANS: PE = *mgh* DIF: L2 OBJ: 15.1.4
38. ANS: chemical DIF: L1 OBJ: 15.1.5
39. ANS: mechanical DIF: L1 OBJ: 15.1.5
40. ANS: potential DIF: L2 OBJ: 15.1.5
41. ANS:
    kinetic
    mechanical
    DIF: L1 OBJ: 15.2.1
42. ANS: conversion DIF: L1 OBJ: 15.2.1
43. ANS: conservation of energy DIF: L1 OBJ: 15.2.2
44. ANS: 0 joules DIF: L2 OBJ: 15.2.2
45. ANS: E DIF: L2 OBJ: 15.2.3
46. ANS: light DIF: L1 OBJ: 15.2.4
47. ANS: nonrenewable DIF: L1 OBJ: 15.3.1
48. ANS: active DIF: L2 OBJ: 15.3.1
49. ANS: nonpolluting DIF: L1 OBJ: 15.3.2
50. ANS: conservation DIF: L2 OBJ: 15.3.3

SHORT ANSWER

51. ANS: The kinetic energy of the golf ball suddenly increases as the club strikes it.
    DIF: L1 OBJ: 15.1.1
52. ANS: $kg \cdot m^2/s^2 = (kg \cdot m/s^2) \cdot m = N \cdot m = J$ DIF: L2 OBJ: 15.1.1
53. ANS: kinetic energy and potential energy
    DIF: L1 OBJ: 15.1.2
54. ANS: Sled B; it has less mass. DIF: L2 OBJ: 15.1.2
55. ANS: Stretch it or compress it. DIF: L2 OBJ: 15.1.3
56. ANS: visible light DIF: L1 OBJ: 15.1.5
57. ANS: because the thermal energy of an object is the kinetic and potential energy of its
    particles
    DIF: L2 OBJ: 15.1.5
58. ANS: Accept either of the following: The potential energy of stored water is converted into
    kinetic energy as the water falls; as the falling water does work on the turbine, it moves the
    turbine's blades (KE). The KE of the rotating blades is converted into electrical energy by the
    generator.
    DIF: L2 OBJ: 15.2.1
59. ANS: The elastic potential energy of the bent bow and string is converted into kinetic energy
    of the arrow.
    DIF: L2 OBJ: 15.2.3
60. ANS: fission and fusion DIF: L1 OBJ: 15.2.4
61. ANS: Accept any two of the following: fossil fuels, such as oil, coal, and natural gas;
    uranium.
    DIF: L1 OBJ: 15.3.1
62. ANS: Accept any two of the following: hydroelectric, solar (passive, active), geothermal,
    wind, biomass, nuclear fusion (future source).
    DIF: L1 OBJ: 15.3.1

63. ANS: Accept either of the following: The resource can be replaced in a relatively short period of time. The resource originates either directly or indirectly from the sun.
DIF: L1   OBJ: 15.3.1

64. ANS: Biomass energy is the chemical energy stored in living things. The chemical energy is produced as plants convert sunlight in the form of electromagnetic energy into chemical energy.
DIF: L2   OBJ: 15.3.1

65. ANS: The refrigerator uses less energy due to its efficiency, so over time, the total cost may be lower.
DIF: L1   OBJ: 15.3.3

PROBLEM

66. ANS: $KE = \frac{1}{2}mv^2 = \frac{1}{2}(74.0\,\text{kg})(52.0\,\text{m/s})^2 = \frac{1}{2}(74\,\text{kg})(2704\,\text{m}^2/\text{s}^2) = 100,000\,\text{J}$
DIF: L2   OBJ: 15.1.2

67. ANS:
$PE = mgh = (0.49\,\text{kg})(9.8\,\text{m/s}^2)(3.6\,\text{m} - 1.5\text{m}) = 10\,\text{J}$
decreased by 10 J
DIF: L2   OBJ: 15.1.4

68. ANS: $(KE)_{beginning} = (PE)_{end}$

$KE = mgh = (7.7\,\text{kg})(9.8\,\text{m/s}^2)(1.1\,\text{m}) = 83\,\text{J}$
DIF: L2   OBJ: 15.2.3

69. ANS: $E = mc^2 = (1.0 \times 10^{-14}\,\text{kg})(3.0 \times 10^8\,\text{m/s})^2 = 9.0 \times 10^2\,\text{J}$
DIF: L2   OBJ: 15.2.4

ESSAY

70. ANS: Biomass energy is energy that is available immediately from the chemical energy stored in living organisms. Biomass is classified as a renewable energy resource. Fossil fuels also contain chemical energy but were formed over a long period of time from once-living organisms. Fossil fuels are classified as nonrenewable energy resources.
DIF: L2   OBJ: 15.3.2

OTHER

71. ANS: 5 J; because the block gained 5 joules of energy, the spring had to do 5 joules of work on the block.
DIF: L1   OBJ: 15.1.1

72. ANS: elastic potential energy   DIF: L1   OBJ: 15.1.3

73. ANS: The elastic potential energy of the spring has decreased.
DIF: L1   OBJ: 15.1.5

74. ANS: The block's kinetic energy would be less. Some of the elastic potential energy of the compressed spring would be converted into thermal energy due to friction. As a result, less of the springs's elastic potential energy would be converted into kinetic energy of the block.
DIF: L1   OBJ: 15.2.2

75. ANS: The block's kinetic energy has increased.
DIF: L1   OBJ: 15.2.3

76. ANS: C   DIF: L2   OBJ: 15.1.3

77. ANS: The gravitational potential energy of the ball is the same at both locations; the height is the same.
DIF: L2   OBJ: 15.1.3

78. ANS: No; since the ball is always moving to the right between locations A and F, at every point between A and F, the ball has kinetic energy. Because the ball has kinetic energy at each point, it has some mechanical energy at each point.
DIF: L2   OBJ: 15.1.5

79. ANS: No; because the ball does not reach the same height each time it bounces, its maximum gravitational potential energy is decreasing from one bounce to the next. Because its gravitational potential energy decreases and its maximum kinetic energy does not increase, the total mechanical energy must be decreasing.
DIF: L2   OBJ: 15.2.2

80. ANS: The kinetic energy is less before the second bounce. Since its gravitational potential energy is zero each time it strikes the floor, its kinetic energy equals its total mechanical energy. Because the total mechanical energy has decreased with the first bounce, its kinetic energy has decreased as it strikes the floor just before the second bounce.
DIF: L2   OBJ: 15.2.3

Name _____ Class _____ Date _____

Chapter 16   Thermal Energy and Heat

Multiple Choice
Identify the letter of the choice that best completes the statement or answers the question.

_____ 1. Which of the following is a unit of temperature?
   a.   Celsius degree   c.   kilogram
   b.   joule   d.   calorie

_____ 2. From his observations of cannon drilling, Count Rumford concluded that heat could NOT be a form of
   a.   kinetic energy.   c.   matter.
   b.   potential energy.   d.   radiation.

_____ 3. Heat is the transfer of thermal energy from one object to another because of a difference in
   a.   specific heat.   c.   temperature.
   b.   phase.   d.   waste heat.

_____ 4. What property of an object is related to the average kinetic energy of the particles in that object?
   a.   specific heat   c.   conductivity
   b.   mass   d.   temperature

_____ 5. As the temperature of an object rises, so does the
   a.   kinetic energy of the object.   c.   thermal energy of the object.
   b.   mass of the object.   d.   potential energy of the object.

_____ 6. Which of the following devices is based on the property of thermal expansion?
   a.   balance   c.   convection oven
   b.   calorimeter   d.   thermometer

_____ 7. Thermal energy depends on an object's
   a.   mass.   c.   temperature.
   b.   phase (solid, liquid, or gas).   d.   all of the above

_____ 8. In the formula $Q = m \times c \times \Delta T$, which quantity represents the specific heat?
   a. c c. Q
   b. m d. ΔT

_____ 9. The specific heat of copper is 0.385 J/g·°C. Which equation would you use to calculate correctly the amount of heat needed to raise the temperature of 0.75 g of copper from 10°C to 25°C?
   a. $Q = 0.385$ J/g·°C $\times (25?C - 10°C)$ c. $Q = 0.75$ g $\times 0.385$ J/g·°C $\times 15°C$
   b. $Q = 0.75$ g $\times 0.385$ J/g·°C $\times 25°C$ d. $Q = 0.75$ g $\times 0.385$ J/g·°C $\times 10°C$

_____ 10. In the formula $Q = m \times c \times \Delta T$, which quantity is measured in units of J/g·°C?
   a. c c. Q
   b. m d. ΔT

____ 11. What does a calorimeter directly measure?
    a.   change in temperature   c.   specific heat
    b.   kinetic energy   d.   radiation

____ 12. How do you know that a sealed calorimeter is a closed system?
    a.   because temperature is conserved
    b.   because the masses of the sample and water are equal
    c.   because thermal energy is not transferred to the environment
    d.   because work is done on the test sample

____ 13. Energy from the sun reaches Earth mostly by
    a.   conduction.   c.   radiation.
    b.   convection.   d.   thermal expansion.

____ 14. Matter is needed to transfer thermal energy by
    a.   conduction.   c.   radiation.
    b.   convection.   d.   both a and b

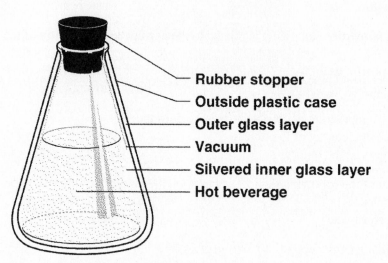

Figure 16-1

____ 15. The vacuum inside the thermos bottle shown in Figure 16-1 stops which type of thermal energy transfer to keep the liquid hot?
    a.   convection   c.   radiation
    b.   conduction   d.   both a and b

____ 16. Which of the following materials conducts heat well?
    a.   glass   c.   metal
    b.   plastic   d.   wood

____ 17. To which of the following does the first law of thermodynamics apply?
    a.   heating objects   c.   doing work on a system
    b.   transferring thermal energy   d.   all of the above

Name _____ Class _____ Date _____

_____ 18. According to the first law of thermodynamics, the amount of work done by a heat engine equals the amount of
 a. work done on the engine.
 b. waste heat it produces.
 c. thermal energy added to the engine minus the waste heat.
 d. thermal energy added to the engine plus the waste heat.

_____ 19. The second law of thermodynamics states that thermal energy can flow from colder objects to hotter objects
 a. by convection.
 c. spontaneously.
 b. only if work is done on the system.
 d. when thermal expansion takes place.

_____ 20. Disorder in the universe increases because
 a. spontaneous changes produce more order in a system.
 b. work produces disorder in a system.
 c. work produces waste heat, which leaves a system.
 d. all of the above

_____ 21. Which of the following states that absolute zero cannot be reached?
 a. the first law of thermodynamics
 b. the second law of thermodynamics
 c. the third law of thermodynamics
 d. the second and third laws of thermodynamics

_____ 22. One consequence of the third law of thermodynamics is that
 a. heat engines have efficiencies less than 100 percent.
 b. in some energy conversions, energy is not conserved.
 c. engines cannot discharge waste heat.
 d. the work a heat engine produces is less than the waste heat it produces.

_____ 23. Which of the following happens in a steam engine?
 a. Fuel is burned outside the engine.
 c. Hot steam pushes a piston.
 b. Heat is converted into work.
 d. all of the above

_____ 24. In most four-stroke internal combustion engines, when does the piston move downward?
 a. during the compression stroke only
 b. during the compression and exhaust strokes
 c. during the intake and exhaust strokes
 d. during the power and intake strokes

_____ 25. Which central heating system involves a furnace and a blower?
 a. electric baseboard
 c. hot-water
 b. forced-air
 d. steam

_____ 26. In forced-air heating systems, where are warm-air vents usually located?
 a. above windows
 c. next to cold-air ducts
 b. near the floor
 d. under radiators

_____ 27. A fluid that vaporizes and condenses inside the tubing of a heat pump is called the
a. compressor.   c. refrigerant.
b. fuel.   d. condenser.

_____ 28. Which of the following happens in a heat pump?
a. The compressor increases the pressure and temperature of the refrigerant.
b. The compressor blows cold refrigerant into the room.
c. The compressor absorbs heat from the refrigerant.
d. none of the above

_____ 29. Which type of central heating system is often used when heating many buildings from a central location?
a. electric baseboard   c. hot-water
b. forced-air   d. steam

_____ 30. Which of the following describes an advantage of radiant heaters?
a. They are portable.
b. They can easily be turned on or off.
c. They direct warm air to where it is needed.
d. all of the above

Completion

Complete each sentence or statement.

31. A measure of how hot or cold an object is compared to a reference point can be measured in units of _____ or _____.

32. Heat is the transfer of thermal energy because of a(an) _____ difference.

33. A hot dinner plate has _____ thermal energy than a similar dinner plate at room temperature.

34. The decrease in volume of a material due to a temperature increase is called _____.

35. If the temperature change of an aluminum nail is negative, thermal energy is transferred _____ the nail _____ the surroundings.

36. In a calorimeter, the increase in the thermal energy of the water and the decrease in the thermal energy of the sample are _____.

37. The transfer of thermal energy with no overall transfer of matter is called _____.

38. The transfer of energy as waves moving through space is called _____.

39. The type of thermal energy transfer that takes place in fluids is mostly
_____.

40. As an object's temperature increases, the _____ at which it radiates energy increases.

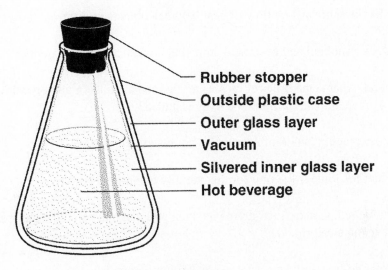

Rubber stopper
Outside plastic case
Outer glass layer
Vacuum
Silvered inner glass layer
Hot beverage

Figure 16-1

41. The thermos bottle in Figure 16-1 has two insulators—the glass layers and the vacuum. The _____ is the better thermal insulator.

42. A material that conducts thermal energy well is called a thermal _____.

43. The study of the conversion between heat and other forms of energy is called
_____.

44. Thermal energy that is not converted into work by a heat engine is called
_____.

45. The statement that absolute _____ cannot be reached is known as the _____ law of thermodynamics.

46. In most automobile engines, the linear motion of the strokes is turned into _____ motion by the crankshaft.

47. A steam-heating system is most similar to a(an) _____ heating system.

48. In a hot-water heating system, room temperature is controlled by a device called a(an) _____.

49. As the fluid in a heat pump evaporates, _____ is transferred from the surroundings to the fluid.

50. Having air cleaned as it passes through _____ near the furnace is an advantage of a(an) _____ heating system.

Short Answer

51. Describe the spontaneous flow of heat between objects at different temperatures.

52. Why does a rubber band become warm when you stretch it repeatedly?

53. In general, what is the order of increasing thermal expansion among solids, liquids, and gases when a given amount of thermal energy is added?

54. How does placing the lid of a jar under hot water help loosen it?

55. Show that the joule is the unit for the quantity equal to $m \times c \times \Delta T$.

56. What three temperature measurements must you make to calculate the specific heat of a sample using a calorimeter?

57. What role do free electrons have in conduction in metals?

58. Explain why the tile on a bathroom floor feels colder than a rug even though both are at the same temperature?

59. Explain how energy is conserved in a heat pump.

60. You add several drops of red food coloring to the water in a beaker without stirring. After a short time, the water has a red color throughout. Was the system of the food coloring and water more organized before or after you added the food coloring to the water? Which law of thermodynamics explains the change in order?

61. A heat engine could reach 100 percent efficiency only if waste heat is transferred to an environment at what temperature?

62. As what type of combustion engine would you classify steam turbines used in power plants? Why?

63. Which type of central heating system involves fans and ducts to circulate warm air?

64. Explain what happens to the surrounding air when a refrigerant condenses and why this happens.

65. How has keeping foods refrigerated helped society?

Problem

66. How many kilojoules of heat must be transferred to a 420-g aluminum pizza pan to raise its temperature from 22°C to 232°C? The specific heat of aluminum in this temperature range is 0.96 J/g·°C. Show your work.

67. As 315 g of hot milk cools in a mug, it transfers 31,000 J of heat to the environment. What is the temperature change of the milk? The specific heat of milk is 3.9 J/g·°C. Show your work.

68. A 410-g cylinder of brass is heated to 95.0°C and placed in a calorimeter containing 335 g of water at 25.0°C. The water is stirred, and its highest temperature is recorded as 32.0°C. From the thermal energy gained by the water, determine the specific heat of brass. The specific heat of water is 4.18 J/g·°C. Show your work.

Essay

On a separate sheet of paper, write an answer to each of the following questions.

69. How do convection currents form in air?

70. How can a heat pump warm a house by causing a refrigerant to evaporate and condense?

Other

USING SCIENCE SKILLS

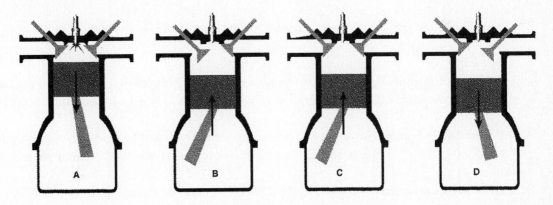

Figure 16-2

71. **Inferring** In Figure 16-2, is the temperature of the material within the cylinder greatest during the intake stroke, compression stroke, power stroke, or exhaust stroke?

72. **Interpreting Visuals** Sequence the four strokes of the engine shown in Figure 16-2 in the following order: intake stroke, compression stroke, power stroke, and exhaust stroke.

Name _____ Class _____ Date _____

73. **Applying Concepts** What is the engine in Figure 16-2 designed to do?

74. **Applying Concepts** According to the second law of thermodynamics, why can't the engine in Figure 16-2 have an efficiency of 100 percent?

75. **Classifying** What type of combustion engine is shown in Figure 16-2?

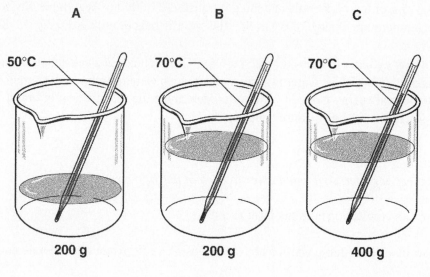

Figure 16-3

76. **Interpreting Data** Compare the average kinetic energy of the water molecules in the three beakers in Figure 16-3.

77. **Applying Concepts** Compare the thermal energy of the water in the three beakers in Figure 16-3.

78. **Applying Concepts** Equal amounts of thermal energy are transferred to the water in each container shown in Figure 16-3. Explain why the water in B has the highest final temperature.

79. **Predicting** In Figure 16-3, what will be the final temperature of the water in each container after 200 g of 70°C water is added? Assume no heat is transferred to the environment.

80. **Drawing Conclusions** The water in the three containers shown in Figure 16-3 is combined with no heat transfer to the environment. Explain whether the temperature of the mixture will be closer to 50°C or 70°C.

Chapter 16   Thermal Energy and Heat
Answer Section

MULTIPLE CHOICE

1. ANS: A	DIF: L1	OBJ: 16.1.1
2. ANS: C	DIF: L2	OBJ: 16.1.1
3. ANS: C	DIF: L2	OBJ: 16.1.1
4. ANS: D	DIF: L1	OBJ: 16.1.2
5. ANS: C	DIF: L2	OBJ: 16.1.2
6. ANS: D	DIF: L1	OBJ: 16.1.3
7. ANS: D	DIF: L2	OBJ: 16.1.3
8. ANS: A	DIF: L1	OBJ: 16.1.4
9. ANS: C	DIF: L1	OBJ: 16.1.4
10. ANS: A	DIF: L1	OBJ: 16.1.4
11. ANS: A	DIF: L1	OBJ: 16.1.5
12. ANS: C	DIF: L2	OBJ: 16.1.5
13. ANS: C	DIF: L1	OBJ: 16.2.1
14. ANS: D	DIF: L2	OBJ: 16.2.1
15. ANS: D	DIF: L2	OBJ: 16.2.1
16. ANS: C	DIF: L1	OBJ: 16.2.2
17. ANS: D	DIF: L1	OBJ: 16.2.3
18. ANS: C	DIF: L2	OBJ: 16.2.3
19. ANS: B	DIF: L1	OBJ: 16.2.4
20. ANS: C	DIF: L2	OBJ: 16.2.4
21. ANS: C	DIF: L1	OBJ: 16.2.5
22. ANS: A	DIF: L2	OBJ: 16.2.5
23. ANS: D	DIF: L1	OBJ: 16.3.1
24. ANS: D	DIF: L2	OBJ: 16.3.1
25. ANS: B	DIF: L1	OBJ: 16.3.2
26. ANS: B	DIF: L2	OBJ: 16.3.2
27. ANS: C	DIF: L1	OBJ: 16.3.3
28. ANS: A	DIF: L2	OBJ: 16.3.3
29. ANS: D	DIF: L1	OBJ: 16.3.4
30. ANS: D	DIF: L2	OBJ: 16.3.4

COMPLETION

31. ANS: kelvins, degrees Celsius	DIF: L1	OBJ: 16.1.1
32. ANS: temperature	DIF: L2	OBJ: 16.1.1
33. ANS: greater	DIF: L1	OBJ: 16.1.2
34. ANS: thermal contraction	DIF: L1	OBJ: 16.1.3
35. ANS: from, to	DIF: L2	OBJ: 16.1.4

36. ANS:
    equal
    the same
    DIF: L2   OBJ: 16.1.5
37. ANS: conduction   DIF: L1   OBJ: 16.2.1
38. ANS: radiation   DIF: L1   OBJ: 16.2.1
39. ANS: convection   DIF: L2   OBJ: 16.2.1
40. ANS: rate   DIF: L2   OBJ: 16.2.1
41. ANS: vacuum   DIF: L1   OBJ: 16.2.2
42. ANS: conductor   DIF: L1   OBJ: 16.2.2
43. ANS: thermodynamics   DIF: L1   OBJ: 16.2.3
44. ANS: waste heat   DIF: L1   OBJ: 16.2.4
45. ANS: zero, third   DIF: L2   OBJ: 16.2.5
46. ANS: rotary   DIF: L1   OBJ: 16.3.1
47. ANS: hot-water   DIF: L1   OBJ: 16.3.2
48. ANS: thermostat   DIF: L2   OBJ: 16.3.2
49. ANS: thermal energy   DIF: L2   OBJ: 16.3.3
50. ANS: filters, forced-air   DIF: L2   OBJ: 16.3.4

SHORT ANSWER

51. ANS: Heat flows spontaneously from hot objects to cold objects.
    DIF: L1   OBJ: 16.1.1
52. ANS: Some of the work you do in stretching the rubber band increases the average kinetic
    energy of the particles in the rubber band, causing its temperature to rise.
    DIF: L2   OBJ: 16.1.2
53. ANS: solids, liquids, gases   DIF: L1   OBJ: 16.1.3
54. ANS: When heated, the metal lid expands at a greater rate than the glass jar. The expanded
    lid is easier to loosen.
    DIF: L1   OBJ: 16.1.3
55. ANS: $m \times c \times \Delta T = g \times \dfrac{J}{g \cdot {}^\circ C} \times {}^\circ C = J$ DIF: L1   OBJ: 16.1.4

56. ANS: beginning temperature of sample, beginning temperature of water, and end temperature
    of sample and water together
    DIF: L1   OBJ: 16.1.5
57. ANS: Free electrons collide with each other and with atoms or ions to transfer thermal
    energy.
    DIF: L2   OBJ: 16.2.1
58. ANS: The tile is a better thermal conductor than the rug and transfers thermal energy quickly
    away from the skin.
    DIF: L1   OBJ: 16.2.2
59. ANS: Energy is conserved in a heat pump because the amount of work done on the pump and
    the amount of thermal energy it transfers from the cold environment equals the amount of
    thermal energy it releases to the hotter environment.
    DIF: L2   OBJ: 16.2.3

60. ANS: more organized before; the second law of thermodynamics
    DIF: L2   OBJ: 16.2.4
61. ANS: absolute zero (0 K)   DIF: L1   OBJ: 16.2.5
62. ANS: external combustion engine; because the steam, which runs the turbine, is produced by fuel, which is burned outside the engine
    DIF: L2   OBJ: 16.3.1
63. ANS: forced-air heating   DIF: L1   OBJ: 16.3.2
64. ANS: The surrounding air is warmed. The refrigerant cools and loses thermal energy as it turns from a gas to a liquid.
    DIF: L1   OBJ: 16.3.3
65. ANS: Keeping foods refrigerated keeps them from spoiling quickly. Since there is less spoilage, there is less chance of diseases from eating spoiled foods.
    DIF: L1   OBJ: 16.3.4

PROBLEM

66. ANS: $Q = m \times c \times \Delta T = 420\,\text{g} \times 0.96\,\text{J/g} \cdot {}^\circ\text{C} \times (232^\circ\text{C} - 22^\circ\text{C})$

    $Q = 420\,\text{g} \times 0.96\,\text{J/g} \cdot {}^\circ\text{C} \times 210^\circ\text{C} = 85{,}000\,\text{J} = 85\,\text{kJ}$
    DIF: L2   OBJ: 16.1.4

67. ANS:
    $Q = m \times c \times \Delta T$

    $\Delta T = \dfrac{Q}{m \times c} = \dfrac{31{,}000\,\text{J}}{315\,\text{g} \times 3.9\,\text{J/g} \cdot {}^\circ\text{C}} = 25^\circ\text{C}$

    The temperature of the milk will decrease by 25°C.
    DIF: L2   OBJ: 16.1.4

68. ANS:
    $Q_{\text{water}} = m_{\text{water}} \times c_{\text{water}} \times \Delta T_{\text{water}} = 335\,\text{g} \times 4.18\,\text{J} \cdot \text{g/}^\circ\text{C} \times (32.0^\circ\text{C} - 25.0^\circ\text{C})$
    $Q_{\text{water}} = 335\,\text{g} \times 4.18\,\text{J/g} \cdot {}^\circ\text{C} \times 7.0^\circ\text{C} = 7000\,\text{J}$
    The heat transferred *from* the brass equals the heat transferred *to* the water.
    $Q_{\text{brass}} = Q_{\text{water}} = m_{\text{brass}} \times c_{\text{brass}} \times \Delta T_{\text{brass}} = Q_{\text{water}}$

    $c_{\text{brass}} = \dfrac{Q_{\text{water}}}{m_{\text{brass}} \times \Delta T_{\text{brass}}} \quad \dfrac{9800\,\text{J}}{410\,\text{g} \times (95.0^\circ\text{C} - 32.0^\circ\text{C})}$

    $c_{\text{brass}} = \dfrac{9800\,\text{J}}{410\,\text{g} \times 63.0^\circ\text{C}} = 0.38\,\text{J/g} \cdot {}^\circ\text{C}$
    DIF: L2   OBJ: 16.1.5

ESSAY

69. ANS: When the air near a heat source is heated, it expands, causing its density to decrease. This less dense, warmer air is buoyed up by the colder air that pushes around and under it. As the warm air is pushed upward, it cools, becomes more dense, and then sinks. It now moves in beneath the air that is being warmed by the heat source and pushes it upward. As parts of the fluid alternately heat and cool, loops of moving fluid form within the fluid itself. These loops are called convection currents.

   DIF: L2   OBJ: 16.2.1

70. ANS: If the pump causes a refrigerant to condense inside the house, the process will release thermal energy to the inside air and warm the air. If the pump releases the cooled refrigerant outside the house, the refrigerant will absorb thermal energy from the warmer surrounding air as the refrigerant evaporates. The absorbed thermal energy can then be used to warm the air inside the house.

   DIF: L2   OBJ: 16.3.3

OTHER

71. ANS: power stroke   DIF: L1   OBJ: 16.1.3

72. ANS: D, C, A, B   DIF: L1   OBJ: 16.3.1

73. ANS: convert heat into work DIF: L1   OBJ: 16.3.1

74. ANS: The efficiency of a heat engine would be 100 percent if the engine could exhaust waste heat (thermal energy) to an outside environment that had a temperature of absolute zero (0 K). However, according the third law of thermodynamics, a temperature of absolute zero cannot be reached.

   DIF: L1   OBJ: 16.3.1

75. ANS: internal combustion engine   DIF: L1   OBJ: 16.3.1

76. ANS: The average kinetic energy of the water molecules in B equals the average kinetic energy of the molecules in C but is greater than the average kinetic energy of the molecules in A.

   DIF: L2   OBJ: 16.1.2

77. ANS: The thermal energy of the water in C is greater than the thermal energy of the water in B, which is greater than the thermal energy of the water in A.

   DIF: L2   OBJ: 16.1.3

78. ANS: B's water has less mass than C's water has, so B's water has a greater temperature change, making B's final water temperature higher. Even though the temperature change for A and B is the same since they have the same mass, B's final water temperature is higher because B's water had a higher beginning temperature.

   DIF: L2   OBJ: 16.1.3

79. ANS:
Temperature$_A$ = 60°C (The thermal energy transferred from the hotter water equals the thermal energy transferred to the warm water.) Because equal masses of water combine, the temperature drop of the hotter water equals the temperature rise of the warm water. The result is that the final temperature of each lies halfway between 50°C and 70°C, which is 60°C. Temprature$_B$ = Temperature$_C$ = 70° (There is no transfer of heat between materials at the same temperature.)
DIF: L2   OBJ: 16.1.4

80. ANS: Heat transferred from the hotter water equals heat transferred to the warm water. Since there are 600 g of hotter water and 200 g of warm water, the temperature change (drop) of the hotter water will be less than the temperature change (rise) of the warm water. As a result, the final temperature of the mixture will be closer to 70°C than to 50°C.
DIF: L2   OBJ: 16.1.4

Chapter 17   Mechanical Waves and Sound

Multiple Choice
Identify the letter of the choice that best completes the statement or answers the question.

_____ 1. A mechanical wave moves through a medium, which can be
    a.   a liquid.   c.   a gas.
    b.   a solid.   d.   all of the above

_____ 2. A mechanical wave generally does NOT
    a.   move the medium from one place to another.
    b.   move through a medium.
    c.   move through solids.
    d.   disturb the medium.

_____ 3. Transverse and longitudinal waves both
    a.   have compressions and rarefactions.
    b.   transfer energy through a medium.
    c.   move at right angles to the vibration of the medium.
    d.   are capable of moving the medium a long distance.

_____ 4. Which type of mechanical wave needs a source of energy to produce it?
    a.   a transverse wave   c.   a surface wave
    b.   a longitudinal wave   d.   all of the above

_____ 5. Which wave causes the medium to vibrate only in a direction parallel to the wave's motion?
    a.   a transverse wave   c.   a longitudinal wave
    b.   a surface wave   d.   none of the above

_____ 6. A disturbance sends ripples across water in a tub. These ripples are an example of a
    a.   rarefaction.   c.   compression.
    b.   longitudinal wave.   d.   surface wave.

_____ 7. When a surfer rides an ocean wave on her surfboard, she is actually riding on
    a.   a crest that is toppling over.   c.   the rest position of the wave.
    b.   a trough of the wave.   d.   a region of rarefaction.

_____ 8. In an earthquake, a P wave is a longitudinal wave. It moves through soil and rock as a
    a.   wavy line.   c.   series of compressions and rarefactions.
    b.   series of faults.   d.   series of crests and troughs.

Name _____ Class _____ Date _____

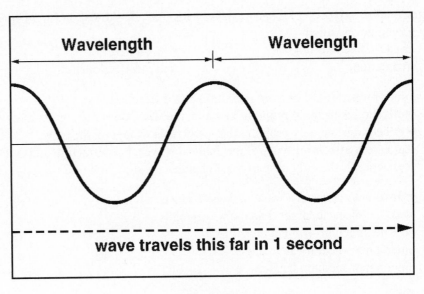

Figure 17-1

_____ 9. Figure 17-1 shows a wave movement during 1 second. What is the frequency of this wave?
  a. 2 hertz
  b. 2 meters/second
  c. 0.5 second
  d. 1 hertz

_____ 10. A period is the length of time it takes for
  a. a disturbance to start a wave.
  b. two complete wavelengths to pass a fixed point.
  c. a wave to travel the length of a rope.
  d. one complete wavelength to pass a fixed point.

_____ 11. To determine the speed of a wave, you would use which of the following formulas?
  a. speed = frequency × amplitude
  b. speed = wavelength × frequency
  c. speed = wavelength × amplitude
  d. speed = wavelength × period

_____ 12. A wave has a wavelength of 15 mm and a frequency of 4.0 hertz. What is its speed?
  a. 60 mm/s
  b. 60 hertz/s
  c. 3.8 mm/s
  d. 0.27 mm/s

_____ 13. To find amplitude, measure
  a. from a trough to the rest position.
  b. from a crest to the rest position.
  c. neither A nor B
  d. either A or B

_____ 14. To what is amplitude related?
  a. the amount of energy carried by the wave
  b. the maximum displacement from the rest position
  c. neither A nor B
  d. both A and B

_____ 15. When a wave strikes a solid barrier, it behaves like a basketball hitting a backboard. This wave behavior is called
    a. constructive interference.
    b. diffraction.
    c. refraction.
    d. reflection.

_____ 16. How does reflection differ from refraction and diffraction?
    a. Reflection is the only property in which the wave does not continue moving forward.
    b. Reflection is the only property that involves a change in the wave.
    c. Reflection affects all types of mechanical waves, but refraction and diffraction do not.
    d. Reflection is the only property that changes the direction of a wave.

_____ 17. For refraction to occur in a wave, the wave must
    a. strike an obstacle larger than the wavelength.
    b. change direction within a medium.
    c. enter a new medium at an angle.
    d. enter a new medium head-on.

_____ 18. In refraction, when two parts of a wave travel through different mediums, the parts move
    a. at different speeds.
    b. in step.
    c. always in the same direction.
    d. in opposite directions.

_____ 19. What is one property of a wave that determines how much it will diffract when it encounters an obstacle?
    a. frequency
    b. amplitude
    c. period
    d. wavelength

_____ 20. Which wave will probably be diffracted the most?
    a. a longitudinal wave
    b. the wave with the highest amplitude
    c. the wave with the longest wavelength
    d. the wave that strikes a solid barrier with the slowest speed

_____ 21. Suppose two waves collide and the temporary combined wave that results is smaller than the original waves. What term best describes this interaction?
    a. diffraction
    b. destructive interference
    c. standing wave formation
    d. constructive interference

_____ 22. The formation of a standing wave requires
    a. the traveling of a wave for a long distance.
    b. constructive interference between two waves of slightly different frequencies.
    c. that refraction and diffraction occur at the same time in a wave.
    d. interference between incoming and reflected waves.

_____ 23. A sound wave is an example of a
    a. transverse wave.
    b. longitudinal wave.
    c. standing wave.
    d. surface wave.

_____ 24. In which medium does sound travel the fastest?
    a. salt water
    b. fresh water
    c. air
    d. cast iron

_____ 25. Sonar equipment sends sound waves into deep water and measures
    a. refraction of the transmitted wave.
    b. only the direction of the reflected wave.
    c. the time delay of the returning echoes.
    d. interference of the transmitted and reflected waves.

_____ 26. A piano, violin, or guitar uses the resonance of a wooden soundboard to
    a. amplify the sound.   c. raise the pitch.
    b. dampen the sound.   d. limit standing waves.

_____ 27. An ambulance siren sounds different as it approaches you than when it moves away from you. What scientific term would you use to explain how this happens?
    a. ultrasound   c. rarefaction
    b. diffraction   d. the Doppler effect

_____ 28. When a sound source approaches you, the pitch you hear is
    a. lower than when the source is stationary.
    b. higher than when the source is stationary.
    c. the same as when the source is stationary.
    d. first higher and then lower than the pitch of the source when stationary.

_____ 29. Which part of the ear amplifies the vibrations from sound waves?
    a. outer ear   c. middle ear
    b. inner ear   d. both a and b

_____ 30. The part of the ear that sends coded nerve signals to the brain is
    a. the outer ear.   c. the middle ear.
    b. the inner ear.   d. the eardrum.

Completion
Complete each sentence or statement.

31. You can make a wave in a rope by adding _____ at one end of the rope.

32. Instead of crests and troughs, as in an ocean wave, a longitudinal wave has compressions and _____.

33. The crest of a transverse wave is most similar to a(an) _____ in a longitudinal wave.

34. A wave in a rope is a transverse wave, but a sound wave is a(an) _____ wave.

35. Waves in a rope are transverse waves because the medium's vibration is _____ to the direction in which the wave travels.

36. A pebble drops straight down into a tub of water, setting off _____ waves that travel between the water and air.

37. In a transverse wave, _____ is measured from crest to crest or from trough to trough.

38. To determine the speed of a wave, you must know the wave's wavelength and _____.

39. If a wave has a wavelength of 2 m and a frequency of 3.0 hertz, its speed is _____.

40. To compare the energy of different waves, measure the _____ of the waves.

41. Amplitude measures the greatest displacement of a wave from the _____.

42. A wave entering a new medium at an angle will undergo _____ as one end of the wave changes speed.

43. Ocean waves will not bend if they approach the shore _____.

44. If two waves collide and form a temporary larger wave, the interference is _____.

45. At the _____ of a standing wave, there is no displacement from the rest position.

46. The standard measure used to compare sound intensities is the _____.

47. When a person plucks a guitar string, the number of half wavelengths that fit into the length of the string determines the _____ of the sound produced.

48. On a piano, striking strings with the hammers sets up _____ between the strings and the soundboard.

49. When a train streaks by blowing its whistle, the changing pitch you hear is due to the _____.

50. The part of the ear that collects sound waves and focuses them inward is the _____ ear.

Short Answer

51. Why is a mechanical wave not always produced when a source vibrates?

52. What is a medium?

53. What type of mechanical wave is produced by pushing sharply on the end of a spring toy?

54. When you shake the end of a rope to make a wave, how can you increase the amplitude of the wave?

55. In what unit is wave frequency measured?

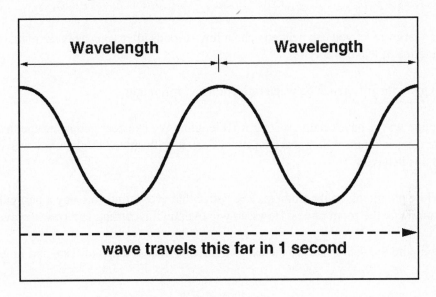

Figure 17-1

56. Consider the properties of a wave—wave speed, amplitude, wavelength, period, and frequency. Which two properties could you determine the numerical values of by using only the information given in Figure 17-1?

57. How can you change the wavelength of a wave in a rope without changing the amplitude?

58. How could you compare the energy carried in two different longitudinal waves?

59. Consider a wave approaching a barrier with a small hole. What change is the wave likely to undergo as it encounters the barrier?

60. Describe how a wave must enter a new medium in order for refraction to occur.

61. Waves X and Y are passing through a hole. Wave X has a relatively large wavelength compared to the hole. Wave Y has a relatively small wavelength. Which wave will diffract more as it passes through the hole?

62. Suppose two waves meet and temporarily cancel each other out. How would you describe the interference?

63. What sounds can damage hearing?

64. How do the frequencies of ultrasound compare to the frequencies that people normally hear?

65. What is the Doppler effect?

Essay

On a separate sheet of paper, write an answer to each of the following questions.

66. In a large cave, you can hear an echo a few seconds after you speak. Explain how this happens in terms of wave properties.

67. Explain the difference between reflection and refraction.

68. Sound waves have relatively long wavelengths. We can hear people around a corner before we can see them. Which wave behavior does this illustrate? Explain how wavelength relates to this behavior.

69. While practicing on the trumpet, you notice that every time you play a particular note, a window in the room rattles. How can you explain this rattling in terms of wave behaviors?

70. Compare the visible part of the ear to a satellite dish in terms of form and function.

Other

USING SCIENCE SKILLS

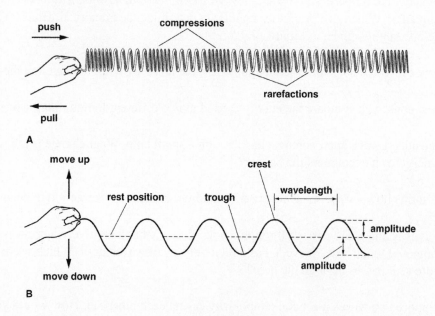

Figure 17-2

71. **Interpreting Illustrations** What kind of wave does A in Figure 17-2 represent? What kind of wave does B represent?

72. **Comparing and Contrasting** Figure 17-2 shows how someone starts the waves. How are these ways of starting waves alike? How are they different?

73. **Inferring** Compare the two waves in Figure 17-2. To what in wave B do the compressions of wave A correspond? To what in wave B do the rarefactions correspond?

74. **Inferring** What represents one wavelength in wave A of Figure 17-2? Define and describe the portion of the wave.

75. **Using Analogies** In Figure 17-2, wave A is produced by a spring toy, representing the concept of a sound wave in air. In sound, what is being squeezed together in the compressions, and what is being released in the rarefactions?

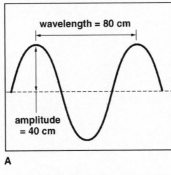

A

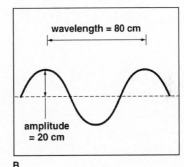

B

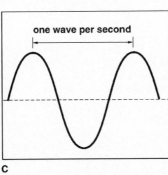

C

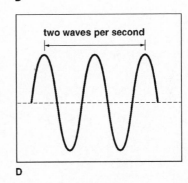

D

Figure 17-3

76. **Analyzing Data** What is the difference between wave A and wave B in Figure 17-3?

77. **Inferring** In Figure 17-3, both wave A and wave B were started by the same type of force—an up-and-down motion. What conclusion can you make about the energy of these two wave-starting forces?

78. **Predicting** Suppose you add the following panel E to the diagram: a wave pattern with a frequency of four waves per second. How will wavelength in this panel compare with the wavelength in panel D? How will it compare with the wavelength in panel C? Assume all the waves travel at the same speed.

79. **Analyzing Data** What is the difference between wave C and wave D in Figure 17-3?

80. **Drawing Conclusions** Consider both frequency and wavelength in Figure 17-3. How does each variable change between wave C and wave D? What is the relationship between the change? Assume the waves travel at the same speed.

Chapter 17   Mechanical Waves and Sound
Answer Section

MULTIPLE CHOICE

1.	ANS: D	DIF:	L1	OBJ:	17.1.1	
2.	ANS: A	DIF:	L2	OBJ:	17.1.1	
3.	ANS: B	DIF:	L2	OBJ:	17.1.2	
4.	ANS: D	DIF:	L1	OBJ:	17.1.2	
5.	ANS: C	DIF:	L1	OBJ:	17.1.3	
6.	ANS: D	DIF:	L2	OBJ:	17.1.3	
7.	ANS: A	DIF:	L1	OBJ:	17.1.4	
8.	ANS: C	DIF:	L2	OBJ:	17.1.4	
9.	ANS: A	DIF:	L1	OBJ:	17.2.1	
10.	ANS: D	DIF:	L2	OBJ:	17.2.1	
11.	ANS: B	DIF:	L1	OBJ:	17.2.2	
12.	ANS: A	DIF:	L2	OBJ:	17.2.2	
13.	ANS: D	DIF:	L1	OBJ:	17.2.3	
14.	ANS: D	DIF:	L2	OBJ:	17.2.3	
15.	ANS: D	DIF:	L1	OBJ:	17.3.1	
16.	ANS: A	DIF:	L2	OBJ:	17.3.1	
17.	ANS: C	DIF:	L2	OBJ:	17.3.2	
18.	ANS: A	DIF:	L1	OBJ:	17.3.2	
19.	ANS: D	DIF:	L1	OBJ:	17.3.3	
20.	ANS: C	DIF:	L2	OBJ:	17.3.3	
21.	ANS: B	DIF:	L1	OBJ:	17.3.4	
22.	ANS: D	DIF:	L2	OBJ:	17.3.4	
23.	ANS: B	DIF:	L1	OBJ:	17.4.1	
24.	ANS: D	DIF:	L2	OBJ:	17.4.1	
25.	ANS: C	DIF:	L1	OBJ:	17.4.2	
26.	ANS: A	DIF:	L2	OBJ:	17.4.2	
27.	ANS: D	DIF:	L1	OBJ:	17.4.3	
28.	ANS: B	DIF:	L2	OBJ:	17.4.3	
29.	ANS: C	DIF:	L1	OBJ:	17.4.4	
30.	ANS: B	DIF:	L2	OBJ:	17.4.4	

COMPLETION

31.	ANS: energy	DIF:	L1	OBJ:	17.1.1
32.	ANS: rarefactions	DIF:	L1	OBJ:	17.1.2
33.	ANS: compression	DIF:	L2	OBJ:	17.1.2
34.	ANS: longitudinal	DIF:	L1	OBJ:	17.1.3

35. ANS:
at right angles
perpendicular
DIF: L2   OBJ: 17.1.3

36. ANS: surface   DIF: L2   OBJ: 17.1.4
37. ANS: wavelength   DIF: L2   OBJ: 17.2.1
38. ANS: frequency   DIF: L1   OBJ: 17.2.2
39. ANS: 2 m/s   DIF: L2   OBJ: 17.2.2
40. ANS: amplitude   DIF: L2   OBJ: 17.2.3
41. ANS: rest position   DIF: L1   OBJ: 17.2.3
42. ANS: refraction   DIF: L2   OBJ: 17.3.2
43. ANS: head-on   DIF: L1   OBJ: 17.3.2
44. ANS: constructive   DIF: L2   OBJ: 17.3.4
45. ANS:
node
nodes
DIF: L1   OBJ: 17.3.4

46. ANS: decibel   DIF: L1   OBJ: 17.4.1
47. ANS:
frequency
pitch
DIF: L1   OBJ: 17.4.2

48. ANS:
standing waves
resonance
DIF: L2   OBJ: 17.4.2

49. ANS: Doppler effect   DIF: L2   OBJ: 17.4.3
50. ANS: outer   DIF: L1   OBJ: 17.4.4

SHORT ANSWER

51. ANS: The vibration has to carry energy through a medium.
DIF: L2   OBJ: 17.1.1
52. ANS: A medium is the material through which a mechanical wave travels.
DIF: L1   OBJ: 17.1.1
53. ANS: a longitudinal wave   DIF: L1   OBJ: 17.1.3
54. ANS: Shake the rope with more force.   DIF: L1   OBJ: 17.1.4
55. ANS:
hertz
cycles per second
1/s
DIF: L1   OBJ: 17.2.1
56. ANS: period and frequency   DIF: L2   OBJ: 17.2.1
57. ANS: Shake the rope faster or slower while using the same force as before.
DIF: L2   OBJ: 17.2.3

58. ANS: The wave with greater compressions has more energy.
    DIF: L2   OBJ: 17.2.3
59. ANS: The wave will bend or diffract.   DIF: L1   OBJ: 17.3.1
60. ANS: The wave must enter the new medium at an angle.
    DIF: L2   OBJ: 17.3.2
61. ANS: Wave X   DIF: L1   OBJ: 17.3.3
62. ANS: It is destructive; troughs of one wave meet crests of the other wave.
    DIF: L1   OBJ: 17.3.4
63. ANS: sounds greater than 90 decibels, such as a jet plane or rock concert
    DIF: L2   OBJ: 17.4.1
64. ANS: Ultrasound frequencies are higher than the sounds that people normally hear.
    DIF: L1   OBJ: 17.4.2
65. ANS: As the source of a sound approaches, you hear a higher frequency, and as the source moves away from you, you hear a lower frequency.
    DIF: L1   OBJ: 17.4.3

ESSAY

66. ANS: Sound waves, like other kinds of waves, reflect, or bounce back, when they strike a solid barrier. It takes time for the echo to return, traveling at the speed of sound, so there is a delay.
    DIF: L2   OBJ: 17.3.1
67. ANS: In reflection, a wave hits a solid barrier that it cannot penetrate, so it reflects, or bounces back, in roughly the same direction from which it came. In refraction, a wave hits a change in the medium, but instead of reflecting (bouncing back), it continues on into the new medium, bending as its speed changes.
    DIF: L2   OBJ: 17.3.1
68. ANS: Diffraction; a wave diffracts more if its wavelength is large compared to the size of the obstacle (the corner people are walking around). Because sound waves have relatively long wavelengths, we hear sound around the corner as the waves diffract, or spread out.
    DIF: L2   OBJ: 17.3.3
69. ANS: The window must have the same natural frequency as that particular note played on the trumpet. When the note is played, resonance causes the window to rattle in much the same way as a soundboard on a musical instrument vibrates as the instrument is played.
    DIF: L2   OBJ: 17.4.2
70. ANS: Both structures are shaped like a funnel to collect waves and focus them into an opening where they can be channeled to a specific location for processing. In the case of the ear, waves are funneled into the middle and inner ear, and then on to the brain. In the case of a satellite dish, waves are funneled into digital circuitry where they can be processed into cable television programs.
    DIF: L2   OBJ: 17.4.4

OTHER

71. ANS: a longitudinal wave; a transverse wave
    DIF: L1   OBJ: 17.1.3

72. ANS: Both waves are started by application of a force. However, wave A, the longitudinal wave, is started by a back-and-forth, or push-and-pull, movement in the same direction as the resulting wave movement, while wave B, the transverse wave, is started by an up-and down movement that is at right angles to the resulting direction in which the wave travels.
DIF: L1   OBJ: 17.1.2

73. ANS: Compressions in wave A correspond to crests in wave B. Rarefactions in wave A correspond to troughs in wave B. Each of these conditions represents an extreme in which the coil is being displaced from its rest position.
DIF: L1   OBJ: 17.1.2, 17.1.3, 17.1.4

74. ANS: In wave A, one wavelength equals the distance between center of a compression in the spring toy and the corresponding location in the next compression. Wavelength is the distance between a point on one wave and the same point on the next cycle of waves.
DIF: L1   OBJ: 17.2.1

75. ANS: In a sound wave in air, the compressions consist of regions of bunched-up air, while the rarefactions consist of regions in which the molecules are more spread out.
DIF: L1   OBJ: 17.4.1

76. ANS: Wave B has an amplitude that is one-half the amplitude of wave A.
DIF: L2   OBJ: 17.2.3

77. ANS: The force that caused wave A added more energy to the wave than the force that caused wave B.
DIF: L2   OBJ: 17.1.2, 17.2.3

78. ANS: The wavelength in E will be one-half that of the wavelength in D; it will be one-fourth that of the wavelength in C.
DIF: L2   OBJ: 17.2.1

79. ANS: Wave D has a frequency twice that of wave C. Also, the wavelength in wave D is about one-half that of wave C.
DIF: L2   OBJ: 17.2.1

80. ANS: Between wave C and wave D, frequency doubles, but wavelength is halved. Wavelength is inversely proportional to frequency.
DIF: L2   OBJ: 17.2.1

Name _____ Class _____ Date _____

Chapter 18   The Electromagnetic Spectrum and Light

Multiple Choice

Identify the letter of the choice that best completes the statement or answers the question.

_____ 1. In 1926, Michelson was able to measure the speed of light using
a. lanterns.   c. mirrors.
b. stars.   d. sunlight.

_____ 2. Electromagnetic waves vary in
a. the speed they travel in a vacuum.   c. the way they reflect.
b. wavelength and frequency.   d. their direction.

_____ 3. To calculate the frequency of an electromagnetic wave, you need to know the speed of the wave and its
a. wavelength.   c. refraction.
b. intensity.   d. amplitude.

_____ 4. An electromagnetic wave in a vacuum has a wavelength of 0.032 m. What is its frequency?
a. $f = 3.00 \times 10^8$ m/s   c. $f = 3.00 \times 10^9$ Hz
b. $f = 9.38 \times 10^9$ Hz   d. $f = 9.38 \times 10^8$ m/s

_____ 5. Light acts like
a. a wave.   c. both a wave and a particle.
b. a particle.   d. neither a wave nor a particle.

_____ 6. Because light travels in a straight line and casts a shadow, Isaac Newton hypothesized that light is
a. radiation.   c. a wave.
b. a stream of particles.   d. heat.

_____ 7. Photons travel outward from a light source in
a. a single straight line.   c. a small, dense area.
b. increasing intensity.   d. all directions.

_____ 8. Which of the following occurs as light travels farther from its source?
a. Far from the source, photons spread through a small area.
b. The intensity of light increases as photons move away from the source.
c. The source gives off less light as photons move away from it.
d. Farther from the source, photons spread over a larger area.

_____ 9. Infrared rays have a shorter wavelength than
a. ultraviolet rays.   c. radar waves.
b. X-rays.   d. gamma rays.

_____ 10. The full range of frequencies of electromagnetic radiation is called
a. visible light.   c. the electromagnetic spectrum.
b. radio waves.   d. invisible radiation.

____ 11. The waves with the longest wavelengths in the electromagnetic spectrum are
      a.   infrared rays.   c.   gamma rays.
      b.   radio waves.   d.   X-rays.

____ 12. The visible light spectrum ranges between
      a.   radar waves and X-rays.   c.   infrared rays and ultraviolet rays.
      b.   television waves and infrared rays.   d.   ultraviolet rays and gamma rays.

____ 13. Cellular telephones utilize
      a.   radar waves.   c.   very low frequency waves.
      b.   very high frequency waves.   d.   microwaves.

____ 14. X-ray photographs show softer tissue
      a.   as invisible.   c.   the same as dense bones.
      b.   as dark, highly exposed areas.   d.   as bright white areas.

____ 15. A translucent material
      a.   scatters some light.   c.   absorbs all light.
      b.   transmits all light.   d.   reflects all light.

____ 16. In order of the light-transmitting capabilities of materials from none to all, which is the correct sequence?
      a.   transparent→opaque→translucent   c.   opaque→translucent→transparent
      b.   opaque→transparent→translucent   d.   translucent→transparent→opaque

____ 17. Which of the following occurs as a light wave bends when it passes from one medium into another?
      a.   constructive interference   c.   destructive interference
      b.   refraction   d.   reflection

____ 18. Polarized sunglasses work by
      a.   blocking light waves that vibrate in one plane.
      b.   gradually refracting light as it passes through the lenses.
      c.   bending light as it passes from air into the lenses.
      d.   reflecting most of the light that strikes the sunglasses.

____ 19. Newton's prism experiments showed that white sunlight is made up of
      a.   the full electromagnetic spectrum.   c.   all the colors of the visible spectrum.
      b.   only blue light when separated by a   d.   only the longest wavelengths.
           prism.

____ 20. When droplets of water in the atmosphere act like prisms, the colors in sunlight undergo
      a.   interference.   c.   polarization.
      b.   absorption.   d.   dispersion.

____ 21. What an object is made of and the color of light that strikes it determines the
      a.   color of the object.   c.   opacity of the object.
      b.   transparency of the object.   d.   translucence of the object.

_____ 22. Blue light and yellow light combine to produce white light because
     a. they absorb each other's wavelengths.
     b. blue, yellow, and white are primary colors.
     c. they are complementary colors of light.
     d. they are both primary colors of light.

_____ 23. The primary colors of light are
     a. green, blue, and black.   c. red, yellow, and blue.
     b. cyan, magenta, and yellow.   d. blue, green, and red.

_____ 24. The primary colors of pigments
     a. are cyan, yellow, and magenta.
     b. are the same as the secondary colors of light.
     c. combine in equal amounts to produce black.
     d. all of the above

_____ 25. An incandescent light bulb produces light when electrons flow through the
     a. air.   c. filament.
     b. glass.   d. vacuum.

_____ 26. Which of the following is NOT true regarding neon lights?
     a. Light is emitted as electrons move through a gas in a tube.
     b. All neon lights are colored by the color of the tubing.
     c. Neon lights may contain other gases, such as helium or krypton.
     d. Each kind of gas produces its own distinctive color.

_____ 27. Many streets and parking lots are illuminated with
     a. laser lights.   c. sodium-vapor lights.
     b. tungsten-halogen lights.   d. fluorescent lights.

_____ 28. Light whose waves all have the same wavelength, direction, and coincidental peaks is called
     a. coherent light.   c. fluorescent light.
     b. incandescent light.   d. neon light.

_____ 29. A fluorescent light bulb usually contains
     a. a vacuum.   c. mercury vapor.
     b. oxygen.   d. fluorescent powder.

_____ 30. Which kind of light is used to carry information through optical fibers?
     a. incandescent   c. sodium-vapor light
     b. fluorescent   d. laser

Completion
Complete each sentence or statement.

31. Electromagnetic waves are _____ waves consisting of changing electric and magnetic fields.

32. Warm objects give off more _____ radiation than cool objects give off.

33. The speed of light in a vacuum is _____ m/s.

34. The farther away you are from a light source, the _____ intense it is.

35. Objects that scatter some of the light that is transmitted through them are _____.

36. When viewed in red light, an object that reflects all the colors of light will appear _____.

37. Combining equal amounts of the three primary pigments produces _____.

38. Electromagnetic waves can travel through a(an) _____.

39. Light is produced when _____ change energy levels in an atom.

40. Visible light waves have a shorter _____ than infrared waves have.

41. A transparent object _____ almost all of the light that strikes it.

42. The electromagnetic waves with the shortest wavelengths are _____ rays.

43. An ultraviolet light wave has a wavelength of 300 nm and a frequency of 7.0×10^{14} Hz. The ultraviolet light is NOT traveling through a(an) _____.

44. In microwave cooking, the food is heated _____ in the areas near the surface of the food than in the center.

45. A mirage, or distorted image, can be caused by the _____ of light as it moves into layers of hotter and hotter air.

46. White light passing through a prism separates into colors because of the differences in the _____ of each color of light.

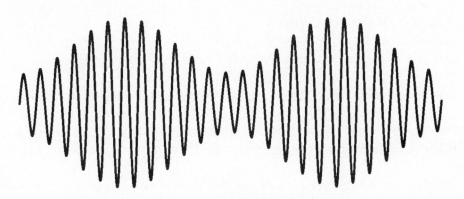

Figure 18-1

47. The electromagnetic waves shown in Figure 18-1 are an example of _____ used in certain radio broadcasts.

48. Light amplification by stimulated emission of radiation is known as _____ light.

49. To form white light from the combination of only two colors of light, the colors must be _____ .

50. The following electromagnetic waves are arranged in order of increasing frequency: infrared, _____ , ultraviolet.

Short Answer

51. What is a basic difference between electromagnetic waves and sound waves?

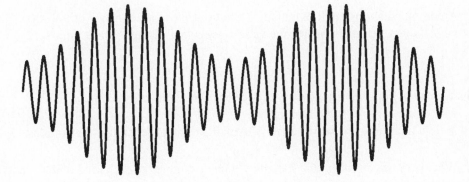

Figure 18-1

52. Why is the amplitude of the radio wave in Figure 18-1 varied?

53. In which medium does light travel faster, air or glass?

54. What is the photoelectric effect?

55. Describe what happens to photons as they travel away from a light source.

56. Which type of electromagnetic wave has the longest wavelength and lowest frequency?

57. Both gamma rays and X-rays are used to see inside the body. Which one is used to make images of bones? How are the other rays used?

58. Which waves have wavelengths longer than those of visible light? Give an example of how each kind of wave is used.

59. How would you describe a translucent material?

60. Use the scattering of light to explain why the sun is red at sunset.

61. What type of light passes through a polarizing filter?

62. What two factors influence the color of an object?

63. Magenta is a secondary color of light. What type of color is magenta when it is a pigment?

64. What is common to all light sources including incandescent, fluorescent, neon, halogen, laser, and sodium-vapor devices?

65. What distinguishes a laser from other common light sources?

Problem

66. A communications satellite transmits a radio wave at a frequency of 9.4×10^9 Hz. What is the signal's wavelength? Assume the wave travels in a vacuum. Show your work.

Essay
On a separate sheet of paper, write an answer to each of the following questions.

67. Is light a particle or a wave? Briefly explain your answer and give examples.

68. What is the electromagnetic spectrum? Give examples of each kind of wave and relate each example to its relative position in the spectrum.

69. What is polarized light? What is unpolarized light? Name at least one familiar kind of polarizing filter and explain how it works.

70. Describe the economic advantage of using sodium-vapor lights and a disadvantage of the color it produces.

Other

USING SCIENCE SKILLS

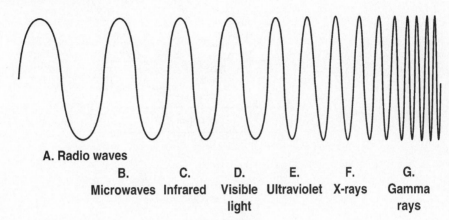

A. Radio waves

B. Microwaves   C. Infrared   D. Visible light   E. Ultraviolet   F. X-rays   G. Gamma rays

Figure 18-2

71. **Comparing and Contrasting** Which waves in Figure 18-2 carry AM and FM signals? How do the frequencies of AM and FM signals compare?

72. **Analyzing Data** How does photon energy change with increasing frequency? Use Figure 18-2 to answer this question.

73. **Interpreting Graphics** Which waves in Figure 18-2 are used to expose heat-sensitive film? Where are these waves located in the electromagnetic spectrum?

74. **Classifying** In Figure 18-2, which waves can be separated into different wavelengths of colored light?

75. **Inferring** Look at Figure 18-2. Without knowing the specific frequencies and wavelengths of the colors of the visible spectrum, at which end of the visible spectrum would you place red? At which end would you place violet? *Hint:* Use the names of the waves outside the visible spectrum to help you.

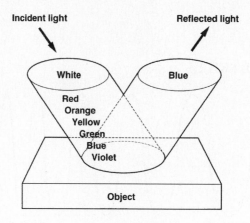

Figure 18-3

76. **Classifying** Examine Figure 18-3, which represents a pencil in a glass container of a liquid. Is the liquid transparent, translucent, or opaque to visible light? Explain.

77. **Applying Concepts** Explain why the pencil in Figure 18-3 appears to be broken.

78. **Interpreting Graphics** Figure 18-3 represents white light striking an object. Explain why the beam of white light is also labeled with colors.

79. **Drawing Conclusions** What color is the object in Figure 18-3? Explain your answer.

80. **Applying Concepts** Suppose the light striking the object in Figure 18-3 was a combination of red and green. What color would the object be when viewed in this light? Explain your answer.

Chapter 18 The Electromagnetic Spectrum and Light
Answer Section

MULTIPLE CHOICE

1.	ANS: C	DIF:	L1	OBJ:	18.1.1
2.	ANS: B	DIF:	L2	OBJ:	18.1.1
3.	ANS: A	DIF:	L1	OBJ:	18.1.2
4.	ANS: B	DIF:	L2	OBJ:	18.1.2
5.	ANS: C	DIF:	L1	OBJ:	18.1.3
6.	ANS: B	DIF:	L2	OBJ:	18.1.3
7.	ANS: D	DIF:	L1	OBJ:	18.1.4
8.	ANS: D	DIF:	L2	OBJ:	18.1.4
9.	ANS: C	DIF:	L1	OBJ:	18.2.1
10.	ANS: C	DIF:	L2	OBJ:	18.2.1
11.	ANS: B	DIF:	L1	OBJ:	18.2.1
12.	ANS: C	DIF:	L2	OBJ:	18.2.1
13.	ANS: D	DIF:	L1	OBJ:	18.2.2
14.	ANS: B	DIF:	L2	OBJ:	18.2.2
15.	ANS: A	DIF:	L1	OBJ:	18.3.1
16.	ANS: C	DIF:	L2	OBJ:	18.3.1
17.	ANS: B	DIF:	L1	OBJ:	18.3.2
18.	ANS: A	DIF:	L2	OBJ:	18.3.2
19.	ANS: C	DIF:	L1	OBJ:	18.4.1
20.	ANS: D	DIF:	L2	OBJ:	18.4.1
21.	ANS: A	DIF:	L1	OBJ:	18.4.2
22.	ANS: C	DIF:	L2	OBJ:	18.4.2
23.	ANS: D	DIF:	L1	OBJ:	18.4.3
24.	ANS: D	DIF:	L2	OBJ:	18.4.3
25.	ANS: C	DIF:	L1	OBJ:	18.5.1
26.	ANS: B	DIF:	L2	OBJ:	18.5.1
27.	ANS: C	DIF:	L1	OBJ:	18.5.2
28.	ANS: A	DIF:	L2	OBJ:	18.5.2
29.	ANS: C	DIF:	L1	OBJ:	18.5.1
30.	ANS: D	DIF:	L2	OBJ:	18.5.3

COMPLETION

31. ANS: transverse   DIF: L1   OBJ: 18.1.1
32. ANS: infrared   DIF: L1   OBJ: 18.2.1
33. ANS:
    3.00×10^8
    300,000,000
    DIF: L1   OBJ: 18.1.3

34.	ANS:	less	DIF:	L1	OBJ:	18.1.4
35.	ANS:	translucent	DIF:	L1	OBJ:	18.3.1
36.	ANS:	red	DIF:	L1	OBJ:	18.4.2
37.	ANS:	black	DIF:	L1	OBJ:	18.4.3
38.	ANS:	vacuum	DIF:	L1	OBJ:	18.1.1
39.	ANS:	electrons	DIF:	L1	OBJ:	18.5.1
40.	ANS:	wavelength	DIF:	L1	OBJ:	18.2.1
41.	ANS:	transmits	DIF:	L2	OBJ:	18.3.1
42.	ANS:	gamma	DIF:	L1	OBJ:	18.2.2
43.	ANS:	vacuum	DIF:	L2	OBJ:	18.1.2
44.	ANS:	more	DIF:	L2	OBJ:	18.2.1
45.	ANS:	refraction	DIF:	L2	OBJ:	18.3.2

46. ANS:
frequency
wavelength
DIF: L2   OBJ: 18.4.1

47.	ANS:	amplitude modulation	DIF:	L2	OBJ:	18.2.2
48.	ANS:	laser	DIF:	L2	OBJ:	18.5.3
49.	ANS:	complementary	DIF:	L1	OBJ:	18.4.3
50.	ANS:	visible light	DIF:	L2	OBJ:	18.2.1

SHORT ANSWER

51. ANS: Electromagnetic waves can travel through a vacuum; sound waves cannot. Also, electromagnetic waves are transverse waves, whereas sound waves are longitudinal waves.
DIF: L2   OBJ: 18.1.1

52. ANS: Amplitude varies with the information coded in it for broadcast.
DIF: L1   OBJ: 18.5.2

53. ANS: air   DIF: L1   OBJ: 18.1.2

54. ANS: the emission of electrons from metal caused by light striking the metal
DIF: L2   OBJ: 18.1.3

55. ANS: Light intensity decreases as distance from the source increases.
DIF: L2   OBJ: 18.1.4

56. ANS: radio waves   DIF: L1   OBJ: 18.2.1

57. ANS: X-rays are used to make images of bones. Gamma rays are used to make images of the brain and to kill cancer cells.
DIF: L2   OBJ: 18.2.2

58. ANS: radio waves (radio and television signals); microwaves and radar waves (microwave ovens); infrared rays (heat lamps)
DIF: L1   OBJ: 18.2.1

59. ANS: If you can see through a material, but the image is blurred or indistinct, it is translucent.
DIF: L1   OBJ: 18.3.1

60. ANS: Blue light is scattered by small particles in the atmosphere, leaving the longer wavelengths such as red and orange to be seen coming from the sun.
    DIF: L1   OBJ: 18.3.2

61. ANS: A polarizing filter transmits light that vibrates only in one plane.
    DIF: L1   OBJ: 18.3.2

62. ANS: what the object is made of and the color of light striking the object
    DIF: L2   OBJ: 18.4.2

63. ANS: Magenta is one of the primary colors of pigments.
    DIF: L1   OBJ: 18.4.3

64. ANS: excited atoms emitting electrons   DIF: L2   OBJ: 18.5.1

65. ANS: A laser emits a straight, narrow, intense beam of coherent light; other light sources produce light that spreads out in all directions as it moves away from the source.
    DIF: L1   OBJ: 18.5.3

PROBLEM

66. ANS: $\text{wavelength} = \dfrac{\text{speed}}{\text{frequency}} \quad \dfrac{3.00 \times 10^8 \text{m/s}}{9.4 \times 10^9 \text{Hz}} = 0.032 \text{ m}$

    DIF: L2   OBJ: 18.1.2

ESSAY

67. ANS: According to modern theory, light is both a particle and a wave. In 1801, Thomas Young proved that light behaves like a wave by showing that light produces interference patterns like a wave. A century later, Albert Einstein proposed that light consists of discrete particles called photons and demonstrated the effects of light striking metal—the photoelectric effect.
    DIF: L2   OBJ: 18.1.3

68. ANS: The full range of wave frequencies of electromagnetic radiation is called the electromagnetic spectrum. In order of increasing frequency, the electromagnetic spectrum includes radio waves (radio, television, microwave ovens, radar), infrared rays (heat lamps), visible light (communication), ultraviolet rays (kill microorganisms), X-rays (medical imaging), and gamma rays (kill cancer cells). Visible light is the only part of the spectrum that we can see, and it is a very small part.
    DIF: L2   OBJ: 18.2.1

69. ANS: Polarized light is light with waves that vibrate in only one plane. Unpolarized light vibrates in all directions. A vertical polarizing filter, such as polarized sunglasses, do not transmit light waves that vibrate in a horizontal plane, thus blocking some glaring light.
    DIF: L2   OBJ: 18.3.2

70. ANS: Sodium-vapor lights are efficient. Where many lights are needed, such as in streets and parking lots, they can be economical to use. They give off a very bright, yellow light. The yellow light can alter the color of the objects it illuminates, which can be a disadvantage.
    DIF: L2   OBJ: 18.5.2

OTHER

71. ANS: Radio waves; FM signals usually have higher frequencies than AM signals have.
    DIF: L1   OBJ: 18.2.1
72. ANS: High frequency waves such as X-rays and gamma rays have higher energy photons than lower frequency waves such as radio waves and infrared rays.
    DIF: L1   OBJ: 18.2.1
73. ANS: infrared rays; between visible light and microwaves
    DIF: L1   OBJ: 18.2.2
74. ANS: visible light   DIF: L1   OBJ: 18.4.1
75. ANS: Red would be at the end of the visible spectrum with the lowest frequency and longest wavelength of all the colors, just above the infrared range. *Infra* means "under," so *infrared* means "under red." In the same way, *ultra* means "beyond," so *ultraviolet* means "beyond violet." Violet would be at the end of the visible spectrum with the shortest wavelength and the highest frequency.
    DIF: L1   OBJ: 18.2.1
76. ANS: Transparent; the submerged portion of the pencil can be seen clearly regardless of the apparent break caused by refraction.
    DIF: L2   OBJ: 18.3.1
77. ANS: Because the light bends as it moves from one medium into another, the image you see appears bent as well.
    DIF: L2   OBJ: 18.3.2
78. ANS: White light is made up of all the frequencies that produce colored light.
    DIF: L2   OBJ: 18.4.1
79. ANS: Blue; all colors are absorbed except blue.
    DIF: L2   OBJ: 18.4.2
80. ANS: Black; there is no blue incident light to reflect.
    DIF: L2   OBJ: 18.4.3

Name _____ Class _____ Date _____

Chapter 19 Optics

Multiple Choice

Identify the letter of the choice that best completes the statement or answers the question.

_____ 1. For reflection off a plane mirror, the angle of incidence
    a. is greater than the angle of reflection.   c. equals the angle of reflection.
    b. is less than the angle of reflection.   d. changes the angle of reflection.

_____ 2. What is the angle of incidence?
    a. the angle that the reflected ray makes with a line drawn perpendicular to the reflecting surface
    b. the angle that the incident ray makes with a line drawn perpendicular to the reflecting surface
    c. the angle the reflecting surface makes with the ground
    d. the angle that is parallel to the reflection angle

_____ 3. The law of reflection states that if the angle of incidence is 45 degrees, the angle of reflection is
    a. 90 degrees.   c. 45 degrees.
    b. 20.25 degrees.   d. 180 degrees.

_____ 4. A mirror with a flat surface is a
    a. plane mirror.   c. concave mirror.
    b. convex mirror.   d. virtual mirror.

_____ 5. In a plane mirror, the light rays appear to come from
    a. in front of the mirror.   c. a distance behind the observer.
    b. an angle above the mirror.   d. behind the mirror.

_____ 6. Unlike a virtual image, a real image
    a. forms at the curvature of a reflecting surface.
    b. can be viewed on a screen.
    c. cannot be viewed on a screen.
    d. is always upright.

Name _____ Class _____ Date _____

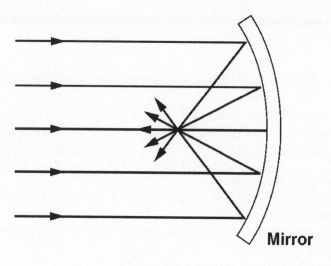

Figure 19-1

_____ 7. What is the point called at which the reflected rays intersect in Figure 19-1?
a. virtual image
b. plane image
c. focal point
d. illumination point

_____ 8. A concave mirror can form
a. only virtual images.
b. only real images.
c. both virtual and real images.
d. none of the above

_____ 9. Why do plane mirrors and convex mirrors form only virtual images?
a. because they both cause light rays to spread out
b. because reflected rays appear to come from behind the mirror
c. because the focal point is in front of the mirror
d. because they both show a wide angle of view

_____ 10. Light refracts when it
a. bounces off a surface.
b. changes speed.
c. comes from a laser.
d. spreads out from its source.

_____ 11. Suppose a light ray traveling in air passes sideways through a glass of water and comes out the other side. How many times will the light ray refract?
a. one time; through the water
b. two times; through the glass and the water
c. three times; through glass, water, and glass again
d. four times; through glass, water, glass, and air

_____ 12. Because air causes light to slow only slightly, air's index of refraction is
a. low.
b. high.
c. moderate.
d. nonexistent.

_____ 13. The speed of light in water is 2.25×10^8 m/s. What is correct about the index of refraction of water?
a. It is 0.
b. It is <1.
c. It is equal to 1.
d. It is >1.

____ 14. Which index of refraction represents the most optically dense material?
   a.   1.77   c.   1.33
   b.   2.42   d.   1.00

____ 15. A concave lens can only form a
   a.   real image.   c.   virtual image.
   b.   reversed image.   d.   magnified image.

____ 16. An object located between a convex lens and its focal point forms a(an)
   a.   reduced virtual image.   c.   reduced real image.
   b.   enlarged virtual image.   d.   enlarged real image.

____ 17. Light can be transmitted through long fiber optic strands because of total
   a.   refraction.   c.   internal reflection.
   b.   external diffraction.   d.   interference.

____ 18. Total internal reflection occurs when the angle of incidence
   a.   is zero.   c.   exceeds the critical angle.
   b.   is less than the critical angle.   d.   equals the angle of reflection.

____ 19. Which optical instrument uses a large concave mirror, a plane mirror, and a convex lens to gather light, focus, and enlarge an image?
   a.   refracting telescope   c.   reflecting telescope
   b.   microscope   d.   film camera

____ 20. Which statement is correct regarding a refracting telescope?
   a.   It produces an enlarged real image.   c.   It produces a reduced-size image.
   b.   It produces an enlarged virtual image. d.   It produces a small, upside-down image.

____ 21. What must be done to a film camera to bring an object into focus on the film?
   a.   The lens must be moved toward or away from the film.
   b.   The diaphragm must be closed.
   c.   The film must be coated with a light-sensitive chemical.
   d.   The film must be developed and printed.

____ 22. What is the function of a diaphragm in a film camera?
   a.   It directs the image to the viewfinder.
   b.   It focuses incoming light rays.
   c.   It opens the shutter.
   d.   It controls the amount of light passing through the film camera.

____ 23. Which part of a film camera focuses incoming light rays?
   a.   diaphragm   c.   shutter
   b.   lens   d.   viewfinder

____ 24. A compound microscope uses
   a.   a mirror to reflect an image of a small object.
   b.   two convex lenses to magnify a small object.
   c.   a convex mirror and a lens to enlarge an image.
   d.   a mirror that flips up to let light through the lens.

_____ 25. Which statement best explains how a compound microscope produces the image you see?
a. The objective lens produces an image that becomes the "object" for the eyepiece lens.
b. The glass slide enlarges the object placed over the light.
c. The objective lens magnifies an image, and the eyepiece lens is used to focus the image.
d. The eyepiece magnifies the object on the slide.

_____ 26. The lens of the human eye focuses light by
a. changing its index of refraction.
b. controlling the amount of light entering the eye.
c. changing color.
d. changing shape.

_____ 27. Which of the following correctly describes the path that light takes when it enters the eye?
a. cornea, pupil, lens, retina
c. lens, cornea, pupil, retina
b. pupil, cornea, lens, retina
d. retina, lens, cornea, pupil

_____ 28. How is the iris of an eye similar to the diaphragm of a film camera?
a. They both control the amount of light passing through.
b. They both focus light rays.
c. They both produce an upside-down image.
d. They both control the movement of the lens.

_____ 29. Farsightedness can be corrected by using eyeglass lenses that are
a. concave in shape and cause light rays entering the eyes to converge.
b. convex in shape and cause light rays entering the eyes to diverge.
c. concave in shape and cause light rays entering the eyes to diverge.
d. convex in shape and cause light rays entering the eyes to converge.

_____ 30. A vision problem that results in seeing blurry images at all distances is called
a. nearsightedness.
c. astigmatism.
b. farsightedness.
d. a blind spot.

Completion
Complete each sentence or statement.

31. The law of reflection states that the angle of reflection is equal to the angle of

_____.

32. The angles of incidence and reflection are the angles that rays make relative to a line drawn
_____ to the surface of a mirror.

33. The image that appears to be behind a plane mirror is a(an) _____ image.

Name _____ Class _____ Date _____

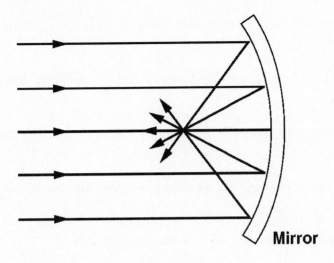

Figure 19-1

34. The mirror in Figure 19-1 is a(an) _____ mirror.

35. The type of image that can be projected on a screen is a(an) _____ image.

36. Mirrors that curve outward and away from the center are called _____ mirrors.

37. A bowl-shape that could hold water can be described as having a(an) _____ shape.

38. When light exits a vacuum and enters any other medium, it _____.

39. A material's index of refraction is a measure of how the speed of light in that material slows compared to the speed of light in a(an) _____.

40. Light rays passing through a convex lens converge at the _____ point on the other side of the lens.

41. Light rays are generally unable to _____ through the sides of curving fiber optic strands.

42. The greater a material's index of refraction, the more likely it is that light passing through the material will be totally _____.

43. Unlike a reflecting telescope, a refracting telescope uses a series of _____ to focus light from distant objects.

44. Like a human eye, a film camera has a convex _____ that forms an upside-down image.

45. The light source for a compound microscope can be either an electric light or light reflected from a(an) _____.

46. The objective of a compound microscope produces an enlarged, upside-down, _____ image.

47. The iris controls the amount of light entering the eye by adjusting the size of the _____.

48. Nerve endings in the retina that are most sensitive to low-intensity light are called _____.

49. Nerves on the retina that are sensitive to color are called _____.

50. Nearsightedness results when light rays from distant objects focus in front of the _____.

Short Answer

51. What is the usual method of graphically analyzing how light rays behave when they strike mirrors or pass through lenses?

52. If you are standing 1 meter in front of a plane mirror, how far does your image appear to be behind the mirror?

53. List two facts about the blind spot in the human eye.

54. Describe how you could focus the light from a bulb into a beam.

55. What determines the type of image produced in a concave mirror?

56. Water has an index of refraction of 1.33, and glass has an index of refraction of 1.50. Which refracts light more and why?

57. How is the index of refraction of a material related to the speed of light?

58. Explain why convex lenses are also called converging lenses.

59. What is the principle that makes fiber optics able to transmit data in the form of light pulses over long distances with little loss in signal strength?

60. What is one basic difference between a reflecting telescope and a refracting telescope in how they collect and focus light?

61. What is the purpose of the diaphragm in a film camera?

62. Why must a microscope slide be made of a transparent material like glass if the glass does not magnify the image?

63. How many and what kind of lenses does a compound microscope use to magnify small objects?

64. What controls the movement of the iris of the human eye?

65. What are two causes of farsightedness?

Essay
On a separate sheet of paper, write an answer to each of the following questions.

66. An incident ray of light strikes a plane mirror at an angle of 45 degrees with the surface of the mirror. What is the angle of reflection? Explain your answer. It may help to sketch a ray diagram.

67. What is refraction? Compare the refraction of light in water with light in diamond.

68. Suppose a beam of light passes straight up through water toward a water-air boundary. Then, the beam is gradually rotated so the angle of incidence becomes larger and larger. What will be observed about the reflection and refraction of the beam of light?

69. Infer why it is necessary, after focusing the image, to control the amount of light that enters a film camera when taking a photograph.

70. Explain the difference between rods and cones in the retina of the human eye. Also, explain the effectiveness of rods and cones in varying light levels.

Name _____ Class _____ Date _____

Other

USING SCIENCE SKILLS

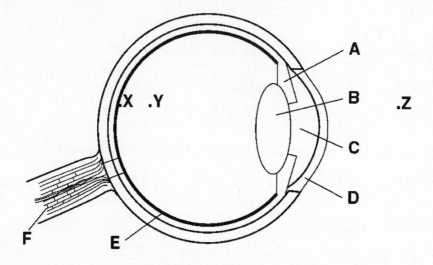

Figure 19-2

71. **Predicting** Figure 19-2 shows the lens of an eye that is focused on a nearby object at point Z. If the eye refocuses on a far object, what happens to the shape of the lens? How?

72. **Applying Concepts** Locate and name the part of the eye in Figure 19-2 that first refracts light. Why does light refract there?

73. **Inferring** In Figure 19-2, a real image is formed at point X. What part of the eye is located at point X? How does the brain interpret the image formed at point X?

74. **Using Models** Examine Figure 19-2. List the structures labeled A–F, and state the function of each structure.

75. **Applying Concepts** Find the location of label Y in Figure 19-2. In an eye exam, the doctor finds that your eyes form images at point Y. What is her diagnosis, and how will she most likely treat it?

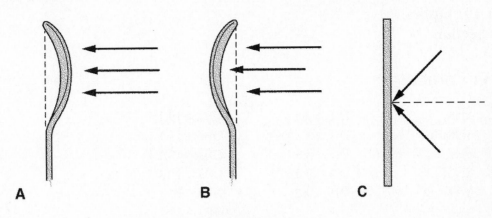

Figure 19-3

76. **Comparing and Contrasting** Compare A, B, and C in Figure 19-3. Which best illustrates the law of reflection? Explain your answer.

77. **Interpreting Graphics** What kind of mirror is C in Figure 19-3? What kind of image does it produce?

78. **Applying Concepts** What type of mirrors are represented by A, B, and C in Figure 19-3? How does each mirror affect parallel light rays that strike it?

79. **Interpreting Graphics** What kind of image does A in Figure 19-3 produce?

80. **Applying Concepts** In an experiment, the three mirrors shown in A, B, and C in Figure 19-3 are placed the same distance from an object so that each mirror produces the same type of image. What type of image do the three mirrors form, and how do the sizes of the images compare? (Assume that the shapes of mirror A and B are similar.)

Chapter 19   Optics
Answer Section

MULTIPLE CHOICE

1.	ANS: C	DIF: L1	OBJ:	19.1.1
2.	ANS: B	DIF: L2	OBJ:	19.1.1
3.	ANS: C	DIF: L1	OBJ:	19.1.1
4.	ANS: A	DIF: L1	OBJ:	19.1.2
5.	ANS: D	DIF: L2	OBJ:	19.1.2
6.	ANS: B	DIF: L1	OBJ:	19.1.3
7.	ANS: C	DIF: L2	OBJ:	19.1.3
8.	ANS: C	DIF: L1	OBJ:	19.1.4
9.	ANS: B	DIF: L2	OBJ:	19.1.4
10.	ANS: B	DIF: L1	OBJ:	19.2.1
11.	ANS: D	DIF: L2	OBJ:	19.2.1
12.	ANS: A	DIF: L1	OBJ:	19.2.2
13.	ANS: D	DIF: L2	OBJ:	19.2.2
14.	ANS: B	DIF: L2	OBJ:	19.2.2
15.	ANS: C	DIF: L1	OBJ:	19.2.3
16.	ANS: A	DIF: L2	OBJ:	19.2.3
17.	ANS: C	DIF: L1	OBJ:	19.2.4
18.	ANS: C	DIF: L2	OBJ:	19.2.4
19.	ANS: C	DIF: L1	OBJ:	19.3.1
20.	ANS: B	DIF: L2	OBJ:	19.3.1
21.	ANS: A	DIF: L1	OBJ:	19.3.2
22.	ANS: D	DIF: L1	OBJ:	19.3.2
23.	ANS: B	DIF: L1	OBJ:	19.3.2
24.	ANS: B	DIF: L1	OBJ:	19.3.3
25.	ANS: A	DIF: L2	OBJ:	19.3.3
26.	ANS: D	DIF: L1	OBJ:	19.4.1
27.	ANS: A	DIF: L2	OBJ:	19.4.1
28.	ANS: A	DIF: L2	OBJ:	19.4.1
29.	ANS: D	DIF: L2	OBJ:	19.4.2
30.	ANS: C	DIF: L1	OBJ:	19.4.2

COMPLETION

31. ANS: incidence   DIF: L1   OBJ: 19.1.1

32. ANS:
    perpendicular
    at right angles
    DIF: L2   OBJ: 19.1.1

33. ANS: virtual   DIF: L2   OBJ: 19.1.2

34.	ANS: concave	DIF: L1	OBJ: 19.1.3
35.	ANS: real	DIF: L2	OBJ: 19.1.3
36.	ANS: convex	DIF: L1	OBJ: 19.1.4
37.	ANS: concave	DIF: L2	OBJ: 19.1.4
38.	ANS: slows down	DIF: L1	OBJ: 19.2.1
39.	ANS: vacuum	DIF: L2	OBJ: 19.2.2
40.	ANS: focal	DIF: L1	OBJ: 19.2.3
41.	ANS: exit	DIF: L1	OBJ: 19.2.4
42.	ANS: internally reflected	DIF: L2	OBJ: 19.2.4
43.	ANS: lenses	DIF: L2	OBJ: 19.3.1
44.	ANS: lens	DIF: L1	OBJ: 19.3.2
45.	ANS: mirror	DIF: L2	OBJ: 19.3.3
46.	ANS: real	DIF: L2	OBJ: 19.3.3
47.	ANS: pupil	DIF: L1	OBJ: 19.4.1
48.	ANS: rods	DIF: L2	OBJ: 19.4.1
49.	ANS: cones	DIF: L2	OBJ: 19.4.2
50.	ANS: retina	DIF: L1	OBJ: 19.4.2

SHORT ANSWER

51. ANS: ray diagrams   DIF: L1   OBJ: 19.1.1

52. ANS: 1 meter   DIF: L1   OBJ: 19.1.2

53. ANS: Student answers may include the following: located on the retina, has no rods or cones, cannot sense light, location where the nerve endings come together to form the optic nerve.
    DIF: L2   OBJ: 19.4.1

54. ANS: When the bulb is placed at the focal point of a concave mirror, the reflected light rays will be parallel.
    DIF: L2   OBJ: 19.1.4

55. ANS: the location of the object relative to the focal point
    DIF: L1   OBJ: 19.1.3

56. ANS: Glass slows and bends light more than water because glass has a greater index of refraction.
    DIF: L1   OBJ: 19.2.1

57. ANS: The index of refraction is a ratio of the speed of light in a vacuum to the speed of light in the material. The greater the index of refraction, the slower is the speed of light in that material.
    DIF: L1   OBJ: 19.2.2

58. ANS: Convex lenses cause incoming parallel rays to come together or converge on the other side of the lens.
    DIF: L1   OBJ: 19.2.3

59. ANS: total internal reflection of light rays
    DIF: L2   OBJ: 19.2.4

60. ANS: A reflecting telescope uses mirrors; a refracting telescope does not.
    DIF: L1   OBJ: 19.3.1

61. ANS: The diaphragm controls the amount of light passing into the film camera.
    DIF: L2   OBJ: 19.3.2
62. ANS: to allow light to pass from the source below the slide up through the lenses of the microscope
    DIF: L2   OBJ: 19.3.3
63. ANS: two convex lenses   DIF: L1   OBJ: 19.3.3
64. ANS: The brain, by responding to the sensed light level in the eye, controls the amount of light in the eye by expanding and contracting the iris.
    DIF: L1   OBJ: 19.4.1
65. ANS: a cornea that is not curved enough and an eyeball that is too short
    DIF: L1   OBJ: 19.4.2

ESSAY

66. ANS: The angle of incidence is 45 degrees because the angle is measured between the incident ray and a line perpendicular to the mirror (not the ray and the mirror). The angle of reflection is equal to the angle of incidence of 45 degrees.
    DIF: L2   OBJ: 19.1.1
67. ANS: Refraction is the bending of the light rays as they enter a new medium at an angle. Because it has a greater index of refraction, a light ray would bend more entering diamond than it would entering air.
    DIF: L2   OBJ: 19.2.1
68. ANS: As the beam rotates and the angle of incidence increases, the amount of light reflected increases and the amount of light refracted decreases. Eventually, the angle of incidence reaches the critical angle, and the light undergoes total internal reflection.
    DIF: L2   OBJ: 19.2.4
69. ANS: The focused light reacts with a light-sensitive chemical coating on the film. In dim light, more light needs to strike the film to record the image. In very bright light, less light is required to keep from overexposing the film. The diaphragm is the part of the film camera that controls light exposure.
    DIF: L2   OBJ: 19.3.2
70. ANS: Rods are nerve endings that are sensitive to low light levels and are more effective at sensing objects at night. They help distinguish black, white, and shades of gray. Cones are sensitive to color, but are not as sensitive as rods in low light. In low light, it is more difficult to distinguish colors.
    DIF: L2   OBJ: 19.4.1

OTHER

71. ANS: The lens becomes longer and thinner. The muscles that control the shape of the lens relax.
    DIF: L2   OBJ: 19.4.1
72. ANS: Light first enters the eye at D, the cornea, and refracts because the index of refraction in the cornea is different from the index of refraction in air.
    DIF: L2   OBJ: 19.2.1

73. ANS: Point X is the retina. The brain interprets the image right-side-up.
    DIF: L2   OBJ: 19.2.3
74. ANS:
    A, iris; controls the amount of light entering the eye
    B, lens; focuses incoming light
    C, pupil; opening that allows light rays to enter the eye
    D, cornea; outer coating of the eye that helps focus light
    E, retina; back of the eye, which has light-sensitive cells that send image messages to the optic nerve
    F, optic nerve; carries image messages to the brain
    DIF: L2   OBJ: 19.4.1
75. ANS: nearsightedness; eyeglasses with diverging lenses to reposition the image on the retina
    DIF: L2   OBJ: 19.4.2
76. ANS: C; the ray diagram shows that the angle of incidence is equal to the angle of reflection.
    DIF: L1   OBJ: 19.1.1
77. ANS: a plane mirror; a virtual image   DIF: L1   OBJ: 19.1.2
78. ANS:
    Possible answers:
    A: convex mirror; a convex mirror causes light rays that are parallel to its optical axis to spread out after reflection.
    B: concave mirror; a concave mirror causes light rays that are parallel to its optical axis to come together after reflection.
    C: plane mirror; a plane mirror causes parallel light to remain parallel after reflection.
    DIF: L2   OBJ: 19.1.3
79. ANS: a virtual image   DIF: L2   OBJ: 19.1.4
80. ANS: Each image is a virtual image. The image formed by A is reduced, the image formed by B is enlarged, and the image formed by C is the same size as the object.
    DIF: L2   OBJ: 19.1.4

Chapter 20   Electricity

Multiple Choice
Identify the letter of the choice that best completes the statement or answers the question.

_____ 1. If an atom loses electrons, it becomes a
    a.   negatively charged ion.   c.   neutral atom.
    b.   positively charged ion.   d.   neutral ion.

_____ 2. The strength of an electric field depends on the
    a.   amount of charge that produced the field.
    b.   distance from the charge.
    c.   amount of charge on a test charge placed in the field.
    d.   both A and B

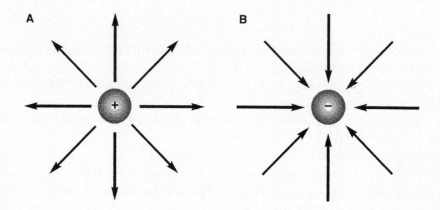

Figure 20-1

_____ 3. If the two charges represented in Figure 20-1 were brought near each other, they would
    a.   attract each other.   c.   cause static discharge.
    b.   repel each other.   d.   have no affect on each other.

_____ 4. What is the SI unit of electric charge?
    a.   ampere   c.   volt
    b.   ohm   d.   coulomb

_____ 5. Walking across a carpet is an example of charge being transferred by
    a.   contact.   c.   static electricity.
    b.   induction.   d.   friction.

_____ 6. If a neutral metal comb is held near an object with a negative charge, the comb will become charged by
    a.   induction.   c.   friction.
    b.   contact.   d.   static discharge.

_____ 7. What type of current is used in a battery?
    a. parallel current
    b. alternating current
    c. direct current
    d. potential current

_____ 8. The type of current in your school is mostly
    a. direct current.
    b. alternating current.
    c. series current.
    d. produced by batteries.

_____ 9. Which of the following materials allows charges to flow easily?
    a. glass
    b. wood
    c. an electrical conductor
    d. an electrical insulator

_____ 10. An electrical insulator has
    a. electrons that freely move.
    b. more protons than electrons.
    c. negatively charged ions.
    d. electrons tightly bound to its atoms.

_____ 11. Resistance is affected by a material's
    a. thickness.
    b. length.
    c. temperature.
    d. all of the above

_____ 12. Which of the following would reduce the resistance of a metal wire?
    a. increasing its thickness
    b. increasing its temperature
    c. increasing its length
    d. all of the above

_____ 13. What is the difference in electrical potential energy between two places in an electric field?
    a. current
    b. resistance
    c. potential difference
    d. induction

_____ 14. Which of the following is maintained across the terminals of a battery?
    a. a potential difference
    b. a voltage drop
    c. an electric charge
    d. both A and B

_____ 15. The current in a clothes iron measures 5.0 amps. The resistance of the iron is 24 ohms. What is the voltage?
    a. 120 V
    b. 4.8 V
    c. 19 V
    d. 600 V

_____ 16. Which of the following represents Ohm's law?
    a. $I = V \times R$
    b. $V = I \times R$
    c. $R = V \times I$
    d. $V = I \div R$

_____ 17. How many paths through which charge can flow would be shown in a circuit diagram of a series circuit?
    a. one
    b. two
    c. none
    d. an unlimited number

_____ 18. Most of the circuits in your home are
    a. series circuits.
    b. parallel circuits.
    c. reversible circuits.
    d. closed circuits.

_____ 19. What is the unit of electric power?
a. ampere
b. volt
c. watt
d. ohm

_____ 20. If you know the power rating of an appliance and the voltage of the line it is attached to, you can calculate the current the appliance uses by
a. multiplying the voltage by the power.
b. subtracting the power from the voltage.
c. dividing the voltage by the power.
d. dividing the power by the voltage.

_____ 21. Which of the following provides electrical safety?
a. circuit breaker
b. fuse
c. ground-fault circuit interrupter
d. all of the above

_____ 22. A ground-fault circuit interrupter shuts down a circuit if it
a. melts.
b. senses an overload.
c. senses unequal currents.
d. senses moisture.

_____ 23. Information sent as patterns and codes in the controlled flow of electrons through a circuit is a(an)
a. electronic signal.
b. digital signal.
c. analog signal.
d. integrated signal.

_____ 24. Electronic signals that are smoothly varying signals produced by continuously changing the voltage or current in a circuit are
a. digital signals.
b. cathode rays.
c. diode signals.
d. analog signals.

_____ 25. A vacuum tube can be used to
a. change alternating current into direct current.
b. increase the strength of a signal.
c. turn a current on or off.
d. all of the above

_____ 26. Which of the following is made from a crystalline solid that conducts a current only under certain circumstances?
a. vacuum tube
b. cathode-ray tube
c. analog devise
d. semiconductor

_____ 27. A solid-state component with three layers of semiconductors is a(an)
a. transistor.
b. diode.
c. vacuum tube.
d. integrated circuit.

_____ 28. A thin slice of silicon that contains many solid-state components is a(an)
a. transistor.
b. integrated circuit.
c. diode.
d. cathode-ray tube.

_____ 29. What do transistors do in a mobile phone?
a. store electric charge
b. maintain proper voltage
c. store data
d. amplify the phone's incoming signal

Name _____ Class _____ Date _____

____ 30. What solid-state component in a mobile phone maintains proper voltage levels in the circuits?
  a. transistors   c. diodes
  b. capacitors   d. microchips

Completion
Complete each sentence or statement.

31. The electric field around a positive charge points _____ the charge.

32. Electric force is _____ proportional to the amount of charge and _____ proportional to the square of the distance between the charges.

33. Like charges _____ and opposite charges _____.

34. When a pathway through which charges can move forms suddenly, _____ occurs.

35. The SI unit of electric current is the _____.

36. Scientists usually define the direction of current as the direction in which _____ charges would flow.

37. Wood, plastic, and rubber are good electrical _____, and copper is a good electrical _____.

38. The SI unit of resistance is the _____.

39. A material that has almost zero resistance when it is cooled to low temperatures is a(an) _____.

40. Potential difference is measured in _____.

41. A complete path through which charge can flow is an electric _____.

42. To calculate power, multiply voltage measured in _____ by _____ measured in amps.

43. The transfer of excess charge through a conductor to Earth is called _____.

44. A(An) _____ signal encodes information as a string of 1's and 0's.

45. A cathode-ray tube is a type of _____ tube.

46. In pure form, germanium and silicon are _____ conductors.

47. A p-type semiconductor is made by adding a trace amount of boron to

   _____.

48. A solid-state component that combines an n-type and a p-type semiconductor is a(an)

   _____.

49. In an electronic device, a diode can be used to change alternating current to

   _____ current.

50. Communication devices use _____ circuits known as

   _____ to make them more portable, reliable, and affordable.

Short Answer

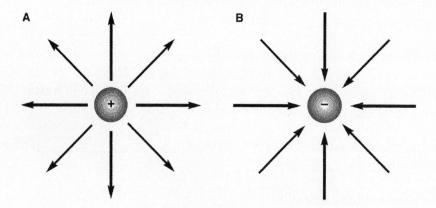

Figure 20-1

51. In Figure 20-1, where is the field of each charge the strongest?

52. What is a charge's electric field?

53. What are three ways that a charge can be transferred?

54. What is the law of conservation of charge?

55. What is the difference between direct current and alternating current?

56. Explain why metal wire coated with plastic or rubber is used in electric circuits.

57. What are three common voltage sources?

58. What is the voltage in a circuit if the current is 3 amps and the resistance is 3 ohms? Explain your answer.

59. If the voltage is 90 volts and the resistance is 30 ohms, what is the current? Explain your answer.

60. How much energy does a 50-watt light bulb use compared to a 100-watt light bulb if both are shining for the same length of time? Explain your answer.

61. What is a circuit breaker?

62. Electric current is used for different purposes. Compare the use of electric current by a computer and by a toaster.

63. What are two types of electronic signals, and how is each produced?

64. What is the difference between n-type and p-type semiconductors?

65. Name three kinds of solid-state components.

Essay
On a separate sheet of paper, write an answer to each of the following questions.

66. How are friction, induction, and static discharge involved in lightning?

67. Explain why a battery causes charge to flow spontaneously when the battery is inserted in a circuit.

68. Suppose you have one light bulb in a simple circuit. If you add a second identical light bulb in series, what would happen to the brightness of the first bulb? If instead you add the second bulb in parallel, what would happen to the brightness of the first bulb? Explain your answers.

69. Why does plugging too many appliances into the same circuit cause too much current to flow through the circuit? What can happen as a result?

70. Explain the flow of electrons in p-type semiconductors and why it looks like positive charges flow.

Name _____ Class _____ Date _____

Other

USING SCIENCE SKILLS

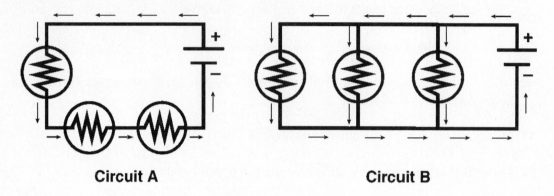

Circuit A   **Circuit B**

Figure 20-2

71. **Classifying** Are both circuits in Figure 20-2 series circuits? Explain your answer.

72. **Comparing and Contrasting** In which direction do the electrons move in Figure 20-2? How does this compare to the direction of the current?

73. **Interpreting Graphics** What objects and how many of each object would you need to draw if symbols were not used in Figure 20-2?

74. **Predicting** Based on the circuit diagrams in Figure 20-2, what would happen if one of the bulbs in Circuit A burned out? What would happen if one of the bulbs in Circuit B burned out? Explain your answers.

75. **Comparing and Contrasting** In Figure 20-2, what device could be added to the circuits to open the circuits? Explain how this device works. Compare this device to safety devices that stop the current in a home.

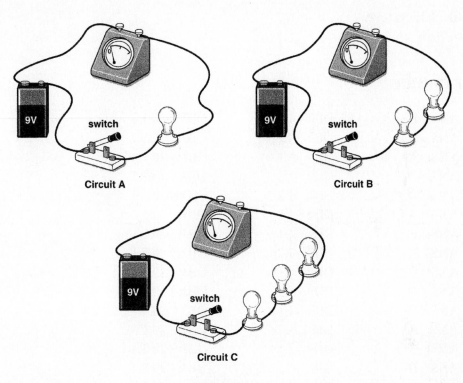

Figure 20-3

76. **Comparing and Contrasting** Compare the resistance in the three circuits shown in Figure 20-3 when the switches are closed. Explain the cause of any differences.

77. **Comparing and Contrasting** In Figure 20-3, how will the current compare in Circuits A, B, and C when the switches are closed? Explain your answer.

78. **Applying Concepts** Explain why the filaments in the light bulbs become hotter than the connecting wires in Figure 20-3.

79. **Predicting** When the switches are closed in Figure 20-3, which bulbs will be the brightest and which will be the dimmest? Assume that all of the light bulbs and batteries are identical. Explain your answer.

80. **Problem Solving** Using the same materials, how could you change the circuits in Figure 20-3 so that all the bulbs would have the same brightness? Explain your answer.

Chapter 20   Electricity
Answer Section

MULTIPLE CHOICE

1.	ANS: B	DIF:	L1	OBJ:	20.1.1
2.	ANS: D	DIF:	L2	OBJ:	20.1.1
3.	ANS: A	DIF:	L1	OBJ:	20.1.2
4.	ANS: D	DIF:	L2	OBJ:	20.1.2
5.	ANS: D	DIF:	L1	OBJ:	20.1.3
6.	ANS: A	DIF:	L2	OBJ:	20.1.3
7.	ANS: C	DIF:	L1	OBJ:	20.2.1
8.	ANS: B	DIF:	L2	OBJ:	20.2.1
9.	ANS: C	DIF:	L1	OBJ:	20.2.2
10.	ANS: D	DIF:	L2	OBJ:	20.2.2
11.	ANS: D	DIF:	L1	OBJ:	20.2.3
12.	ANS: A	DIF:	L2	OBJ:	20.2.3
13.	ANS: C	DIF:	L1	OBJ:	20.2.4
14.	ANS: D	DIF:	L2	OBJ:	20.2.4
15.	ANS: A	DIF:	L2	OBJ:	20.2.5
16.	ANS: B	DIF:	L1	OBJ:	20.2.5
17.	ANS: A	DIF:	L2	OBJ:	20.3.1
18.	ANS: B	DIF:	L2	OBJ:	20.3.1
19.	ANS: C	DIF:	L1	OBJ:	20.3.2
20.	ANS: D	DIF:	L2	OBJ:	20.3.2
21.	ANS: D	DIF:	L1	OBJ:	20.3.3
22.	ANS: C	DIF:	L2	OBJ:	20.3.3
23.	ANS: A	DIF:	L1	OBJ:	20.4.1
24.	ANS: D	DIF:	L1	OBJ:	20.4.1
25.	ANS: D	DIF:	L1	OBJ:	20.4.2
26.	ANS: D	DIF:	L2	OBJ:	20.4.2
27.	ANS: A	DIF:	L1	OBJ:	20.4.3
28.	ANS: B	DIF:	L1	OBJ:	20.4.3
29.	ANS: D	DIF:	L2	OBJ:	20.4.4
30.	ANS: C	DIF:	L2	OBJ:	20.4.4

COMPLETION

31.	ANS: away from	DIF:	L1	OBJ:	20.1.1
32.	ANS: directly, inversely	DIF:	L2	OBJ:	20.1.1
33.	ANS: repel, attract	DIF:	L1	OBJ:	20.1.2

34. ANS:
    static discharge
    electric discharge
    DIF: L2   OBJ: 20.1.3
35. ANS:
    ampere
    amp
    DIF: L1   OBJ: 20.2.1
36. ANS: positive   DIF: L2   OBJ: 20.2.1
37. ANS: insulators, conductor   DIF: L1   OBJ: 20.2.2
38. ANS: ohm   DIF: L1   OBJ: 20.2.3
39. ANS: superconductor   DIF: L2   OBJ: 20.2.3
40. ANS:
    volts
    joules per coulomb
    DIF: L2   OBJ: 20.2.4
41. ANS: circuit   DIF: L1   OBJ: 20.3.1
42. ANS: volts, current   DIF: L1   OBJ: 20.3.2
43. ANS: grounding   DIF: L1   OBJ: 20.3.3
44. ANS: digital   DIF: L1   OBJ: 20.4.1
45. ANS: vacuum   DIF: L1   OBJ: 20.4.2
46. ANS: poor   DIF: L2   OBJ: 20.4.2
47. ANS:
    silicon
    germanium
    DIF: L2   OBJ: 20.4.2
48. ANS: diode   DIF: L1   OBJ: 20.4.3
49. ANS: direct   DIF: L1   OBJ: 20.4.4
50. ANS: integrated, microchips   DIF: L2   OBJ: 20.4.4

SHORT ANSWER

51. ANS: Both fields are strongest nearest the charge, where the lines representing the field are closest together.
    DIF: L2   OBJ: 20.1.1
52. ANS: the effect an electric charge has on other charges in the space around it
    DIF: L2   OBJ: 20.1.2
53. ANS: by friction, contact, and induction   DIF: L1   OBJ: 20.1.3
54. ANS: It is a law that states that the total charge in an isolated system is constant.
    DIF: L2   OBJ: 20.1.3
55. ANS: In direct current, the charge flows only in one direction. In alternating current, the charge regularly reverses its direction.
    DIF: L1   OBJ: 20.2.1

56. ANS: The wire is a conductor and carries the charges. The plastic or rubber is an insulator and does not carry the charges. The coating helps control the current and keep it where it is needed.
DIF: L2   OBJ: 20.2.2

57. ANS: batteries, solar cells, and generators
DIF: L1   OBJ: 20.2.4

58. ANS: 9 volts; because voltage is equal to the current multiplied by the resistance
DIF: L1   OBJ: 20.2.5

59. ANS: 3 amps, or amperes; because current is equal to voltage (90 volts) divided by resistance (30 ohms)
DIF: L2   OBJ: 20.2.5

60. ANS: A 50-watt light bulb uses half the energy that a 100-watt light bulb uses. Energy equals power (watts) multiplied by time. The time is the same, and the power of a 50-watt bulb is half as much, so the energy used by the 50-watt bulb is half as much.
DIF: L2   OBJ: 20.3.2

61. ANS: a switch that opens when current in a circuit is too high
DIF: L1   OBJ: 20.3.3

62. ANS: A computer uses electric current to process or transmit information, while a toaster uses electric current to change electrical energy into thermal energy.
DIF: L1   OBJ: 20.4.1

63. ANS: Analog signals are produced by continuously varying the voltage or current, and digital signals are produced by turning the current on and off.
DIF: L2   OBJ: 20.4.1

64. ANS: In n-type semiconductors, electrons flow, and in p-type semiconductors, positively charged "holes" flow.
DIF: L2   OBJ: 20.4.2

65. ANS: diodes, transistors, and integrated circuits
DIF: L2   OBJ: 20.4.3

ESSAY

66. ANS: Charges can build up in a storm cloud from friction between moving air masses. Negative charge in the lower part of the cloud induces a positive charge in the ground below the cloud. As the amount of charge in the cloud increases, the force of attraction between the charges in the cloud and charges in the ground increases. Eventually, the air becomes charged, forming a pathway for electrons to travel from the cloud to the ground. The sudden discharge that follows is lightning.
DIF: L2   OBJ: 20.1.3

67. ANS: The battery is a source of electrical energy. A voltage drop, or potential difference, is maintained across the negative and positive terminals of a battery. Charge flows spontaneously from a higher electrical potential energy to a lower electrical potential energy.
DIF: L2   OBJ: 20.2.4

68. ANS: The brightness of the first bulb decreases if a second bulb is added in series but does not change if a second bulb is added in parallel. By adding a second bulb in series, the overall current is reduced because the resistance of the circuit increases. With less current, the brightness of the first bulb decreases because $P = IV$, and I decreases, while V is unchanged. By adding a second bulb in parallel, the total current increases, but the current through the first bulb is unchanged, so its brightness is unchanged.
    DIF: L2   OBJ: 20.3.1

69. ANS: The amount of current in a circuit can increase if the devices are connected in parallel. Each device that is turned on increases the current. If the current exceeds safety limits, the wire many overheat and start a fire unless a fuse melts or the circuit breaker switches off.
    DIF: L2   OBJ: 20.3.3

70. ANS: A p-type semiconductor is made by adding trace amounts of boron to silicon. A space, called a hole, occurs at each boron atom. The holes are positively charged. When charge flows, electrons are attracted toward the positively charged holes in the p-semiconductor. As electrons jump from hole to hole, it looks like a flow of positive charge because the locations of the holes change.
    DIF: L2   OBJ: 20.4.2

OTHER

71. ANS: No; only Circuit A is a series circuit. In Circuit A, the current can follow only one path through all three bulbs. Circuit B is a parallel circuit because the current can follow a separate path through each of the three bulbs.
    DIF: L1   OBJ: 20.3.1

72. ANS: The electrons move from the negative terminal of the battery to the positive terminal of the battery. This is opposite the direction in which the current moves.
    DIF: L1   OBJ: 20.3.1

73. ANS: For each circuit, three bulbs and a battery would need to be drawn.
    DIF: L1   OBJ: 20.3.1

74. ANS: If a bulb in Circuit A burned out, the path for a charge is broken, and the other two light bulbs will go out. If a bulb in Circuit B burned out, the charge can still flow through the paths with the other two bulbs, and the other bulbs stay lit.
    DIF: L1   OBJ: 20.3.1

75. ANS: A switch could be added. When the switch is open, the circuit is not a complete loop, and the current immediately stops. A person must manually open and close the switch. In a home, fuses and circuit breakers are safety devices that automatically stop the current if too much current flows through the circuit.
    DIF: L1   OBJ: 20.3.3

76. ANS: The light bulbs are sources of resistance, so Circuit A has the least resistance because the electrons pass through only one light bulb. Circuit B has more resistance than A has because Circuit B has two light bulbs. Circuit C has three light bulbs and the most resistance. Although other parts of the circuits, such as the wire, are sources of resistance, they are the same in all three circuits.
    DIF: L2   OBJ: 20.2.5

77. ANS: Circuit A will have more current flowing through it than Circuit B will, and Circuit C will have the least current flowing through it. More current can flow when there is less resistance, and, since light bulbs are a source of resistance, Circuit A has the least resistance and the most current.

DIF: L2   OBJ: 20.2.5

78. ANS: In the filament, which is a thin wire, the resistance is high. The electrons collide more often in the filament, so the filaments become hotter than the connecting wires.

DIF: L2   OBJ: 20.2.5

79. ANS: The bulb in Circuit A will be the brightest. The bulbs in Circuit C will be the dimmest. Each bulb is a source of resistance, and as resistance increases, current decreases. Bulbs shine less brightly as the current decreases.

DIF: L2   OBJ: 20.2.5

80. ANS: All the bulbs would have the same brightness if Circuits B and C were rewired as parallel circuits. Some wires would need to be cut in half to do this. Then, the current would have a separate path through each bulb and would not be affected by the resistance of another bulb.

DIF: L2   OBJ: 20.2.5

Name _____ Class _____ Date _____

Chapter 21   Magnetism

Multiple Choice
Identify the letter of the choice that best completes the statement or answers the question.

_____ 1. The force a magnet exerts on another magnet, on iron or a similar metal, or on moving charges is
a.   an electric force.
b.   a magnetic force.
c.   proportional to the charge of the magnet.
d.   proportional to the mass of the magnet.

_____ 2. Which of the following statements describes the interaction between magnetic poles?
a.   Like poles attract each other.
b.   Like poles repel each other, and opposite poles attract each other.
c.   Opposite poles repel each other.
d.   Like poles attract each other, and opposite poles repel each other.

_____ 3. How does the magnetic force exerted by a magnet change as the distance between two magnets increases?
a.   The magnetic force increases.
b.   The magnetic force stays the same.
c.   The magnetic force decreases.
d.   The magnetic force does not change with distance.

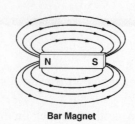

Bar Magnet

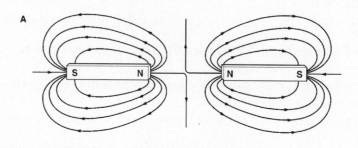

A

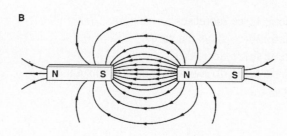

B

Figure 21-1

_____ 4. In Figure 21-1, what magnetic poles are shown on the two bar magnets in A and B?
   a. A: north and south; B: both north
   b. A: both south; B: both north
   c. A: both north; B: both south
   d. A: north and south; B: both south

_____ 5. Which statement describes magnetic field lines at the north pole and south pole of a bar magnet?
   a. Field lines begin near the magnet's south pole and extend toward its north pole.
   b. Field lines begin near both the magnet's north and south poles and meet in the middle.
   c. Field lines begin near the center of the magnet and extend toward the north and south poles.
   d. Field lines begin near the magnet's north pole and extend toward its south pole.

_____ 6. What is the name of the area surrounding Earth that is influenced by Earth's magnetic field?
   a. magnetosphere
   b. atmosphere
   c. magnetic domain
   d. magnetic declination

_____ 7. Which of the following statements is true about Earth's magnetic poles?
   a. They are located at Earth's geographic poles.
   b. They are the areas where Earth's magnetic field is weakest.
   c. They are the areas where Earth's magnetic field is strongest.
   d. Earth has four magnetic poles.

____ 8. A region that has a large number of atoms whose magnetic fields are lined up parallel to a magnet's field is
    a.   the magnetosphere.   c.   a magnetic domain.
    b.   the magnetic declination.   d.   a ferromagnetic region.

____ 9. Which of the following statements is true about ferromagnetic materials?
    a.   All ferromagnetic materials are permanent magnets.
    b.   Ferromagnetic materials that are permanent magnets have domains that are randomly oriented.
    c.   Ferromagnetic materials that are permanent magnets have domains that remain aligned for long periods of time.
    d.   Ferromagnetic materials do not have domains and cannot be magnetized.

____ 10. A ferromagnetic material that has domains that remain aligned for a long period of time is called
    a.   a neutral object.   c.   a permanent magnet.
    b.   nonmagnetic.   d.   a temporary magnet.

____ 11. How can a permanent magnet be demagnetized?
    a.   Cut the magnet in half.   c.   Strike the magnet with a heavy blow.
    b.   Heat the magnet up.   d.   both b and c

____ 12. What creates a magnetic field?
    a.   charged particles that do not move   c.   gravity
    b.   moving electric charges   d.   an isolated magnetic pole

____ 13. If the current in a wire is directed upward, what is the direction of the magnetic field produced by the current?
    a.   counterclockwise in the horizontal plane   c.   in the same direction as the current
    b.   clockwise in the horizontal plane   d.   in the opposite direction to the current

____ 14. If a current-carrying wire is in a magnetic field, in what direction will a force be exerted on the wire?
    a.   perpendicular to the magnetic field and parallel to the current direction
    b.   parallel to both the current direction and the magnetic field
    c.   perpendicular to the current direction and parallel to the magnetic field
    d.   perpendicular to both the magnetic field and the current direction

____ 15. Which of the following statements is true about a current-carrying wire in a magnetic field?
    a.   Reversing the current direction will cause the force deflecting the wire to be parallel to the magnetic field.
    b.   Reversing the current direction will cause the force deflecting the wire to be perpendicular to the magnetic field but in the opposite direction.
    c.   Reversing the current direction will cause the force deflecting the wire to be parallel to the velocity of the charge.
    d.   Reversing the current direction will not affect the force deflecting the wire.

____ 16. A coil of wire that is carrying a current and produces a magnetic field is
    a.   a galvanometer.   c.   a magnetic domain.
    b.   a solenoid.   d.   an electric motor.

_____ 17. Which of the following is the reason "soft" iron is used for the cores of electromagnets?
     a.   It is difficult to magnetize.   c.   It has no magnetic domains.
     b.   It is easily magnetized.   d.   It is a permanent magnet.

_____ 18. The device that measures current in a wire by using the deflections of an electromagnet in an external magnetic field is
     a.   a galvanometer.   c.   an electric motor.
     b.   a solenoid.   d.   a loudspeaker.

_____ 19. The electromagnet in a galvanometer
     a.   increases the voltage in a circuit.
     b.   moves a pointer along a numbered scale in response to a current.
     c.   induces an electric current.
     d.   increases the current in a circuit.

_____ 20. In an electric motor, periodically changing the direction of current in the electromagnet can cause the axle to spin because
     a.   the electromagnet loses its magnetism.
     b.   mechanical energy is converted to electric energy.
     c.   the moving electrons push the electromagnet in the opposite direction.
     d.   the magnetic field reverses direction.

_____ 21. How can the voltage in a coil of wire be increased in the process of electromagnetic induction?
     a.   Move the magnet inside the coil of wire more slowly.
     b.   Hold the magnet stationary.
     c.   Move the coil of wire slowly, and keep the magnet stationary.
     d.   Move the magnet inside the coil of wire more rapidly.

_____ 22. The process of generating an electric current by moving an electrical conductor relative to a magnetic field is called
     a.   magnetization.   c.   electromagnetic induction.
     b.   electromagnetic force.   d.   alternating current.

_____ 23. A device that changes mechanical energy to electric energy by rotating a coil of wire through a magnetic field is called a(an)
     a.   transformer.   c.   electromagnet.
     b.   generator.   d.   current meter.

_____ 24. A DC generator is similar to an AC generator except that in
     a.   DC generators, slip rings produce direct current.
     b.   DC generators, commutators produce direct current.
     c.   AC generators, commutators produce alternating current.
     d.   AC generators, no commutators or slip rings are used.

_____ 25. The strength of the output voltage and current of a transformer are determined by the
     a.   number of turns in the primary and secondary coils.
     b.   strength of the DC current in the primary coil.
     c.   ferromagnetic material of the rings connecting the coils.
     d.   direction of the current in the primary coil.

_____ 26. A transformer has a primary coil with 500 turns and a secondary coil with 250 turns. If the output voltage is 240 volts, what is the input voltage?
   a. 96 volts
   b. 120 volts
   c. 480 volts
   d. 500 volts

_____ 27. If a step-up transformer has a primary coil with 10 turns, how many turns would be required in the secondary coil in order to increase the voltage from 60 volts to 120 volts?
   a. 5 turns
   b. 20 turns
   c. 60 turns
   d. 120 turns

_____ 28. How are step-up transformers used in the transmission of electrical energy?
   a. They increase the voltage and the current for a home.
   b. They decrease the voltage before it leaves a power plant.
   c. They increase the voltage for efficient long-distance transmission.
   d. all of the above

_____ 29. Before electric current in power lines can be safe for your home, it must pass through a
   a. turbine.
   b. step-down transformer.
   c. step-up transformer
   d. generator.

_____ 30. How are fossil fuels used to generate electrical energy?
   a. Heat from burning fuel spins magnets inside an electric motor.
   b. Heat from burning fuel creates steam that spins a turbine.
   c. Heat from burning fuel causes an electric motor to produce a current.
   d. Heat from burning fuel creates steam that turns a transformer.

Completion
Complete each sentence or statement.

31. The region around a magnet that exerts magnetic force is called a(an)

    _____.

32. The region where a magnet's force is strongest is at the _____.

33. The magnetic field lines of a bar magnet begin near the magnet's

    _____.

34. In most materials, the magnetic fields of _____ cancel their effects.

35. The _____ are caused by charged particles from the sun entering Earth's magnetic field.

36. The angle between the direction a compass points and geographic north is called

    _____.

37. In ferromagnetic materials, regions with large numbers of atoms with aligned magnetic fields are called _____.

38. Magnetic domains aligned with an external field _____ as a ferromagnetic material is magnetized.

39. A charged particle moving in a magnetic field will be deflected in a direction _____ to the magnetic field.

40. When the current direction of a current-carrying wire is reversed, the wire will be deflected perpendicular to the magnetic field in the _____ direction.

41. In a solenoid, there will be no magnetic field if there is no _____ in the wires of the coil.

42. The strength of a(an) _____ depends on the current in the solenoid, the number of coils, and the type of ferromagnetic material in the core.

43. A(An) _____ converts electrical energy into mechanical energy.

44. The statement that a voltage can be induced in a conductor by a changing magnetic field is known as _____ law.

45. Moving a magnet through a wire coil can produce a(an) _____ in the coil.

46. A(An) _____ converts mechanical energy into electric energy.

47. Large power plants in the United States currently use _____ generators.

48. _____ transformers decrease the current and increase the voltage in the output circuit.

49. Transformers only work with _____ current.

50. The energy source used to produce most of the electrical energy in the United States is _____.

Short Answer

51. What are magnetic poles?

52. Describe the force between two magnets if you bring a pole of one magnet near the middle of the other magnet.

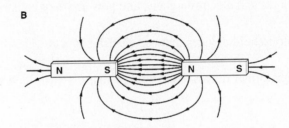

Bar Magnet

A

B

Figure 21-1

53. In Figure 21-1, what do the lines around the bar magnets represent?

54. How does magnetic declination vary?

55. Explain why Earth's magnetic North Pole would be a south pole of a bar magnet.

56. What is the difference between a temporary magnet and a permanent magnet in terms of the magnetic domains?

57. How does a vibrating electric charge produce an electromagnetic wave?

58. How does the charge of a particle affect the direction in which the particle is deflected in a magnetic field?

59. How does the strength of an electromagnet depend on the current and the number of turns in the coil?

60. How does a galvanometer use a magnetic field to indicate the strength of an electric current?

61. Does movement of a conducting wire in a magnetic field always produce a current? Explain your answer.

62. What is a generator and how does it work?

63. Compare generators and electric motors.

64. List five energy sources that are used in the United States to produce electrical energy.

65. How is water used to produce electric energy in a hydroelectric power plant?

Essay

On a separate sheet of paper, write an answer to each of the following questions.

66. Why does a compass point to the east or west of true north in different locations?

67. What are solenoids and electromagnets, and how are they constructed?

68. Describe two household devices that use electromagnets.

69. How does a transformer decrease the voltage that is transmitted across power lines before it enters homes?

70. Explain how a step-up transformer is different from a step-down transformer.

Name _____ Class _____ Date _____

Other

USING SCIENCE SKILLS

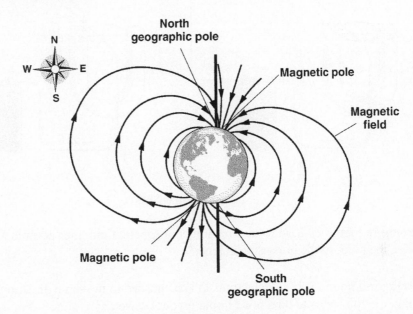

Figure 21-2

71. **Interpreting Graphics** In Figure 21-2, use the direction of the magnetic field lines to determine what type of magnetic pole is located at the magnetic South Pole.

72. **Predicting** Use Figure 21-2 to predict where Earth's magnetic field is strongest. Explain your answer.

73. **Inferring** Use Figure 21-2 to determine in what direction the north magnetic pole of the compass will point. What type of magnetic pole is the compass pointing toward?

74. **Applying Skills** A scientist studying Earth's magnetic field found that at Hot Springs, Arkansas, her compass pointed 5° east of true north. In Durango, Colorado, she took another reading and found that her compass pointed 14° east of true north. Use Figure 21-2 to explain why the two readings were different.

75. **Interpreting Graphics** In Figure 21-2, where is the magnetic field the weakest?

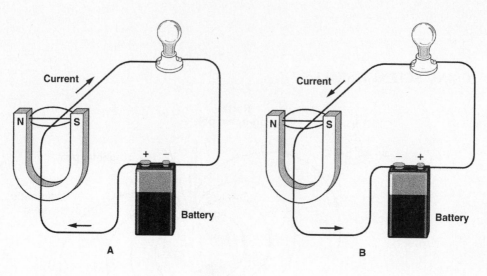

Figure 21-3

76. **Inferring** In Figure 21-3, in what direction do magnetic field lines point in A in the area between the poles of the horseshoe magnet?

77. **Inferring** In Figure 21-3, will electrons in B be pushed in the same direction as the wire is pushed or in the opposite direction? Explain your answer.

78. **Using Models** Use Figure 21-3 to determine whether the current flows toward the negative or positive connection on a battery.

79. **Interpreting Graphics** In Figure 21-3, in what direction is the force deflecting the wire in B?

80. **Interpreting Graphics** In Figure 21-3, in what direction is the force deflecting the wire in A? How does this compare with the force deflecting the wire in B?

Chapter 21   Magnetism
Answer Section

MULTIPLE CHOICE

1.	ANS: B	DIF:	L1	OBJ:	21.1.1
2.	ANS: B	DIF:	L1	OBJ:	21.1.1
3.	ANS: C	DIF:	L1	OBJ:	21.1.1
4.	ANS: A	DIF:	L2	OBJ:	21.1.2
5.	ANS: D	DIF:	L2	OBJ:	21.1.2
6.	ANS: A	DIF:	L1	OBJ:	21.1.3
7.	ANS: C	DIF:	L2	OBJ:	21.1.3
8.	ANS: C	DIF:	L1	OBJ:	21.1.4
9.	ANS: C	DIF:	L2	OBJ:	21.1.4
10.	ANS: C	DIF:	L1	OBJ:	21.1.4
11.	ANS: A	DIF:	L2	OBJ:	21.1.4
12.	ANS: B	DIF:	L1	OBJ:	21.2.1
13.	ANS: A	DIF:	L2	OBJ:	21.2.1
14.	ANS: D	DIF:	L1	OBJ:	21.2.2
15.	ANS: B	DIF:	L2	OBJ:	21.2.2
16.	ANS: B	DIF:	L1	OBJ:	21.2.3
17.	ANS: B	DIF:	L1	OBJ:	21.2.3
18.	ANS: A	DIF:	L1	OBJ:	21.2.4
19.	ANS: B	DIF:	L2	OBJ:	21.2.3
20.	ANS: D	DIF:	L2	OBJ:	21.2.4
21.	ANS: D	DIF:	L2	OBJ:	21.3.1
22.	ANS: C	DIF:	L1	OBJ:	21.3.1
23.	ANS: B	DIF:	L1	OBJ:	21.3.2
24.	ANS: B	DIF:	L2	OBJ:	21.3.2
25.	ANS: A	DIF:	L1	OBJ:	21.3.3
26.	ANS: C	DIF:	L2	OBJ:	21.3.3
27.	ANS: B	DIF:	L2	OBJ:	21.3.3
28.	ANS: C	DIF:	L2	OBJ:	21.3.4
29.	ANS: B	DIF:	L1	OBJ:	21.3.4
30.	ANS: B	DIF:	L2	OBJ:	21.3.4

COMPLETION

31. ANS: magnetic field   DIF: L1   OBJ: 21.1.1
32. ANS:
magnetic poles
poles
    DIF: L2   OBJ: 21.1.1
33. ANS: north pole   DIF: L2   OBJ: 21.1.2

34. ANS:
    electrons
    unpaired electrons
    DIF: L1   OBJ: 21.1.2
35. ANS: aurora   DIF: L1   OBJ: 21.1.3
36. ANS: magnetic declination   DIF: L2   OBJ: 21.1.3
37. ANS:
    magnetic domains
    domains
    DIF: L1   OBJ: 21.1.4
38. ANS: grow larger   DIF: L2   OBJ: 21.1.4
39. ANS:
    perpendicular
    at right angles
    DIF: L1   OBJ: 21.2.1
40. ANS: opposite   DIF: L2   OBJ: 21.2.2
41. ANS: current   DIF: L1   OBJ: 21.2.3
42. ANS: electromagnet   DIF: L2   OBJ: 21.2.3
43. ANS: electric motor   DIF: L2   OBJ: 21.2.4
44. ANS: Faraday's   DIF: L2   OBJ: 21.3.1
45. ANS:
    electric current
    current
    voltage
    DIF: L1   OBJ: 21.3.1
46. ANS: generator   DIF: L1   OBJ: 21.3.1
47. ANS:
    AC
    alternating current
    DIF: L1   OBJ: 21.3.2
48. ANS: Step-up   DIF: L1   OBJ: 21.3.3
49. ANS: alternating   DIF: L2   OBJ: 21.3.3
50. ANS: coal   DIF: L2   OBJ: 21.3.4

SHORT ANSWER

51. ANS: areas of a magnet where the magnetic force is strongest
    DIF: L1   OBJ: 21.1.1
52. ANS: The force will be very weak.   DIF: L1   OBJ: 21.1.2
53. ANS: The lines are field lines representing the magnetic field around the magnets.
    DIF: L1   OBJ: 21.1.2
54. ANS: Magnetic declination varies with your location on Earth.
    DIF: L2   OBJ: 21.1.3
55. ANS: Opposite poles of magnets will attract each other, so the magnetic North Pole must be
    a south pole because it attracts the north pole of a compass needle.
    DIF: L2   OBJ: 21.1.3

56. ANS: In a temporary magnet, the magnetic domains only remain aligned for a short time, but in a permanent magnet, the domains remain aligned for a long time.
    DIF: L1   OBJ: 21.1.4

57. ANS: A vibrating electric charge induces a changing magnet field, which induces a changing electric field. The changing electric and magnetic fields regenerate each other, producing an electromagnetic wave.
    DIF: L2   OBJ: 21.2.1

58. ANS: Positive and negative charges are both deflected perpendicular to the magnetic field and to their direction of motion by the magnetic field but in opposite directions.
    DIF: L1   OBJ: 21.2.2

59. ANS: As current in the solenoid and the number of turns in the coil increase, the strength of the electromagnet increases.
    DIF: L1   OBJ: 21.2.3

60. ANS: An electromagnet on a spring is placed between the poles of a permanent magnet. When there is current in the coil, the resulting magnetic field lines up with the field of the permanent magnet and indicates the strength of the current by deflecting a needle on a dial.
    DIF: L2   OBJ: 21.2.4

61. ANS: No; current is only induced if the conductor is part of a complete circuit.
    DIF: L1   OBJ: 21.3.1

62. ANS: A generator is a device that induces an electric current by rotating a coil of wire in a magnetic field.
    DIF: L1   OBJ: 21.3.2

63. ANS: Generators convert mechanical energy into electrical energy, while electric motors convert electrical energy into mechanical energy.
    DIF: L2   OBJ: 21.3.2

64. ANS: Accept any five of the following: coal, oil, natural gas, hydroelectric, nuclear, wind, solar.
    DIF: L1   OBJ: 21.3.4

65. ANS: Falling water pushes the blades of a turbine, which turns the axle of a generator or spins magnets around coils of wire.
    DIF: L1   OBJ: 21.3.4

ESSAY

66. ANS: The magnetic poles of Earth are not at the same position as the geographic poles. A compass will point along field lines towards the magnetic poles, not the geographic poles. Therefore, the compass direction will vary depending on where you are. The angle between the direction to geographic north and the direction a compass points is called the magnetic declination.
    DIF: L2   OBJ: 21.1.3

67. ANS: A solenoid is a coil of current-carrying wire that produces a magnetic field. A solenoid can be constructed by coiling a length of wire, then connecting either end to a battery. An electromagnet is a solenoid with a core of ferromagnetic material, such as an iron bar. To build an electromagnet, wrap wire around a nail and connect the ends of the wire to a battery or other source of electric current.
    DIF: L2   OBJ: 21.2.3

68. ANS: With an electromagnet, the magnetic field can be turned on and off, which can control a diaphragm to make sounds in a loudspeaker (for example, in a telephone). The strength and direction of the magnetic field can be controlled by modifying the current. This can be used to control the speed with which a motor operates in a device such as a fan.
   DIF: L2   OBJ: 21.2.4

69. ANS: A step-down transformer is used, which has a primary coil with a large number of turns and a secondary coil with fewer turns, so the ratio of the number of secondary coil turns to the primary coil turns is the same as the ratio of the output voltage to the input voltage. This will decrease the voltage.
   DIF: L2   OBJ: 21.3.3

70. ANS: A step-up transformer increases voltage and decreases current. A step-up transformer has a primary coil with fewer turns than in the secondary coil. A step-down transformer increases current and decreases voltage. A step-down transformer has a primary coil with more turns than the secondary coil has.
   DIF: L2   OBJ: 21.3.3

OTHER

71. ANS: The magnetic pole near the magnetic South Pole is a north magnetic pole.
   DIF: L1   OBJ: 21.1.1

72. ANS: Earth's magnetic field is strongest at the magnetic North Pole and at the magnetic South Pole. The field lines are closest together in these regions.
   DIF: L1   OBJ: 21.1.3

73. ANS: The north pole of a compass will point along Earth's magnetic field lines in the general direction of the magnetic pole near the geographic North Pole. This pole is a south magnetic pole.
   DIF: L1   OBJ: 21.1.3

74. ANS: The difference in the angle between the direction toward true north and the direction toward the magnetic pole is called magnetic declination. It varied because the two readings were taken in different locations.
   DIF: L1   OBJ: 21.1.3

75. ANS: midway between the poles, and far from Earth's surface
   DIF: L1   OBJ: 21.1.3

76. ANS: The magnetic field lines point from the north pole to the south pole.
   DIF: L2   OBJ: 21.2.1

77. ANS: The same direction; the direction of current associated with the electron flow is the same as the direction of the current in the wire.
   DIF: L2   OBJ: 21.2.1

78. ANS: The current always flows from the positive connection toward the negative connection on a battery.
   DIF: L2   OBJ: 21.2.1

79. ANS: The force is perpendicular to the direction of the current, in an upward direction.
   DIF: L2   OBJ: 21.2.2

80. ANS: The force is perpendicular to the direction of the current, in a downward direction. The force is in the opposite direction as it would be on the wire in B.
   DIF: L2   OBJ: 21.2.2

Name _____ Class _____ Date _____

Chapter 22 Earth's Interior

Multiple Choice
Identify the letter of the choice that best completes the statement or answers the question.

_____ 1. The study of Earth's composition, structure, and history is called
 a. seismology.
 b. physics.
 c. chemistry.
 d. geology.

_____ 2. Forces that shape Earth's surface can be divided into
 a. constructive and physical.
 b. constructive and destructive.
 c. chemical and destructive.
 d. chemical and physical.

_____ 3. The two layers that make up the lithosphere are the
 a. upper mantle and lower mantle.
 b. oceanic crust and continental crust.
 c. inner core and outer core.
 d. crust and upper mantle.

_____ 4. The three main layers of Earth's interior are the
 a. crust, core, and lithosphere.
 b. crust, mantle, and core.
 c. mantle, inner core, and outer core.
 d. crust, mantle, and asthenosphere.

_____ 5. A naturally occurring, inorganic solid with a crystal structure and a characteristic chemical composition is a
 a. rock.
 b. fossil.
 c. mineral.
 d. piece of granite.

_____ 6. What is a mineral's cleavage?
 a. the resistance of a mineral to scratching
 b. a type of fracture in which a mineral breaks along regular, well-defined planes
 c. the color of a mineral's powder
 d. a type of fracture in which a mineral breaks along a curved surface

_____ 7. Rocks are classified as
 a. sandstone, limestone, or granite.
 b. organic, intrusive, or clastic.
 c. igneous, metamorphic, or sedimentary.
 d. sedimentary, intrusive, or metamorphic.

_____ 8. Intense heat, intense pressure, or reactions with hot water can modify a pre-existing rock to form a(an)
 a. metamorphic rock.
 b. sedimentary rock.
 c. igneous rock.
 d. organic rock.

_____ 9. A series of processes in which rocks are continuously changed from one type to another is called
 a. a volcanic eruption.
 b. the rock cycle.
 c. geology.
 d. melting.

_____ 10. What changes are involved when mud from a lake bottom turns into a sedimentary rock, then into a metamorphic rock?
  a. compaction and cementation, then melting
  b. heat and pressure, then weathering
  c. compaction and cementation, then heat and pressure
  d. melting, then compaction and cementation

_____ 11. The hypothesis that the continents move slowly over Earth's surface and once were joined into one supercontinent is called
  a. plate tectonics.   c. sea-floor spreading.
  b. continental drift.   d. subduction.

_____ 12. Why was Wegener's hypothesis of continental drift originally rejected by geologists?
  a. Wegener did not have any data to support his hypothesis.
  b. The continents of South America and Africa do not fit well together.
  c. Wegener could not explain how the continents could move through the ocean floor.
  d. Wegener's data was incorrect.

_____ 13. New ocean crust is formed along
  a. mid-ocean ridges.   c. mountain belts.
  b. subduction zones.   d. trenches.

_____ 14. A subducting oceanic plate
  a. is less dense than the plate it moves under.
  b. is pushed up and over the continental crust.
  c. sinks into the mantle, forming a trench.
  d. moves horizontally in the opposite direction past the other plate.

_____ 15. The heat that drives mantle convection comes from the cooling of Earth's interior and
  a. the sun.   c. sea-floor spreading.
  b. the decay of radioactive isotopes.   d. trenches.

_____ 16. Plates slide pass each other, and crust is neither created nor destroyed at a
  a. convergent boundary.   c. mid-ocean ridge.
  b. divergent boundary.   d. transform boundary.

_____ 17. What is a break in a rock mass along which movement occurs?
  a. fold   c. fault
  b. earthquake   d. epicenter

_____ 18. Stress in Earth's crust is caused by
  a. folds.   c. earthquakes.
  b. plate movements.   d. faults.

_____ 19. What is the name of the location within Earth where an earthquake begins?
  a. fold   c. epicenter
  b. focus   d. core

_____ 20. P waves
    a. cause Earth to vibrate in the direction of the wave's motion.
    b. cause Earth to vibrate at right angles to the direction the wave moves.
    c. travel along Earth's surface.
    d. move in a rolling motion similar to ocean waves.

_____ 21. The amount of energy released by an earthquake is measured on the
    a. Richter scale.
    b. moment magnitude scale.
    c. modified Mercalli scale.
    d. seismic scale.

_____ 22. Geologists have inferred that Earth's outer core is liquid because
    a. P waves cannot pass through the outer core.
    b. S waves speed up in the outer core.
    c. S waves are bent downward as they travel through the outer core.
    d. S waves cannot pass through the outer core.

_____ 23. The area where magma collects inside a volcano before an eruption is called
    a. the crater.
    b. a caldera.
    c. a vent.
    d. the magma chamber.

_____ 24. What causes the magna inside a volcano to rise towards the surface?
    a. It is a thick liquid, denser than the surrounding rock.
    b. It does not contain dissolved gases.
    c. It is less dense than the surrounding rock.
    d. It is cooler than the surrounding rock.

_____ 25. What determines whether a volcano erupts quietly or explosively?
    a. the size of the volcano
    b. the age of the volcano
    c. the characteristics of the magma
    d. the magnitude of nearby earthquakes

_____ 26. Volcanoes that erupt quietly have what type of magma?
    a. very hot, low-silica magma
    b. high-silica magma
    c. hot, high-silica magma
    d. low temperature magma

_____ 27. Shield volcanoes are produced by
    a. explosive eruptions of lava and ash.
    b. quiet eruptions of lava.
    c. explosive eruptions of ash and cinders.
    d. quiet eruptions that alternate with explosive eruptions.

_____ 28. A steep-sided volcano formed entirely of ash and cinders is a
    a. shield volcano.
    b. composite volcano.
    c. cinder cone.
    d. hot spot.

_____ 29. The largest type of intrusive igneous feature is a
    a. sill.
    b. dike.
    c. volcanic neck.
    d. batholith.

____ 30. A sequence of rock layers consists of horizontal layers of sandstone, granite, and limestone. What type of intrusive igneous feature does the granite layer represent?
   a. a sill
   b. a dike
   c. a batholith
   d. a volcanic neck

Completion
Complete each sentence or statement.

31. The study of the composition, structure, and the history of Earth is called _____.

32. The crust and upper mantle together form the _____.

33. The color of the powder a mineral leaves on an unglazed porcelain tile is called the mineral's _____.

34. Igneous rocks that form at Earth's surface are called _____ rocks.

35. The process by which oceanic plates sink into the mantle through a trench is called _____.

36. The sinking of dense slabs of lithosphere and _____ from within Earth drive the mantle convection current.

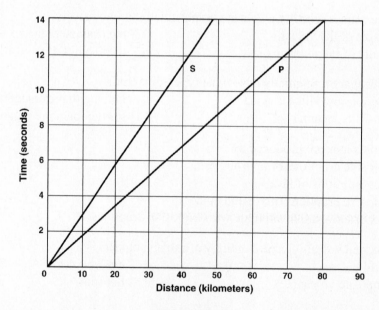

Figure 22-1

37. In Figure 22-1, the P wave will reach a seismograph located 40 kilometers from the earthquake epicenter in _____ seconds.

38. A(An) _____ is a device that is used to detect and record seismic waves.

Name _____ Class _____ Date _____

39. A(An) _____ is the bowl-shaped pit at the top of a volcano.

40. A(An) _____ volcano is created by alternating lava flows and explosive eruptions.

41. The type of sedimentary rock that forms when fragments of pre-existing rocks are cemented together is called a(an) _____ rock.

42. Alfred Wegener proposed that a continent was formed by continental drift. This supercontinent was called _____.

43. Due to sea-floor spreading, the youngest rocks in the ocean floor are found near a(an) _____.

44. Faults and folds are caused by _____. This is a force that squeezes rocks together, pulls them apart, or pushes them in different directions.

45. The _____ scale is used to indicate the energy released by an earthquake.

46. Magma with a(an) _____ viscosity results in explosive volcanic eruptions.

47. The structure that remains when the softer rock around the hardened pipe of a volcano erodes away is called a(an) _____.

48. Subduction occurs at _____ plate boundaries.

49. The seismic waves that compress and expand the ground are called _____ waves.

50. The mineral pyrite has a metallic _____.

Short Answer

51. By what three ways can metamorphic rocks form?

52. What theory explains how Earth's plates form and move?

53. What three factors determine magma viscosity?

54. How does an igneous dike form?

55. What feature is formed when rocks bend under stress but do not break?

56. What part of Earth's core is liquid?

57. What is uniformitarianism?

58. How do geologists classify rocks as igneous, sedimentary, or metamorphic?

59. How do calderas form?

60. In what two types of locations do most volcanoes occur?

61. How is the streak of a mineral obtained?

62. Describe the physical properties of the three layers of the mantle.

63. What is the difference between how an intrusive rock and an extrusive rock forms?

64. Why did most geologists initially reject Alfred Wegener's hypothesis of continental drift?

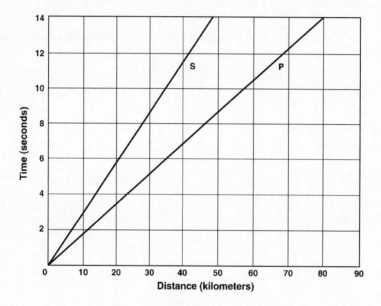

Figure 22-1

65. Use Figure 22-1 to determine when the P waves and S waves reached a seismograph station located 40 km from the earthquake epicenter.

Essay

On a separate sheet of paper, write an answer to each of the following questions.

66. How does the subduction of an oceanic plate result in the formation of a volcano?

67. Describe the rock cycle.

68. Use plate tectonics to explain where mountains form.

69. How can earthquakes be used to map the location of a plate boundary?

70. Your teacher provides you with two white mineral samples. One is quartz and one is calcite. Describe the tests you could use to identify the samples.

Other

USING SCIENCE SKILLS

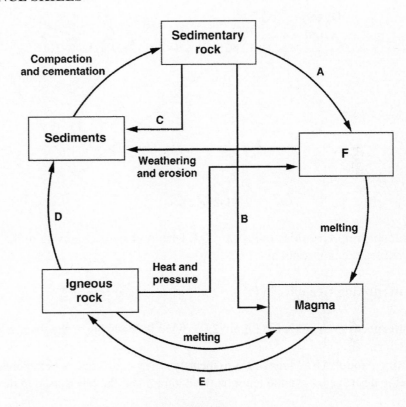

Figure 22-2

71. **Classifying** What type of rock would fit into Figure 22-2 at the location shown by the letter F?

72. **Interpreting Graphics** In Figure 22-2, what processes are represented by the arrow labeled A?

73. **Interpreting Graphics** In Figure 22-2, what process is represented by the arrow labeled E?

74. **Drawing Conclusions** Use Figure 22-2 to describe how an igneous rock could turn into a sedimentary rock and then into a metamorphic rock.

75. **Using Models** Use Figure 22-2 to describe the process involved in the formation of a sedimentary rock.

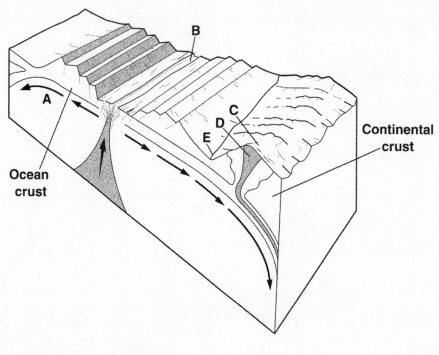

Figure 22-3

76. **Interpreting Graphics** In Figure 22-3, what process is occurring in the area labeled D, and what feature will result at C?

77. **Interpreting Graphics** In Figure 22-3, what is occurring at A?

78. **Interpreting Graphics** In Figure 22-3, what is occurring at the feature labeled B?

79. **Using Models** Use Figure 22-3 to identify where new crust is being created and where it is being destroyed. Give the letter on the diagram and the terms used to describe these areas.

80. **Classifying** In Figure 22-3, what type of plate boundary is illustrated at E?

Chapter 22   Earth's Interior
Answer Section

MULTIPLE CHOICE

1.	ANS: D	DIF:	L1	OBJ:	22.1.1
2.	ANS: D	DIF:	L2	OBJ:	22.1.1
3.	ANS: D	DIF:	L2	OBJ:	22.1.2
4.	ANS: B	DIF:	L1	OBJ:	22.1.2
5.	ANS: C	DIF:	L1	OBJ:	22.2.1
6.	ANS: B	DIF:	L2	OBJ:	22.2.1
7.	ANS: C	DIF:	L1	OBJ:	22.3.1
8.	ANS: A	DIF:	L2	OBJ:	22.3.1
9.	ANS: B	DIF:	L1	OBJ:	22.3.2
10.	ANS: C	DIF:	L2	OBJ:	22.3.2
11.	ANS: B	DIF:	L1	OBJ:	22.4.1
12.	ANS: C	DIF:	L2	OBJ:	22.4.1
13.	ANS: A	DIF:	L1	OBJ:	22.4.2
14.	ANS: C	DIF:	L2	OBJ:	22.4.2
15.	ANS: B	DIF:	L2	OBJ:	22.4.3
16.	ANS: D	DIF:	L1	OBJ:	22.4.3
17.	ANS: C	DIF:	L1	OBJ:	22.5.1
18.	ANS: B	DIF:	L2	OBJ:	22.5.1
19.	ANS: B	DIF:	L1	OBJ:	22.5.2
20.	ANS: A	DIF:	L2	OBJ:	22.5.2
21.	ANS: B	DIF:	L1	OBJ:	22.5.3
22.	ANS: D	DIF:	L2	OBJ:	22.5.3
23.	ANS: D	DIF:	L1	OBJ:	22.6.1
24.	ANS: C	DIF:	L2	OBJ:	22.6.1
25.	ANS: C	DIF:	L1	OBJ:	22.6.2
26.	ANS: A	DIF:	L2	OBJ:	22.6.2
27.	ANS: B	DIF:	L1	OBJ:	22.6.3
28.	ANS: C	DIF:	L2	OBJ:	22.6.3
29.	ANS: D	DIF:	L1	OBJ:	22.6.4
30.	ANS: A	DIF:	L2	OBJ:	22.6.4

COMPLETION

31.	ANS: geology	DIF:	L1	OBJ:	22.1.1
32.	ANS: lithosphere	DIF:	L1	OBJ:	22.1.2
33.	ANS: streak	DIF:	L1	OBJ:	22.2.1
34.	ANS: extrusive	DIF:	L1	OBJ:	22.3.1
35.	ANS: subduction	DIF:	L1	OBJ:	22.4.2
36.	ANS: heat	DIF:	L1	OBJ:	22.4.3

37.	ANS: 7	DIF: L1	OBJ: 22.5.2
38.	ANS: seismograph	DIF: L1	OBJ: 22.5.3
39.	ANS: crater	DIF: L1	OBJ: 22.6.1
40.	ANS: composite	DIF: L1	OBJ: 22.6.3
41.	ANS: clastic	DIF: L2	OBJ: 22.3.2
42.	ANS: Pangaea	DIF: L2	OBJ: 22.4.1
43.	ANS: mid-ocean ridge	DIF: L2	OBJ: 22.4.2
44.	ANS: stress	DIF: L2	OBJ: 22.5.1
45.	ANS: moment magnitude	DIF: L2	OBJ: 22.5.3
46.	ANS: high	DIF: L2	OBJ: 22.6.2
47.	ANS: volcanic neck	DIF: L2	OBJ: 22.6.4
48.	ANS: convergent	DIF: L2	OBJ: 22.4.3
49.	ANS: P	DIF: L2	OBJ: 22.5.2
50.	ANS: luster	DIF: L2	OBJ: 22.2.1

SHORT ANSWER

51. ANS: by heat, pressure, or reactions with hot water
    DIF: L1   OBJ: 22.3.2
52. ANS: the theory of plate tectonics   DIF: L1   OBJ: 22.4.2
53. ANS: water content, silica content, and temperature
    DIF: L1   OBJ: 22.6.2
54. ANS: Magma hardens in a fracture that cuts across other rock layers.
    DIF: L1   OBJ: 22.6.4
55. ANS: a fold   DIF: L1   OBJ: 22.5.1
56. ANS: the outer core   DIF: L1   OBJ: 22.1.2
57. ANS: the idea that the geologic processes operating today also operated in the past
    DIF: L1   OBJ: 22.1.1
58. ANS: by how the rocks form   DIF: L1   OBJ: 22.3.1
59. ANS: After an eruption, the empty magma chamber or main vent of a volcano may collapse, forming a large depression at the top of the volcano.
    DIF: L1   OBJ: 22.6.1
60. ANS: at plate boundaries and at hot spots
    DIF: L1   OBJ: 22.6.3
61. ANS: by scraping the mineral on a piece of unglazed porcelain called a streak plate
    DIF: L2   OBJ: 22.2.1
62. ANS: The lithosphere is cool and rigid; the aesthenosphere is a layer of soft, weak rock that can flow slowly; and the mesosphere is the strong, lowest layer.
    DIF: L2   OBJ: 22.1.2
63. ANS: An intrusive rock cools from magma inside Earth, and an extrusive rock cools from lava at Earth's surface.
    DIF: L2   OBJ: 22.3.1
64. ANS: Wegener could not explain how the continents could move through the solid rock of the ocean floor or what force could move entire continents.
    DIF: L2   OBJ: 22.4.1

65. ANS: The P wave arrived in about 7 seconds, and the S wave arrived in about 11.9 seconds.
    DIF: L2   OBJ: 22.5.2

ESSAY

66. ANS: As the oceanic plate sinks into the mantle in the subduction zone, the plate causes melting. Magma forms and rises to the surface, where it erupts and forms volcanoes.
    DIF: L2   OBJ: 22.6.1

67. ANS: The rock cycle is a series of processes in which rocks continuously change from one type to another. These processes include erosion, weathering, melting, cooling, heat and pressure, and compaction and cementation.
    DIF: L2   OBJ: 22.3.2

68. ANS: Some mountains form at convergent plate boundaries where two plates collide. Other mountains form at divergent plate boundaries along the mid-ocean ridge systems.
    DIF: L2   OBJ: 22.4.2

69. ANS: Earthquake epicenters can occur anywhere, but most earthquakes occur at plate boundaries. Earthquake epicenters commonly follow along a plate boundary and can be used to map the location of the boundary.
    DIF: L2   OBJ: 22.5.3

70. ANS: You could use the hardness test. Quartz would scratch glass, but calcite would not. Calcite also reacts with dilute hydrochloric acid. Place a drop of acid on both samples. The sample that bubbles is calcite.
    DIF: L2   OBJ: 22.2.1

OTHER

71. ANS: metamorphic rock   DIF: L1   OBJ: 22.3.1
72. ANS: heat and pressure   DIF: L1   OBJ: 22.3.2
73. ANS: cooling   DIF: L1   OBJ: 22.3.2
74. ANS: An igneous rock would undergo weathering and erosion to form sediment. The sediment would undergo compaction and cementation to form a sedimentary rock. Heat and pressure would change the sedimentary rock to a metamorphic rock.
    DIF: L2   OBJ: 22.3.1

75. ANS: Weathering and erosion form sediment, which piles up. Over time, this sediment is squeezed and cemented together to form sedimentary rock.
    DIF: L1   OBJ: 22.3.1

76. ANS: melting; volcanoes   DIF: L2   OBJ: 22.4.2
77. ANS: An ocean plate is being subducted beneath a continental plate.
    DIF: L2   OBJ: 22.4.2

78. ANS: New ocean crust is being added as sea-floor spreading is occurring.
    DIF: L2   OBJ: 22.4.2

79. ANS: New crust is being created at B, at a mid-ocean ridge. Crust is being destroyed at A and E in subduction zones.
    DIF: L2   OBJ: 22.4.3

80. ANS: a convergent boundary   DIF: L2   OBJ: 22.4.3

Chapter 23   Earth's Surface

Multiple Choice
Identify the letter of the choice that best completes the statement or answers the question.

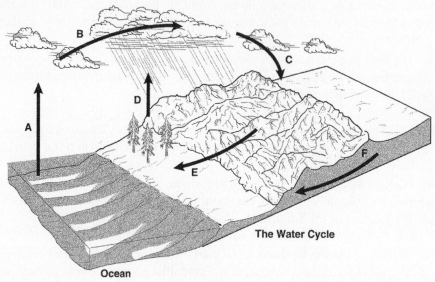

Figure 23-1

_____ 1. In Figure 23-1, what process does the arrow labeled A represent?
    a. transpiration   c. evaporation
    b. condensation   d. precipitation

_____ 2. Which processes are involved in erosion?
    a. precipitation, evaporation, and condensation
    b. weathering, runoff, and transpiration
    c. weathering, evaporation, and runoff
    d. weathering, the force of gravity, and wind

_____ 3. In the water cycle, the process that changes a liquid into a gas is called
    a. transpiration.   c. condensation.
    b. evaporation.   d. precipitation.

_____ 4. Most of Earth's liquid fresh water is found in
    a. groundwater.   c. reservoirs.
    b. lakes and streams.   d. glaciers.

_____ 5. A permeable layer of rock that is saturated with water is called a(an)
    a. water table.   c. watershed.
    b. lake.   d. aquifer.

6. Which of the following is an example of erosion?
   a. to wear down and carry away rock and soil through the force of gravity
   b. to wear down and carry away rock and soil through the action of wind
   c. to wear down and carry away rock and soil through the action of water
   d. all of the above

7. Which of the following is NOT an agent of chemical weathering?
   a. rainwater   c. frost wedging
   b. oxidation   d. carbonic acid

8. Which of the following rock types and conditions would result in the highest rate of chemical weathering?
   a. granite in a cold and dry area   c. slate in a hot and rainy area
   b. limestone in a hot and rainy area   d. granite in a hot and dry area

9. A rapid mass movement of large amounts of rock and soil down a slope is called a
   a. landslide.   c. creep.
   b. slump.   d. mudflow.

10. Tilted telephone poles and fences curving in a downward direction on a hillside are evidence of
   a. a landslide.   c. a slump.
   b. a mudflow.   d. creep.

11. A stream's ability to erode depends mainly on
   a. its temperature.   c. its speed.
   b. the size of the sediment in the stream. d. the shape of its valley.

12. Meanders, V-shaped valleys, and oxbow lakes are all features formed by
   a. glaciers.   c. water deposition.
   b. water erosion.   d. groundwater erosion.

13. A sediment deposit formed when a stream flows into a lake or the ocean is called a(an)
   a. alluvial fan.   c. meander.
   b. delta.   d. natural levee.

14. The portion of a stream that flows through gently sloping flood plains is often characterized by
   a. V-shaped valleys and waterfalls.   c. meanders and oxbow lakes.
   b. steep valleys and rapids.   d. meanders and waterfalls.

15. Caves are formed by erosion from
   a. glaciers.   c. wind.
   b. streams.   d. groundwater.

16. Groundwater forms caves and sinkholes by the process of
   a. chemical weathering.   c. condensation.
   b. physical weathering.   d. mineral deposition.

_____ 17. Unsorted sediment deposited by a glacier is called
    a.   a cirque.   c.   a horn.
    b.   till.   d.   an erratic.

_____ 18. What pyramid-shaped glacial formation is a combination of several connected ridges?
    a.   a horn   c.   a moraine
    b.   a U-shaped valley   d.   a cirque

_____ 19. Wind erodes the land by
    a.   deflation and oxidation.   c.   deflation and plucking.
    b.   abrasion and chemical weathering.   d.   deflation and abrasion.

_____ 20. Deposits formed from windblown dust are called
    a.   moraines.   c.   loess.
    b.   dunes.   d.   cirques.

_____ 21. Which of the following describes the changing conditions in the ocean as depth increases?
    a.   pressure increases, light decreases, and temperature decreases
    b.   pressure decreases, light decreases, and temperature decreases
    c.   pressure increases, light increases, and temperature decreases
    d.   pressure increases, light increases, and temperature increases

_____ 22. Why do most ocean organisms live above a water depth of 500 meters?
    a.   Pressure below that depth is too great.   c.   Pressure below that depth is too low.
    b.   Temperature below that depth is too high.   d.   Light below that depth is too bright.

_____ 23. Surface currents in the ocean are caused by
    a.   deep upwelling.   c.   density differences of ocean water.
    b.   salinity changes with depth.   d.   wind blowing across the ocean surface.

_____ 24. What type of ocean current brings cold water from the deep ocean to the surface?
    a.   a density current   c.   a surface current
    b.   upwelling   d.   a current caused by wind

_____ 25. What is the process that moves sand along a shore?
    a.   abrasion   c.   a spit
    b.   hydraulic action   d.   longshore drift

_____ 26. Which of the following is an example of a feature caused by wave erosion?
    a.   a delta   c.   a sea stack
    b.   an alluvial fan   d.   a spit

_____ 27. The absolute age of an igneous rock found on a beach can be determined by using
    a.   radioactive isotopes.   c.   the law of superposition.
    b.   fossils.   d.   relative dating.

_____ 28. Geologists could use which of the following to compare the age of sedimentary rock layers in Bryce Canyon with sedimentary rock layers in the Grand Canyon?
    a.   radioactive isotopes   c.   relative dating
    b.   index fossils   d.   all of the above

_____ 29. The Triassic, Jurassic, and Cretaceous periods are divisions of
   a. Precambrian time.
   b. the Cenozoic Era.
   c. the Paleozoic Era.
   d. the Mesozoic Era.

_____ 30. When did the first land plants and animals appear in the fossil record?
   a. in the Mesozoic Era
   b. in the Paleozoic Era
   c. during the Triassic period
   d. during the Carboniferous period

Completion

Complete each sentence or statement.

31. A rock that allows water to flow through it is said to be _____.

32. Fresh water on Earth occurs in lakes, ponds, rivers, streams, in groundwater, in the atmosphere as water vapor, and in _____.

33. _____ is the process by which rocks are chemically altered or physically broken down into fragments at or near Earth's surface.

34. The main agent of chemical weathering is _____.

35. Slumping, landslides, mudflows, and _____ are all forms of mass movement.

36. _____ is the process in which particles move in a stream by bouncing along the bottom.

37. A(An) _____ glacier is a thick sheet of ice that covers large areas of land.

38. Deposits of windblown dust are called _____.

39. The process by which sand is moved along a shore is called _____.

40. Humans evolved during the _____ Era.

41. When a stream flows out of a mountain range onto a flat area of land, it deposits sediments in a(an) _____.

42. The carbonic acid that is involved in the formation of caves is formed when rainwater combines with _____ in the air.

43. The _____ is a gently sloping plain covered with shallow water along the edges of continents.

44. Currents in the deep ocean are caused by density differences in ocean water. These density differences are caused by temperature and _____ differences.

Name _____ Class _____ Date _____

45. The _____ is used by geologists to determine the relative ages of sedimentary rock layers.

46. Life on Earth first occurred in _____ time.

47. The top of the region where pore spaces in rock and soil are filled with groundwater is referred to as the _____.

48. An area where there are large variations between high and low temperatures during a 24-hour period should have higher rates of _____ weathering.

49. In mountainous areas, valley glaciers cut _____ valleys.

50. Wave erosion is caused by abrasion and the _____ of waves.

Short Answer

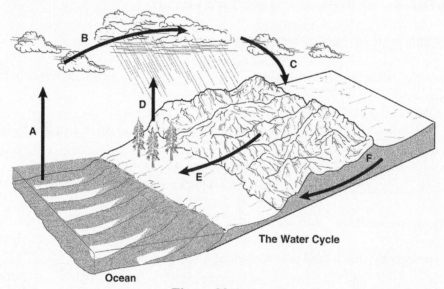

The Water Cycle

Ocean

Figure 23-1

51. In Figure 23-1, what process is labeled C in the diagram?

52. What are three common features of fast-moving streams in mountainous areas?

53. What are two features formed by deposition that are often found in caves?

54. Describe the changes in amount of light, temperature, and pressure as depth in the ocean increases.

55. Briefly describe how upwelling occurs in the ocean.

56. What is the relative age of a sedimentary rock layer?

57. What is the water cycle?

58. What is the land area that contributes water to a river system called?

59. List at least four agents of erosion.

60. What are the four largest divisions of the geologic time scale?

61. What are the processes that make up the water cycle?

62. Compare and contrast weathering and erosion.

63. How are landslides and mudflows alike?

64. Describe three ways that wind erosion moves sediment.

65. Describe how a glacier erodes the land.

Essay
On a separate sheet of paper, write an answer to each of the following questions.

66. Describe the two types of glaciers.

67. Explain how a stream transports sediment of various sizes.

68. Describe the journey of a water molecule through the water cycle.

69. Describe and discuss what causes surface currents and deep currents in the ocean.

70. In order to be useful, an index fossil must be easy to identify, have been widespread, and lived during a short, well-defined period of time. Explain why each of these three factors is important to the usefulness of index fossils in the relative dating of sedimentary rocks.

Name _____ Class _____ Date _____

Other

USING SCIENCE SKILLS

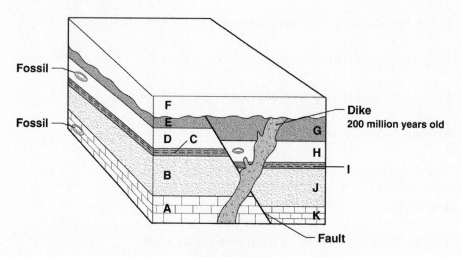

Figure 23-2

71. **Inferring** Which rock layer is the youngest layer shown in Figure 23-2?

72. **Analyzing Data** In Figure 23-2, would a fossil in layer D be younger or older than fossils found in layer B?

73. **Analyzing Data** In Figure 23-2, is the fault older or younger than the dike? Explain.

74. **Interpreting Graphics** In Figure 23-2, on either side of the fault, which rock layers were a single layer before the faulting?

75. **Drawing Conclusions** In Figure 23-2, what can be concluded about the relative ages of the rock layers below layer F? What can be concluded about the absolute ages of these layers?

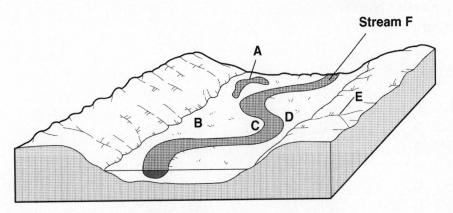

Figure 23-3

76. **Inferring** In Figure 23-3, is the stream flow moving faster at point C or at point D? Explain your answer.

77. **Interpreting Graphics** What is the feature labeled A in Figure 23-3?

78. **Inferring** In Figure 23-3, what process is occurring at C? What process is occurring at D?

79. **Interpreting Graphics** Use Figure 23-3 to describe the area that forms the floodplain for stream F.

80. **Inferring** In Figure 23-3, what are the smaller streams, which are labeled E, called?

Chapter 23   Earth's Surface
Answer Section

MULTIPLE CHOICE

1.	ANS: C	DIF:	L2	OBJ:	23.1.1
2.	ANS: D	DIF:	L2	OBJ:	23.2.1
3.	ANS: B	DIF:	L1	OBJ:	23.1.1
4.	ANS: A	DIF:	L1	OBJ:	23.1.2
5.	ANS: D	DIF:	L1	OBJ:	23.1.1
6.	ANS: D	DIF:	L1	OBJ:	23.2.1
7.	ANS: C	DIF:	L1	OBJ:	23.2.2
8.	ANS: B	DIF:	L2	OBJ:	23.2.2
9.	ANS: A	DIF:	L1	OBJ:	23.2.3
10.	ANS: D	DIF:	L2	OBJ:	23.2.3
11.	ANS: C	DIF:	L1	OBJ:	23.3.1
12.	ANS: B	DIF:	L2	OBJ:	23.3.1
13.	ANS: B	DIF:	L1	OBJ:	23.3.2
14.	ANS: C	DIF:	L2	OBJ:	23.3.2
15.	ANS: D	DIF:	L1	OBJ:	23.3.3
16.	ANS: A	DIF:	L2	OBJ:	23.3.3
17.	ANS: B	DIF:	L1	OBJ:	23.4.1
18.	ANS: A	DIF:	L2	OBJ:	23.4.1
19.	ANS: D	DIF:	L1	OBJ:	23.4.2
20.	ANS: C	DIF:	L1	OBJ:	23.4.2
21.	ANS: A	DIF:	L1	OBJ:	23.5.1
22.	ANS: A	DIF:	L2	OBJ:	23.5.1
23.	ANS: D	DIF:	L1	OBJ:	23.5.2
24.	ANS: B	DIF:	L2	OBJ:	23.5.2
25.	ANS: D	DIF:	L1	OBJ:	23.5.3
26.	ANS: C	DIF:	L2	OBJ:	23.5.3
27.	ANS: A	DIF:	L1	OBJ:	23.6.1
28.	ANS: D	DIF:	L2	OBJ:	23.6.1
29.	ANS: D	DIF:	L1	OBJ:	23.6.2
30.	ANS: B	DIF:	L2	OBJ:	23.6.2

COMPLETION

31.	ANS: permeable	DIF:	L1	OBJ:	23.1.1
32.	ANS: glaciers	DIF:	L1	OBJ:	23.1.2
33.	ANS: Weathering	DIF:	L1	OBJ:	23.2.1
34.	ANS: water	DIF:	L1	OBJ:	23.2.2
35.	ANS: creep	DIF:	L1	OBJ:	23.2.3
36.	ANS: Saltation	DIF:	L1	OBJ:	23.3.1

37.	ANS:	continental	DIF:	L1	OBJ:	23.4.1
38.	ANS:	loess	DIF:	L1	OBJ:	23.4.2
39.	ANS:	longshore drift	DIF:	L1	OBJ:	23.5.3
40.	ANS:	Cenozoic	DIF:	L1	OBJ:	23.6.2
41.	ANS:	alluvial fan	DIF:	L2	OBJ:	23.3.2
42.	ANS:	carbon dioxide	DIF:	L2	OBJ:	23.3.3
43.	ANS:	continental shelf	DIF:	L2	OBJ:	23.5.1
44.	ANS:	salinity	DIF:	L2	OBJ:	23.5.2
45.	ANS:	law of superposition	DIF:	L2	OBJ:	23.6.1
46.	ANS:	Precambrian	DIF:	L2	OBJ:	23.6.2
47.	ANS:	water table	DIF:	L2	OBJ:	23.1.2
48.	ANS:	mechanical	DIF:	L2	OBJ:	23.2.2
49.	ANS:	U-shaped	DIF:	L2	OBJ:	23.4.1
50.	ANS:	hydraulic action	DIF:	L2	OBJ:	23.5.3

SHORT ANSWER

51. ANS: precipitation   DIF: L1   OBJ: 23.1.1

52. ANS: waterfalls, rapids, and V-shaped valleys
    DIF: L1   OBJ: 23.3.2

53. ANS: stalactites and stalagmites   DIF: L1   OBJ: 23.3.3

54. ANS: The amount of light decreases, temperature decreases, and pressure increases.
    DIF: L1   OBJ: 23.5.1

55. ANS: Winds blow warm surface water away from coastal areas, and cold, deep water rises
    up to the surface to take the place of the warmer surface water.
    DIF: L1   OBJ: 23.5.2

56. ANS: the age of the rock layer compared to the ages of other rock layers in a sequence of
    sedimentary rock layers
    DIF: L1   OBJ: 23.6.1

57. ANS: the movement of water between Earth's atmosphere, oceans, land surface, and
    underground
    DIF: L1   OBJ: 23.1.1

58. ANS: a watershed   DIF: L1   OBJ: 23.1.2

59. ANS: Accept any four of the following: wind, glaciers, gravity, groundwater, waves, streams,
    weathering.
    DIF: L1   OBJ: 23.2.1

60. ANS: Precambrian time, Paleozoic Era, Mesozoic Era, and Cenozoic Era
    DIF: L1   OBJ: 23.6.2

61. ANS: precipitation, evaporation, condensation, transpiration, and the return of water to the
    ocean via runoff or groundwater flow
    DIF: L2   OBJ: 23.1.1

62. ANS: Weathering breaks down or chemically alters rocks, while erosion wears down and
    carries away rock and soil. Weathering contributes to erosion.
    DIF: L2   OBJ: 23.2.1

63. ANS: Both occur rapidly on steep slopes.
    DIF: L2   OBJ: 23.2.3
64. ANS: Fine particles are suspended in the air and blown about by the wind. Larger particles bounce along the ground by saltation. The largest particles are pushed along the ground by the wind.
    DIF: L2   OBJ: 23.4.2
65. ANS: As the glacier moves, it grinds and scrapes the bedrock and soil at its base and sides.
    DIF: L2   OBJ: 23.4.1

ESSAY

66. ANS: The two types of glaciers are continental glaciers and valley glaciers. A continental glacier is a thick sheet of ice that covers a very large area. A valley glacier occurs high in a mountain valley. Valley glaciers are much smaller than continental glaciers.
    DIF: L2   OBJ: 23.4.1
67. ANS: Fine sediment is carried in suspension. Some material is carried in solution by the water. Larger particles slide or are pushed along the bottom. Some medium-sized particles move by bouncing along the bottom. This process is called saltation.
    DIF: L2   OBJ: 23.3.1
68. ANS: Possible answer: A molecule of water falls as precipitation; it flows as runoff along the surface; it then soaks into the soil to become groundwater. The groundwater flows toward the coast, where the water molecule flows into the ocean. It then evaporates and travels up into the atmosphere. As it travels up, it cools and condenses. It is joined by other water molecules and then falls back to the surface as precipitation.
    DIF: L2   OBJ: 23.1.1
69. ANS: Surface currents are large streams of ocean water that move continuously over the ocean surface in about the same path. Surface currents are caused by wind blowing across the ocean's surface. Deep currents are caused by differences in the density of ocean water. These density differences can be caused by differences in water temperature or salinity. Cold temperatures or high salinity cause water to become denser.
    DIF: L2   OBJ: 23.5.2
70. ANS: The fossil must be easy to identify so it can be identified by geologists who are not experts in that particular fossil group. In order to date rock layers over large distances, the index fossil must have occurred in a widespread area. If the fossil occurred only in a small, restricted area it will not be useful for matching up or relatively dating rock layers over large regions. If the fossil lived for a long period of time, it would not be very useful in narrowing down the relative age of a rock layer.
    DIF: L2   OBJ: 23.6.1

OTHER

71. ANS: Layer F   DIF: L2   OBJ: 23.6.1
72. ANS: younger   DIF: L2   OBJ: 23.6.1
73. ANS: The fault is older than the dike. The fault must be older than the dike because the fault is cut by the dike.
    DIF: L2   OBJ: 23.6.2

74. ANS: layers A and K, layers B and J, layers C and I, layers D and H, and layers E and G
    DIF: L2   OBJ: 23.6.1
75. ANS: The layers are older than layer F, with layer A–K being the oldest, and E–G the youngest. All of the layers are older than 200 million years because they are cut by the dike, which is 200 million years old.
    DIF: L2   OBJ: 23.6.1
76. ANS: At point D; the stream flow is faster because water moves faster on the outside of the curve in a meander.
    DIF: L1   OBJ: 23.3.2
77. ANS: an oxbow lake   DIF: L1   OBJ: 23.3.2
78. ANS: deposition; erosion   DIF: L1   OBJ: 23.3.1
79. ANS: The flat area around stream F, between the steeper walls of the main valley, is the floodplain.
    DIF: L1   OBJ: 23.3.2
80. ANS: tributaries   DIF: L1   OBJ: 23.3.2

Chapter 24   Weather and Climate

Multiple Choice
Identify the letter of the choice that best completes the statement or answers the question.

____   1.   What gas makes up about 78 percent of dry air?
    a.   oxygen   c.   hydrogen
    b.   nitrogen   d.   carbon dioxide

____   2.   As altitude increases,
    a.   air pressure decreases and density increases.
    b.   air pressure increases and density decreases.
    c.   air pressure and density increase.
    d.   air pressure and density decrease.

____   3.   Most weather takes place in the
    a.   stratosphere.   c.   troposphere.
    b.   thermosphere.   d.   mesosphere.

____   4.   The ozone layer is located in the
    a.   lower troposphere.   c.   upper ionosphere.
    b.   lower thermosphere.   d.   upper stratosphere.

____   5.   Day and night are caused by Earth's
    a.   rotation.   c.   orbit.
    b.   revolution.   d.   tilt.

____   6.   As Earth completes one orbit around the sun, it has completed one
    a.   rotation.   c.   revolution.
    b.   year.   d.   both b and c

____   7.   Which region usually has temperatures cooler than temperatures near the equator?
    a.   tropic zone   c.   temperate zone
    b.   polar zone   d.   both b and c

____   8.   Which of the following lists all the zones in the correct order, starting at the North Pole and ending at the South Pole?
    a.   polar, temperate, tropic, polar   c.   polar, tropic, temperate, polar
    b.   polar, temperate, tropic, temperate, polar   d.   polar, tropic, temperate, tropic, polar

____   9.   About how much of the solar energy that reaches Earth passes through the atmosphere and is absorbed by the surface of Earth?
    a.   20 percent   c.   50 percent
    b.   30 percent   d.   80 percent

____ 10.   Earth's atmosphere is heated mainly by
    a.   heat that travels directly from the sun.   c.   reflected sunlight.
    b.   visible light as it passes through the air.   d.   energy reradiated by Earth's surface.

_____ 11. Which of the following is NOT an example of a global wind?
   a. westerlies
   b. trade winds
   c. polar easterlies
   d. sea breezes

_____ 12. The daily breezes that occur in a city that is located near a large body of water are examples of
   a. local winds.
   b. monsoons.
   c. global winds.
   d. westerlies.

_____ 13. A cloud is a dense, visible mass of
   a. tiny water droplets.
   b. ice crystals.
   c. water vapor.
   d. both a and b

_____ 14. Low, flat layers of clouds that often cover much of the sky and produce steady and widespread rain are
   a. cumulonimbus clouds.
   b. cirrus clouds.
   c. nimbostratus clouds.
   d. altostratus clouds.

_____ 15. Which of the following forms of precipitation falls as a liquid?
   a. rain
   b. freezing rain
   c. hail
   d. both a and b

_____ 16. Round, solid pieces of ice more than 5 millimeters in diameter fall as
   a. hail.
   b. sleet.
   c. snow.
   d. freezing rain.

_____ 17. A maritime tropical air mass that affects weather in the Unites States might form over
   a. the Gulf of Mexico.
   b. Mexico.
   c. Canada.
   d. the North Atlantic ocean.

_____ 18. Which of the following air masses forms over land north of 50° north latitude?
   a. maritime polar
   b. temperate continental
   c. continental polar
   d. continental tropical

_____ 19. What type of front forms when two unlike air masses form a boundary but neither is moving?
   a. warm
   b. cold
   c. stationary
   d. occluded

_____ 20. A cold front forms when a cold air mass
   a. collides with a warm air mass and pushes the warm air up.
   b. collides with a warm air mass and slides over the warm air.
   c. collides with another cold air mass.
   d. stops moving over a particular area.

_____ 21. Which of the following is a weather system with a center of low pressure?
   a. cyclone
   b. anticyclone
   c. warm front
   d. cold front

_____ 22. Which of the following is a characteristic of an anticyclone?
   a.   has a center of high pressure
   b.   has clockwise winds in the Northern Hemisphere
   c.   is generally associated with clear weather
   d.   all of the above

_____ 23. A tropical storm with sustained winds of at least 119 kilometers per hour is called a
   a.   tornado.   c.   monsoon.
   b.   thunderstorm.   d.   hurricane.

_____ 24. A small, intense storm formed when a vertical cylinder of rotating air develops is a
   a.   thunderstorm.   c.   monsoon.
   b.   tornado.   d.   hurricane.

Front A

Front C

Front B

Front D

Figure 24-1

_____ 25. Which of the symbols in Figure 24-1 represents a warm front?
   a.   Front A   c.   Front C
   b.   Front B   d.   Front D

_____ 26. Lines on a weather map that connect points that have the same air temperature are called
   a.   millibars.   c.   isotherms.
   b.   isobars.   d.   front lines.

_____ 27. A description of the pattern of weather over many years is a region's
   a.   weather forecast.   c.   climate.
   b.   air mass.   d.   weather system.

_____ 28. Which of the following factors affect a region's temperature?
   a.   latitude and altitude   c.   ocean currents
   b.   distance from large bodies of water   d.   all of the above

_____ 29. An example of a long-term climate change that occurs naturally is
   a.   an ice age.   c.   global warming.
   b.   an El Niño.   d.   the greenhouse effect.

_____ 30. Which of the following climate changes may be affected by human activities?
   a.   ice age   c.   global warming
   b.   El Niño   d.   monsoon

Completion

Complete each sentence or statement.

31. The _____ forms a protective boundary between Earth and space and provides conditions that are suitable for life.

32. Plants need _____ from the air for photosynthesis, and many animals need _____ from the air to breathe.

33. Of the four layers of the atmosphere, the _____ has the hottest temperatures.

34. The seasons are caused by the _____ of Earth's _____ as Earth moves around the sun.

35. On the two days each year when the sun is directly overhead at noon at latitude 23.5° north or 23.5° south, a(an) _____ occurs.

36. The latitude of the equator is _____, and the latitude of the North Pole is _____.

37. The _____ zones are located from 23.5° north to 66.5° north and from 23.5° south to 66.5° south.

38. Energy is transferred within the troposphere in three ways—radiation, _____, and _____.

39. Wind is air blowing from an area of _____ pressure to an area of _____ pressure.

40. A belt of high-speed wind in the upper troposphere is called the _____.

41. The three basic cloud forms are _____, _____, and _____.

42. Rain, sleet, and snow are types of _____.

43. The size and shape of snowflakes depends on the _____ at which they form.

44. Air masses that form over water tend to have more _____ in them than air masses that form over land.

45. The sharply defined boundary that forms where two unlike air masses meet is called a(an) _____.

46. Air spirals in toward the center of a cyclone but flows away from the center of a(an) _____.

47. A major type of storm associated with lightning, strong winds, and heavy rain or hail is called a(an) _____.

48. _____ works by bouncing radio waves off particles of precipitation in moving storms and then measuring the frequency of the waves that return.

49. The two main factors that determine a region's climate are _____ and _____.

50. _____ is a short-term variation in climate that is caused by a change in the normal direction of winds, which causes ocean currents to shift direction.

Short Answer

51. Describe what the temperatures on Earth would be like during the day and at night if the atmosphere did not exist.

52. List the four layers of the atmosphere, starting with the layer closest to Earth.

53. Why is Earth generally warmer near the equator and colder toward the poles?

54. What is the greenhouse effect?

55. What causes the differences in pressure that result in winds?

56. Explain why sea breezes occur during the day.

57. Why do solid particles such as dust need to be present for clouds to form?

58. How does hail form?

59. What is the difference between sleet and freezing rain?

60. What physical properties of an air mass are affected by where the air mass forms?

61. What weather is associated with a cyclone?

62. How does a thunderstorm form?

Name _____ Class _____ Date _____

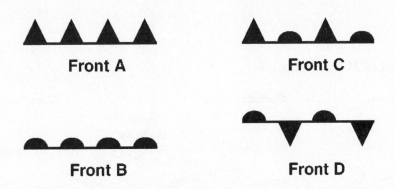

Figure 24-1

63. What is the name of each type of front represented by the symbols in Figure 24-1?

64. What are three factors that affect a region's pattern of precipitation?

65. What are some ways that people could limit the effects of global warming? Explain how these ways would help.

Essay
On a separate sheet of paper, write an answer to each of the following questions.

66. Explain why temperate zones in the Northern Hemisphere and the Southern Hemisphere have the same seasons but are six months apart.

67. What are trade winds and what causes them? How are trade winds in the Northern Hemisphere different from those in the Southern Hemisphere?

68. What are humidity, relative humidity, and dew point? Explain what happens to each if the temperature of the air decreases.

69. Compare the weather that might occur in an area as a warm front passes through, after the warm front has passed through, as a cold front passes through, and after the cold front has passed through.

70. What information can meteorologists obtain from Doppler radar, automated weather stations, and weather satellites? How do high-speed computers help meteorologists?

Name _____ Class _____ Date _____

Other

USING SCIENCE SKILLS

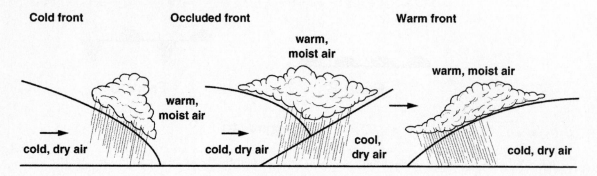

Figure 24-2

71. **Inferring** What causes clouds to form in the three fronts in Figure 24-2?

72. **Interpreting Graphics** Explain what is happening to the two air masses in the cold front in Figure 24-2.

73. **Comparing and Contrasting** Based on your observations of Figure 24-2, how are a cold front and a warm front alike?

74. **Comparing and Contrasting** Based on your observations of Figure 24-2, how are a cold front and a warm front different?

75. **Interpreting Graphics** What has happened to the warm air mass in the occluded front in Figure 24-3?

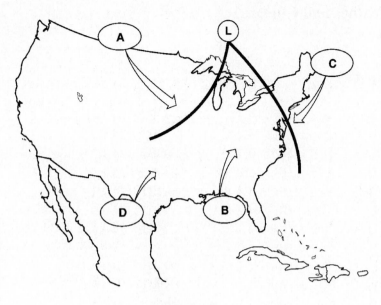

Figure 24-3

76. **Inferring** What factors are used to classify the air masses in Figure 24-3?

77. **Classifying** Based on their locations in Figure 24-3, name the types of air masses represented by A and D and describe the characteristics of each.

78. **Comparing and Contrasting** Based on their locations in Figure 24-3, name the types of air masses represented by B and C. How are they similar, and how are they different?

79. **Predicting** Based on Figure 24-3, what would you expect weather conditions to be like in the southeastern section of the United States at the time this map was drawn? Explain your answer.

80. **Applying Concepts** What does the symbol L represent in Figure 24-3, and what type of weather system is it the center of? What are the characteristics of this weather system?

Chapter 24   Weather and Climate
Answer Section

MULTIPLE CHOICE

1.	ANS: B	DIF: L1	OBJ: 24.1.1
2.	ANS: D	DIF: L2	OBJ: 24.1.1
3.	ANS: C	DIF: L1	OBJ: 24.1.2
4.	ANS: D	DIF: L2	OBJ: 24.1.2
5.	ANS: A	DIF: L1	OBJ: 24.2.1
6.	ANS: D	DIF: L2	OBJ: 24.2.1
7.	ANS: D	DIF: L1	OBJ: 24.2.2
8.	ANS: B	DIF: L2	OBJ: 24.2.2
9.	ANS: C	DIF: L1	OBJ: 24.3.1
10.	ANS: D	DIF: L2	OBJ: 24.3.1
11.	ANS: D	DIF: L1	OBJ: 24.3.2
12.	ANS: A	DIF: L2	OBJ: 24.3.2
13.	ANS: D	DIF: L1	OBJ: 24.4.1
14.	ANS: C	DIF: L2	OBJ: 24.4.1
15.	ANS: D	DIF: L1	OBJ: 24.4.2
16.	ANS: A	DIF: L2	OBJ: 24.4.2
17.	ANS: A	DIF: L1	OBJ: 24.5.1
18.	ANS: C	DIF: L2	OBJ: 24.5.1
19.	ANS: C	DIF: L1	OBJ: 24.5.2
20.	ANS: A	DIF: L2	OBJ: 24.5.2
21.	ANS: A	DIF: L1	OBJ: 24.5.3
22.	ANS: D	DIF: L2	OBJ: 24.5.3
23.	ANS: D	DIF: L1	OBJ: 24.5.4
24.	ANS: B	DIF: L2	OBJ: 24.5.4
25.	ANS: B	DIF: L1	OBJ: 24.6.1
26.	ANS: C	DIF: L2	OBJ: 24.6.1
27.	ANS: C	DIF: L1	OBJ: 24.7.1
28.	ANS: D	DIF: L2	OBJ: 24.7.1
29.	ANS: A	DIF: L1	OBJ: 24.7.2
30.	ANS: C	DIF: L2	OBJ: 24.7.2

COMPLETION

31.	ANS: atmosphere	DIF: L1	OBJ: 24.1.1
32.	ANS: carbon dioxide, oxygen	DIF: L2	OBJ: 24.1.1
33.	ANS: thermosphere	DIF: L2	OBJ: 24.1.2
34.	ANS: tilt, axis	DIF: L1	OBJ: 24.2.1
35.	ANS: solstice	DIF: L2	OBJ: 24.2.1

36. ANS: 0°, 90°   DIF: L1   OBJ: 24.2.2
37. ANS: temperate   DIF: L2   OBJ: 24.2.2
38. ANS: convection, conduction   DIF: L2   OBJ: 24.3.1
39. ANS: high, low   DIF: L1   OBJ: 24.3.2
40. ANS: jet stream   DIF: L2   OBJ: 24.3.2
41. ANS: stratus, cumulus, cirrus   DIF: L1   OBJ: 24.4.1
42. ANS: precipitation   DIF: L1   OBJ: 24.4.2
43. ANS: temperature   DIF: L2   OBJ: 24.4.2
44. ANS: moisture   DIF: L2   OBJ: 24.5.1
45. ANS: front   DIF: L1   OBJ: 24.5.2
46. ANS: anticyclone   DIF: L2   OBJ: 24.5.3
47. ANS: thunderstorm   DIF: L1   OBJ: 24.5.4
48. ANS: Doppler radar   DIF: L1   OBJ: 24.6.1
49. ANS: temperature, precipitation   DIF: L1   OBJ: 24.7.1
50. ANS: El Niño   DIF: L2   OBJ: 24.7.2

SHORT ANSWER

51. ANS: During the day, temperatures would be boiling hot, and at night, they would be
    freezing cold.
    DIF: L2   OBJ: 24.1.1
52. ANS: troposphere, stratosphere, mesosphere, thermosphere
    DIF: L1   OBJ: 24.1.2
53. ANS: Regions near the equator receive more direct sunlight than regions near the poles
    receive.
    DIF: L1   OBJ: 24.2.2
54. ANS: the process by which gases, including water vapor and carbon dioxide, absorb energy,
    radiate energy, and warm the lower atmosphere
    DIF: L1   OBJ: 24.3.1
55. ANS: the uneven heating of Earth's surface
    DIF: L1   OBJ: 24.3.2
56. ANS: During the day, land heats up faster than water does, so the air above the land is
    warmer than the air above the water. The warm air above the land rises and then lowers the air
    pressure, and the cool air over the water flows toward the land, causing a sea breeze.
    DIF: L1   OBJ: 24.3.2
57. ANS: The water vapor in the air needs something to condense upon.
    DIF: L1   OBJ: 24.4.1
58. ANS: Small ice pellets in cumulonimbus clouds are tossed up and down by rising and falling
    air. As they are tossed about, they collide and combine with water droplets that freeze and add
    more layers to the ice. Eventually the pellets become heavy enough to fall to the ground.
    DIF: L1   OBJ: 24.4.2
59. ANS: Sleet is rain that freezes as it falls. Freezing rain falls as rain and freezes after hitting
    the surface.
    DIF: L2   OBJ: 24.4.2

60. ANS: The amount of water vapor in the air mass and the temperature of the air mass are affected by the land or water over which the air mass forms.
DIF: L1   OBJ: 24.5.1

61. ANS: clouds, precipitation, and stormy weather
DIF: L1   OBJ: 24.5.3

62. ANS: A thunderstorm forms when columns of air rise within a cumulonimbus cloud. If the rising air is cooled to the dew point and the convection is strong enough, a thunderstorm results.
DIF: L2   OBJ: 24.5.4

63. ANS: Front A is a cold front, Front B is a warm front, Front C is an occluded front, and Front D is a stationary front.
DIF: L2   OBJ: 24.6.1

64. ANS: latitude, the distribution of air pressure systems and global winds, and the existence of a mountain barrier
DIF: L2   OBJ: 24.7.1

65. ANS: Conserving energy and a greater reliance on solar, nuclear, or geothermal power could limit the effects of global warming because they would reduce the amount of carbon dioxide released.
DIF: L1   OBJ: 24.7.2

ESSAY

66. ANS: As Earth revolves around the sun, the north end of Earth's axis points in the same direction, which is toward the North Star. But the orientation of the axis changes relative to the sun over the course of a year. When the north end of Earth's axis is tilted toward the sun, the south end is tilted away from the sun. At this time, the temperate zone in the Northern Hemisphere has summer, and the temperate zone in the Southern Hemisphere has winter. Six months later, Earth has reached the opposite side of its orbit, and the north end of its axis tilts away from the sun. The temperate zone in the Northern Hemisphere has winter, and the temperate zone in the Southern Hemisphere has summer.
DIF: L2   OBJ: 24.2.1

67. ANS: Trade winds are wind belts or convection cells just north and south of the equator. They are caused by temperature variations across Earth's surface. At the equator, temperatures tend to be warmer than at other latitudes. Warm air rises at the equator, creating a low-pressure region. This warm air is replaced by cooler air brought by global winds blowing near the surface. Higher in the atmosphere, the air blows away from the equator toward the poles. The winds curve because of the Coriolis effect caused by Earth's rotation. Trade winds in the Northern Hemisphere curve to the right and blow from the northeast to the southwest. Trade winds in the Southern Hemisphere curve to the left and blow from the southeast to the northwest.
DIF: L2   OBJ: 24.3.2

68. ANS: Humidity is the amount of water vapor in the air. The humidity stays the same if the temperature decreases. Relative humidity is a ratio of the amount of water vapor in the air compared to the maximum amount of water vapor that can exist at that temperature. The maximum amount of water vapor that can exist in air is greater at high temperatures than at low temperatures. If the temperature decreases, the relative humidity increases even though the amount of water vapor stays the same. The temperature at which air becomes saturated, which is when the relative humidity is 100 percent, is the dew point. If the temperature decreases to the dew point, water vapor will condense.
    DIF: L2   OBJ: 24.4.1

69. ANS: As a warm front passes through, the area might have stratus clouds, steady rain, and occasionally heavy showers or thunderstorms. After the warm front passes through, the skies are mostly clear, there may be some cumulus clouds, and temperatures rise. As a cold front passes through, the area might have cumulus or cumulonimbus clouds, strong winds, severe thunderstorms, and large amounts of precipitation, which usually lasts for only a short time. After the cold front passes through, the skies clear and temperatures drop.
    DIF: L2   OBJ: 24.5.2

70. ANS: Meteorologists use Doppler radar to obtain information about the speed of storms and to track the path of storms. Automated weather stations gather data such as temperature, precipitation, and wind speed and direction. Weather satellites provide information such as cloud cover, humidity, temperature, and wind speed. High-speed computers help meteorologists compile and analyze the large amount of weather data and make forecasts.
    DIF: L2   OBJ: 24.6.1

OTHER

71. ANS: Because cold, dry air is denser than warm, moist air, the cold air pushes the warm air up. As warm air rises, it cools, and water vapor in the air condenses and forms clouds.
    DIF: L1   OBJ: 24.4.1

72. ANS: A cold, dry air mass is overtaking a warm, moist air mass, and the warm air mass is being lifted up by the cold air.
    DIF: L1   OBJ: 24.5.2

73. ANS: Both a cold front and a warm front have a cold, dry air mass and a warm, moist air mass colliding. In both fronts, the cold air is under the warm air, and in both fronts, precipitation can occur.
    DIF: L1   OBJ: 24.5.2

74. ANS: At a cold front, a cold air mass is overtaking a warm air mass and lifting it up. At a warm front, a warm air mass is overtaking a cold air mass and rising over the cold air.
    DIF: L1   OBJ: 24.5.2

75. ANS: The warm air mass has been trapped between two cold air masses, which have forced it to rise, cutting it off from the ground.
    DIF: L1   OBJ: 24.5.2

76. ANS: Air masses are classified by whether they form over land or over water and the latitude at which they form.
    DIF: L2   OBJ: 24.5.1

77. ANS: A is a continental polar air mass and has cold, dry air. D is a continental tropical air mass and has warm, dry air.
    DIF: L2   OBJ: 24.5.1

78. ANS: B is a maritime tropical air mass, and C is a maritime polar air mass. They both form over water and contain moist air. B has warm air and C has cool air.
    DIF: L2   OBJ: 24.5.1

79. ANS: Possible answer: The weather is warm and humid because a maritime tropical air mass, which has warm, moist air, is moving into the area.
    DIF: L2   OBJ: 24.5.1

80. ANS: L represents a center of low pressure or a low. A weather system with an area of low pressure at its center is called a cyclone. This weather system is associated with clouds, precipitation, and stormy weather.
    DIF: L2   OBJ: 24.5.3

Chapter 25   The Solar System

Multiple Choice
Identify the letter of the choice that best completes the statement or answers the question.

____ 1. In a diagram depicting the solar system as heliocentric, what is located at the center?
a. Earth
b. the sun
c. the moon
d. Mars

____ 2. Which of the following is the most likely reason that ancient observers believed that Earth was the center of the universe?
a. The Earth seemed to move on its axis.
b. Earth's motions are only recently known because of high-powered telescopes.
c. Objects in the sky appear to circle around Earth.
d. Ancient observers believed the universe was stationary.

____ 3. The orbit of a planet around the sun is a(an)
a. ellipse.
b. straight line.
c. circle.
d. parabola.

____ 4. Which of the following helps explain why the planets remain in motion around the sun?
a. density
b. gravity
c. inertia
d. both b and c

____ 5. Which of the following objects does NOT orbit directly around the sun?
a. planets
b. comets
c. moons
d. all of the above

____ 6. What led to the discovery of three more planets than those that the ancient observers knew about?
a. the invention of the telescope in 1600
b. the Hubble telescope launched in 1990
c. space missions in the Apollo program
d. observations by *Sputnik 1* in 1957

____ 7. Who was the first American in space?
a. Yuri Gargarin
b. Alan Shepard
c. Chuck Yeager
d. Neil Armstrong

____ 8. Which of the following are currently operating the space station?
a. Soviet cosmonauts
b. a cooperative team of scientists from 16 countries
c. American astronauts
d. a cooperative team of scientists from Russia and the United States

____ 9. Why does Earth's moon have no atmosphere?
a. The average temperature is too high.
b. There are no plants to release oxygen.
c. The moon is too far from Earth.
d. The moon's gravity is too weak to hold onto gas molecules.

____ 10. How might a nitrogen-oxygen atmosphere on the moon affect the range of temperatures on the moon?
   a. An atmosphere might hold heat in, making the moon very hot.
   b. An atmosphere might block heat radiating from the sun, making the moon very cold.
   c. An atmosphere might moderate temperatures, making them more even, such as on Earth.
   d. An atmosphere would have no effect on the range of temperatures on the moon.

____ 11. On the moon, maria are
   a. meteoroid craters.
   b. low, flat plains.
   c. rough mountains.
   d. lunar seas filled with water.

____ 12. What is meant by the statement "The moon is geologically dead"?
   a. The moon has little erosion and no plate movement.
   b. The moon is devoid of living things.
   c. The moon has no atmosphere.
   d. The moon has no air currents or weather patterns.

____ 13. The moon most likely formed
   a. from a collision with a Mars-sized object.
   b. in another region of space and drifted toward Earth.
   c. from material in the solar system that came together.
   d. in the same way as Earth was formed.

____ 14. Soon after the collision with Earth, the materials that eventually formed the moon
   a. orbited Earth in a large, irregular clump.
   b. were bits of Earth's mantle encircling Earth.
   c. were mostly broken pieces of the object that hit Earth.
   d. none of the above

____ 15. Ocean tides are the result of
   a. the rotation of the Earth.
   b. the sun's gravitational pull on Earth.
   c. changes in Earth's orbital position around the sun.
   d. differences in both the sun's and moon's gravitational pull on Earth.

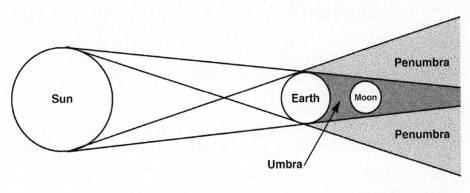

NOT TO SCALE

Figure 25-1

_____ 16. Study Figure 25-1. Suppose you are an astronaut on the side of the moon facing Earth during a total lunar eclipse. Which would you see as you look toward Earth?
   a. Nothing; there would be total darkness.
   b. The normal view; there is always reflected light from the moon's surface.
   c. You could not see the sun because Earth blocks its light.
   d. The light from the sun behind Earth would be blinding.

_____ 17. The four terrestrial planets are so called because they
   a. are the nearest planets to Earth.
   b. were all once part of Earth.
   c. are similar in structure to Earth.
   d. can all be seen from Earth without a telescope.

_____ 18. Which characteristic of the inner planets increases with increasing distance from the sun?
   a. equatorial diameter   c. average temperature
   b. period of rotation   d. period of revolution

_____ 19. Asteroids are mainly found
   a. in the asteroid belt beyond Mars.   c. throughout the solar system.
   b. in orbit around Jupiter.   d. beyond the farthest known planet.

_____ 20. What evidence suggests that asteroids are like rubble heaps and not solid like rock?
   a. They are held together by weak gravity.
   b. They have not shattered on impact with other objects.
   c. They mostly have irregular shapes.
   d. They are remnants of a shattered planet.

_____ 21. Which of the gas giants has the largest diameter?
   a. Jupiter   c. Saturn
   b. Uranus   d. Neptune

_____ 22. Which characteristic of the gas giants decreases with increasing distance from the sun?
   a. equatorial diameter   c. number of moons
   b. period of rotation   d. both a and c

_____ 23. Comets are made mostly of
    a.   iron.
    b.   ice and rock.
    c.   hydrogen and helium.
    d.   methane.

_____ 24. What is the difference between a meteoroid and a meteorite?
    a.   A meteoroid is made of metal; a meteorite is made of rock.
    b.   A meteoroid is larger than a meteorite.
    c.   A meteoroid is located in space; it becomes a meteorite when it hits Earth.
    d.   A meteoroid has a tail like a comet; a meteorite burns up in Earth's atmosphere.

_____ 25. Which of the following is a sparse sphere of comets that surrounds the sun and planets?
    a.   the asteroid belt
    b.   the Kuiper belt
    c.   the Oort cloud
    d.   none of the above

_____ 26. In astronomical units (AU), what is the approximate distance of the outer edge of the Oort cloud from the outer edge of the Kuiper belt?
    a.   100 AU
    b.   20,000 AU
    c.   30,000 AU
    d.   more than 49,000 AU

_____ 27. According to the nebula theory, the solar system formed from
    a.   accretion of protoplanets.
    b.   a large, thin cloud of dust and gas.
    c.   colliding planetesimals.
    d.   all of the above

_____ 28. In the formation of our solar system, nearly all of the mass of the solar nebula became
    a.   the terrestrial planets.
    b.   the gas giants.
    c.   the sun.
    d.   the Oort cloud.

_____ 29. Which of the following statements explains why the terrestrial planets are small and rocky instead of large and less dense like the gas giants?
    a.   The inner planets were exposed to much higher temperatures.
    b.   Ice-forming compounds vaporize at high temperatures.
    c.   Rock-forming materials can condense at high temperatures.
    d.   all of the above

_____ 30. Which evidence provides support for the nebular theory?
    a.   Scientists have observed the formation of a distant solar system.
    b.   The nebular theory has been proven mathematically.
    c.   Astronomers have observed protoplanetary disks around distant newborn stars.
    d.   none of the above

Completion
Complete each sentence or statement.

31. The force of gravity that the sun exerts on a planet is directed _____.

32. Because Earth's orbit around the sun is an ellipse, and Earth is not always the same distance from the sun, one AU is defined as the _____ distance from Earth to the sun.

Name ________________________ Class ______________________ Date ________

33. All of the planets in our solar system have ____________________ with the exception of Mercury and Venus.

34. The beginning of the "space race" occurred when the ____________________ launched the first artificial satellite in 1957.

35. Because there is no ____________________ on the moon, any liquid water would have evaporated long ago.

36. A person weighing 600 newtons (about 120 pounds) on Earth would weigh about ____________________ newtons on the moon.

37. The model of the universe in which Earth is stationary is the ____________________ model.

38. On Earth's moon, there are fewer ____________________ within the maria than in the highlands.

39. The collision from which the moon formed ejected a huge amount of Earth's crust into space including part of Earth's ____________________.

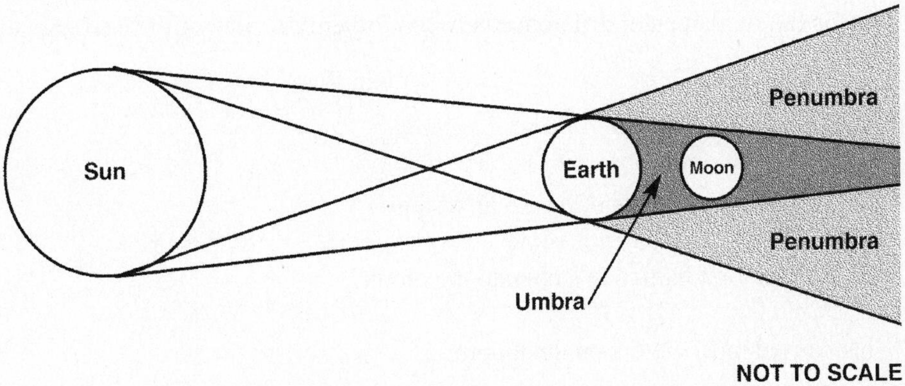

Figure 25-1

40. The total lunar eclipse shown in Figure 25-1 is occurring during the ____________________ phase of the moon.

41. The length of a planet's day is determined by its ________________________.

42. On Venus, a day is ____________________ than an Earth year.

43. The large, irregular objects mostly located between Mars and Jupiter are ____________________.

44. The ________________________ is so great inside the gas giants that hydrogen and helium exist in liquid form.

45. The rings around the gas giants have not clumped to form moons because of large _____ forces.

46. Icy objects that mostly travel in long, elliptical orbits around the sun are _____.

47. The _____ belt contains perhaps tens of thousands of objects orbiting within about 100 AU of the sun.

48. The great reservoir of comets beyond the Kuiper belt is called the _____.

49. The material that formed our solar system originated from a solar _____.

50. The difference in the composition of the terrestrial planets and the gas giants can be explained by the different condensation _____ in the regions near and far from the sun during the formation of the solar system.

Short Answer

51. What is the fundamental difference between Ptolemy's view of the universe and that of Aristarchus?

52. What is the ecliptic plane?

53. What are the components of our solar system?

54. Who was the first human to step onto the moon?

55. What caused most craters on the moon?

56. What formed the moon's maria?

57. At about what time in Earth's history did the formation of the moon begin?

58. What is the difference between a full moon and a new moon?

59. Explain why Mars is called the most Earthlike of all the other planets.

60. Explain the odd and irregular shapes of most asteroids.

61. What first provided evidence in the early 1800s that another planet existed beyond Uranus?

62. How has radioactive dating of certain meteoroids enabled scientists to estimate the age of the universe?

73. **Using Models** Look at Figure 25-2. Where would you mark the position of the asteroid belt?

74. **Applying Concepts** During the time the solar system was forming, which region had sufficiently cool temperatures for ice crystals to form? Use Figure 25-2 to indicate the location.

75. **Drawing Conclusions** Given that Pluto is about 39.5 AU from the sun, where would you locate the Kuiper belt on Figure 25-2? What would be the location of the Oort cloud?

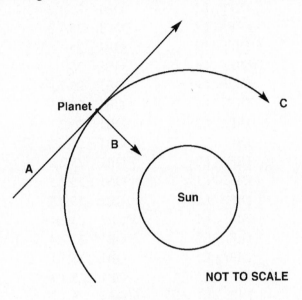

NOT TO SCALE

Figure 25-3

76. **Applying Concepts** If a planet is orbiting along path C in Figure 25-3, explain why it stays in orbit. Refer to Figure 25-3 in your explanation.

77. **Inferring** Based on Figure 25-3, describe the path that the planet would follow if the sun did not exist. Why would this happen?

78. **Formulating Hypotheses** In Figure 25-3, why would you expect B to lie in the planet's orbital plane?

79. **Drawing Conclusions** Saturn is the least dense of all the planets. Why does Saturn remain in orbit instead of drifting away in space or crashing into the sun?

80. **Applying Concepts** The period of revolution of the planet shown in Figure 25-3 is 1.88 Earth years. What planet is it? How does the period of an asteroid in the asteroid belt compare with the period of the planet shown?

Chapter 25   The Solar System
Answer Section

MULTIPLE CHOICE

1. ANS: B   DIF: L1   OBJ: 25.1.1
2. ANS: C   DIF: L2   OBJ: 25.1.1
3. ANS: A   DIF: L1   OBJ: 25.1.2
4. ANS: D   DIF: L2   OBJ: 25.1.2
5. ANS: C   DIF: L1   OBJ: 25.1.3
6. ANS: A   DIF: L2   OBJ: 25.1.3
7. ANS: B   DIF: L1   OBJ: 25.1.4
8. ANS: B   DIF: L2   OBJ: 25.1.4
9. ANS: D   DIF: L1   OBJ: 25.2.1
10. ANS: C   DIF: L2   OBJ: 25.2.1
11. ANS: B   DIF: L1   OBJ: 25.2.2
12. ANS: A   DIF: L2   OBJ: 25.2.2
13. ANS: A   DIF: L1   OBJ: 25.2.3
14. ANS: B   DIF: L2   OBJ: 25.2.3
15. ANS: D   DIF: L1   OBJ: 25.2.4
16. ANS: C   DIF: L2   OBJ: 25.2.4
17. ANS: C   DIF: L1   OBJ: 25.3.1
18. ANS: D   DIF: L2   OBJ: 25.3.1
19. ANS: A   DIF: L1   OBJ: 25.3.2
20. ANS: B   DIF: L2   OBJ: 25.3.2
21. ANS: A   DIF: L1   OBJ: 25.4.1
22. ANS: D   DIF: L2   OBJ: 25.4.1
23. ANS: B   DIF: L1   OBJ: 25.4.2
24. ANS: C   DIF: L2   OBJ: 25.4.2
25. ANS: C   DIF: L1   OBJ: 25.4.3
26. ANS: D   DIF: L2   OBJ: 25.4.3
27. ANS: D   DIF: L1   OBJ: 25.5.1
28. ANS: C   DIF: L2   OBJ: 25.5.1
29. ANS: D   DIF: L1   OBJ: 25.5.2
30. ANS: C   DIF: L2   OBJ: 25.5.2

COMPLETION

31. ANS: toward the sun   DIF: L1   OBJ: 25.1.2
32. ANS: average   DIF: L2   OBJ: 25.1.2
33. ANS: moons   DIF: L2   OBJ: 25.1.3
34. ANS: Soviet Union   DIF: L1   OBJ: 25.1.4
35. ANS: atmosphere   DIF: L1   OBJ: 25.2.1
36. ANS: 100   DIF: L2   OBJ: 25.2.1

37.	ANS: geocentric	DIF: L1	OBJ: 25.2.2
38.	ANS: craters	DIF: L2	OBJ: 25.2.2
39.	ANS: mantle	DIF: L2	OBJ: 25.2.3
40.	ANS: full moon	DIF: L1	OBJ: 25.2.4
41.	ANS: period of rotation	DIF: L1	OBJ: 25.3.1
42.	ANS: longer	DIF: L2	OBJ: 25.3.1
43.	ANS: asteroids	DIF: L1	OBJ: 25.3.2

44. ANS:
pressure
atmospheric pressure
DIF: L2   OBJ: 25.4.1

45.	ANS: gravitational	DIF: L2	OBJ: 25.4.1
46.	ANS: comets	DIF: L1	OBJ: 25.4.2
47.	ANS: Kuiper	DIF: L2	OBJ: 25.4.3
48.	ANS: Oort cloud	DIF: L1	OBJ: 25.4.3
49.	ANS: nebula	DIF: L1	OBJ: 25.5.1
50.	ANS: temperatures	DIF: L2	OBJ: 25.5.2

SHORT ANSWER

51. ANS: Ptolemy's view was geocentric. Aristarchus' view was heliocentric.
DIF: L2   OBJ: 25.1.1

52. ANS: the plane of Earth's orbit   DIF: L2   OBJ: 25.1.2

53. ANS: the sun, planets and their moons, and a variety of smaller objects, such as asteroids, meteoroids, and comets
DIF: L1   OBJ: 25.1.3

54. ANS: Neil Armstrong   DIF: L1   OBJ: 25.1.4

55. ANS: the impact of high speed meteoroids
DIF: L1   OBJ: 25.2.1

56. ANS: ancient lunar lava flows   DIF: L1   OBJ: 25.2.2

57. ANS: 4.6 billion years ago when Earth was still forming
DIF: L1   OBJ: 25.2.3

58. ANS: A full moon occurs when the side of the moon facing Earth is fully lit by the sun, and Earth is between the sun and the moon. A new moon occurs when the moon is between the sun and Earth, and the moon's dark side faces Earth.
DIF: L2   OBJ: 25.2.4

59. ANS: Mars is most similar to Earth of all the planets in size, mass, and density. It has distinct seasons and shows evidence of once having a great deal of water.
DIF: L2   OBJ: 25.3.1

60. ANS: The weak gravity of small asteroids and impacts with other objects caused these shapes.
DIF: L2   OBJ: 25.3.2

61. ANS: Uranus did not follow its predicted orbit. It was affected by gravity from another unseen planet.
DIF: L1   OBJ: 25.4.1

62. ANS: Certain meteoroids are unaltered remnants of the early solar system.
    DIF: L1   OBJ: 25.4.2
63. ANS: tens of thousands of objects, mostly made of ice, dust, and rock
    DIF: L1   OBJ: 25.4.3
64. ANS: remnants of previous stars   DIF: L1   OBJ: 25.5.1
65. ANS: Planetesimals grew larger because more gas condensed in the outer solar system. The gravity of these larger planetesimals could attract and capture hydrogen and helium, which were abundant.
    DIF: L2   OBJ: 25.5.2

ESSAY

66. ANS: Possible answers: Space probes, or unpiloted vehicles, are being used to photograph and measure parameters of the planets, moons, and other objects, and then transmit information back to Earth. The Hubble telescope in orbit around Earth and others telescopes provide views and information about the solar system and beyond. The space shuttle is a reusable vehicle that sends humans into orbit around Earth to do scientific research. The International Space Station is a permanent laboratory designed for research in space.
    DIF: L2   OBJ: 25.1.4
67. ANS: Most of that material of this mass has already joined a solar-system component, such as a planet, or is already in orbit.
    DIF: L2   OBJ: 25.2.3
68. ANS: Two moons, Ganymede and Callisto, are about the size of Mercury. Io and Europa are about the size of Earth's moon. Unlike Jupiter, Ganymede, Io, and Europa have metal cores and rocky mantles. Io is the most volcanically active body in the solar system. Europa has an icy crust that appears to rest on a liquid-water ocean. Ganymede and Callisto are covered with ice.
    DIF: L2   OBJ: 25.4.1
69. ANS: Comets are dusty pieces of ice and rock that have no tails in the regions of space far from the sun. Comets travel in highly elliptical orbits around the sun. A comet develops two tails as it approaches the sun. The bluish tail is an ion tail comprised of charged gas particles pushed away from the comet by the solar wind. The dust tail is white and is produced by dust that is pushed away from the sun by photons. The ion tail of a comet can be millions of kilometers long and always faces away from the sun.
    DIF: L2   OBJ: 25.4.2
70. ANS: Any theory must explain the following: 1) why the planets lie in a single plane, 2) why all the planets orbit the sun in a single direction, and 3) the difference in size and composition between the terrestrial planets and the gas giants. The nebular theory satisfies all three criteria.
    DIF: L2   OBJ: 25.5.2

OTHER

71. ANS: Heliocentric; the sun is shown at the center, and other bodies are indicated in orbit around the sun.
    DIF: L1   OBJ: 25.1.1

72. ANS: Planets; 1. Mercury, terrestrial; 2. Venus, terrestrial; 3. Earth, terrestrial; 4. Mars, terrestrial; 5. Jupiter, gas giant; 6. Saturn, gas giant; 7. Uranus, gas giant; 8. Neptune, gas giant; 9. Pluto, neither (can't be classified as either terrestrial or gas giant)
DIF: L1   OBJ: 25.1.3

73. ANS: The asteroid belt lies mostly between Mars and Jupiter, so the diagram could be marked anywhere between 4 and 5.
DIF: L1   OBJ: 25.3.2

74. ANS: Sufficiently cool temperatures for ice-forming compounds to condense must occur beyond Mars (4). Mars is the last terrestrial planet before the first of the gas giants, Jupiter. Cool temperatures had to exist in this region for the gas giants to form.
DIF: L1   OBJ: 25.4.1

75. ANS: The Kuiper belt would have to be drawn extending from Pluto (9) to a little more than twice the distance of Pluto from the sun. The Oort cloud could not be drawn on this scale because it extends out to 50,000 AU.
DIF: L1   OBJ: 25.4.3

76. ANS: Newton's first law of motion states that an object in motion will continue to move in a straight line unless acted upon by a force. A planet in orbit C would move approximately along path A if another force—gravity—was not acting on it. The planet has inertia, which carries it in direction A, but force B pulls the planet in a curved path C. The planet stays in orbit because of the balance between inertia and the gravitational pull of the sun.
DIF: L2   OBJ: 25.1.2

77. ANS: The planet's inertia would carry it forward in a straight-line path, such as A. Because there would be no gravitational force on the planet from the sun, the net force on the planet would be zero. As a result, there would be no change in the planet's speed or direction.
DIF: L2   OBJ: 25.2.1

78. ANS: Arrow B represents the gravitational force between the planet and the sun. The force acts between the center of the planet and the center of the sun, and both the center of the planet and the center of the sun lie in the orbital plane. Therefore, the force of attraction between the centers must also lie in the same plane.
DIF: L2   OBJ: 25.2.1

79. ANS: Saturn is not dense, but it still has mass, so inertia and gravity balance to keep Saturn in orbit.
DIF: L2   OBJ: 25.4.1

80. ANS: Mars; the period of the asteroid would be greater than 1.88 years because the asteroid belt is beyond the orbit of Mars, and orbital periods increase as distance from the sun increases.
DIF: L2   OBJ: 25.4.1

Chapter 26 Exploring the Universe

Multiple Choice
Identify the letter of the choice that best completes the statement or answers the question.

_____ 1. The sun's energy is produced by
   a.   the sun burning fuel.
   c.   an ordinary chemical reaction.
   b.   nuclear fission.
   d.   nuclear fusion.

_____ 2. What will happen to the relative amounts of hydrogen and helium in the sun over the next few billion years?
   a.   Hydrogen will increase and helium will decrease.
   b.   Hydrogen will decrease and helium will increase.
   c.   Both hydrogen and helium will decrease.
   d.   Both hydrogen and helium will remain the same.

_____ 3. The sun remains stable over time because
   a.   its supply of hydrogen is inexhaustible.
   b.   the product of fusion, helium, is a stable element.
   c.   the inward pull of gravity and outward push of thermal pressure are balanced.
   d.   nuclear fusion is a stabilizing process.

_____ 4. For the sun to be stable, the inward and outward forces within the sun must be
   a.   in equilibrium.
   c.   focused in the core.
   b.   part of the fusion reaction.
   d.   balanced with temperature and density.

_____ 5. The stream of electrically charged particles sent into space by the sun is called
   a.   a solar flare.
   c.   a solar prominence.
   b.   a sunspot.
   d.   the solar wind.

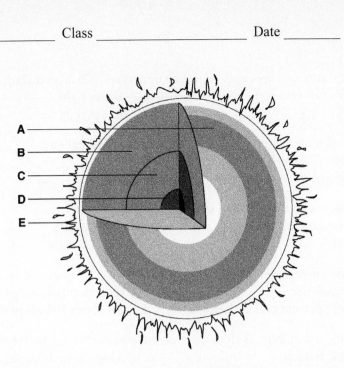

Figure 26-1

_____ 6. Examine Figure 26-1. Which area is the convection zone?

    a. A   c. C

    b. B   d. D

_____ 7. The distance between stars is typically measured in

    a. light-years.   c. astronomical units.

    b. kilometers.   d. miles.

_____ 8. The parallax of a star is observed because

    a. all stars have the same apparent brightness.

    b. parallax increases with distance.

    c. stars do not move.

    d. the observer moves.

_____ 9. Astronomers classify stars according to their

    a. distance from Earth.   c. age and parallax.

    b. color, size, and absolute brightness.   d. all of the above

_____ 10. The apparent brightness of a star

    a. varies with the position from which it is viewed.

    b. can be calculated from its absolute brightness and mass.

    c. is greater as distance from the sun increases.

    d. is a measure of its light viewed from any position.

_____ 11. An H-R diagram

    a. is a map of the positions of the stars.

    b. graphs stars according to their size and distance.

    c. lists every known star.

    d. graphs a sample of stars according to surface temperature and absolute brightness.

_____ 12. A cool, bright star would appear in which section of an H-R diagram?
   a. lower left   c. upper right
   b. upper left   d. lower right

_____ 13. The life cycle of a star begins with a cloud of gas and dust called a
   a. protoplanet.   c. nebula.
   b. constellation.   d. protosun.

_____ 14. Both high-mass and low-mass adult stars are classified as
   a. main-sequence stars.   c. supernovas.
   b. white dwarfs.   d. neutron stars.

_____ 15. All stars remain on the main sequence
   a. until they stabilize.   c. until they become protostars.
   b. for about 90 percent of their lifetimes.   d. for about 10 billion years.

_____ 16. Which kind of star will most likely remain on the main sequence the longest?
   a. a low-mass, red star   c. a high-mass blue star
   b. a yellow star like the sun   d. a bright white star

_____ 17. Low-mass and medium-mass stars eventually
   a. grow into supergiants.   c. become neutron stars.
   b. become supernovas.   d. turn into white dwarfs.

_____ 18. What is a pulsar?
   a. the remains of a low-mass star after it explodes
   b. a spinning neutron star emitting radio waves
   c. another name for a protostar
   d. the stage before a dying star becomes a supernova

_____ 19. Which of the following is true about more than half of all stars?
   a. They are dying red giants.   c. They are members of a star system.
   b. They are visible to the unaided eye.   d. They are high-mass stars.

_____ 20. Why is studying star clusters useful?
   a. because there is such a large diversity of stars in a cluster
   b. because they are about the same age and distance from Earth
   c. because they are all about the same size and temperature
   d. because all of them are always young, bright stars

_____ 21. How do open star clusters differ from associations?
   a. Associations are usually larger and have fewer stars.
   b. Open clusters are organized into constellations.
   c. Associations are usually smaller and have more stars.
   d. Open clusters typically contain loose groupings of old stars.

_____ 22. A large group of older stars would be found in which of the following star clusters?
   a. open cluster   c. globular cluster
   b. association   d. both a and b

_____ 23. Galaxies are classified into four groups based on their
      a. shapes.
      b. sizes.
      c. number of stars.
      d. brightness.

_____ 24. Older stars are most likely found in
      a. the arms of spiral and barred-spiral galaxies.
      b. elliptical galaxies.
      c. irregular galaxies.
      d. both a and b

_____ 25. When the absorption lines of a galaxy shift toward the red end of the spectrum, it means that the galaxy is
      a. moving closer to Earth.
      b. small and young.
      c. moving away from Earth.
      d. large and old.

_____ 26. Hubble's Law states that the speed at which a galaxy is moving away is proportional to the
      a. mass of the galaxy.
      b. number of stars in the galaxy.
      c. galaxy's distance from Earth.
      d. age of the galaxy.

_____ 27. The big bang theory explains the
      a. origin of the universe.
      b. life cycle of a star.
      c. Doppler effect.
      d. arrangement of constellations.

_____ 28. Which of the following provides support for the big bang theory?
      a. red shift
      b. cosmic microwave background radiation
      c. elliptical galaxies
      d. both a and b

_____ 29. Dark matter can be detected by its
      a. cosmic microwave background radiation.
      b. red shift.
      c. gravitational effects on visible matter.
      d. velocity.

_____ 30. Much of the mass of the universe may be composed of
      a. electromagnetic waves.
      b. cosmic microwaves.
      c. background radiation.
      d. dark matter.

Completion
Complete each sentence or statement.

31. The sun's major source of fuel is _____.

32. The two forces that are balanced when a star is in equilibrium are outward pressure and _____.

33. Nuclear fusion within the sun takes place within the _____.

34. The apparent change in position of an object with respect to a distant background is called _____.

Name _____ Class _____ Date _____

35. By using a spectrograph, a star's absorption lines can identify the different _____ that a star is composed of.

36. In an H-R diagram, most stars are found in a diagonal band from the upper left to the lower right, which is called the _____.

37. A contracting cloud of dust and gas with enough mass to form a star is called a(an) _____.

38. A young star forms when the pressure from _____ supports the star against the tremendous inward pull of gravity.

39. The main sequence lifetime of a star is dependent upon the star's _____.

40. The sun will end its life as a red giant and eventually end up as a(an) _____.

41. A group of two or more stars held together by gravity is called a(an) _____.

42. A large spherical group of older stars is called a(an) _____.

43. New stars are not forming in older _____ galaxies.

44. The apparent change in frequency and wavelength of a sound or light source as it moves toward or away from an observer is called the _____.

45. The theory that the universe came into being in a single moment with an enormous explosion is the _____ theory.

46. Matter that does not give off any radiation is called _____.

47. As a star stabilizes as a red giant, it produces carbon, oxygen, and other elements from the fusion of _____.

48. The characteristic of the radiation observed from a pulsar is caused by the neutron star's _____.

49. A binary system in which one star passes in front of the other, blocking some light from reaching Earth is called a(an) _____ binary.

50. The observation that cosmic microwave background radiation is detected n all directions in the universe supports the hypothesis that the universe is _____.

Name _____ Class _____ Date _____

Short Answer

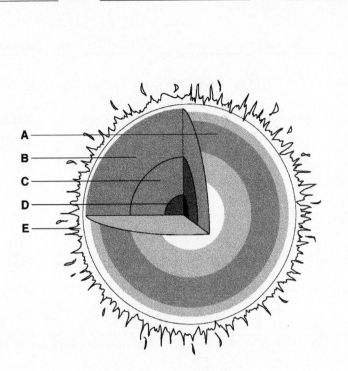

Figure 26-1

51. In Figure 26-1, name and describe area C and tell how it differs from area B in the way it transfers energy.

52. At least how much longer is the sun expected to remain a stable main sequence star?

53. What is the innermost layer of the sun's atmosphere called?

54. Why do astronomers measure the parallax of nearby stars?

55. What characteristic of a star's spectrum do astronomers use to determine the different elements in the star?

56. What are the very bright stars in the upper right of an H-R diagram called?

57. What two factors cause a nebula to develop into a star?

58. How long will a yellow star like the sun remain on the main sequence?

59. How are elements other than helium produced?

60. What is a group of stars called that appears to form a pattern when seen from Earth?

61. Why do globular clusters generally contain only old stars?

62. What does recent evidence suggest is at the center of our galaxy?

63. How can an object's red shift tell us how fast the object is moving away from Earth?

64. How have scientists used Hubble's Law to estimate the age of the universe?

65. To what do astronomers attribute the increasing rate of expansion of the universe?

Essay

On a separate sheet of paper, write an answer to each of the following questions.

66. Describe the process of nuclear fusion in the sun's core.

67. What is the difference between the apparent brightness and the absolute brightness of a star?

68. The astronomer Carl Sagan once said that we are all made of "star stuff." Explain what he meant.

69. Besides shape, what is the difference between an elliptical galaxy and an irregular galaxy?

70. Discuss the hypothetical role of the amount of dark matter and dark energy in predicting the future of the universe.

Other

USING SCIENCE SKILLS

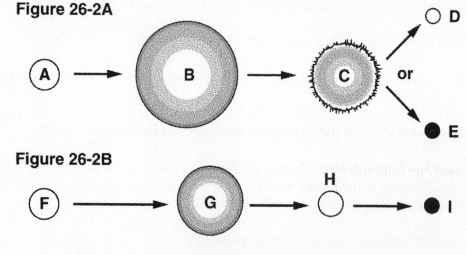

Figure 26-2A

Figure 26-2B

Figure 26-2

71. **Applying Concepts** Would you expect to find helium fusion occurring in stage F or stage G of the star shown in Figure 26-2B? Explain your answer.

72. **Using Models** Which figure—26-2A or 26-2B—models the evolution of a high-mass star? Explain how you know.

73. **Inferring** Which figure—26-2A or 26-2B—can you infer is a model of a star formed from a small nebula? Explain your answer.

74. **Interpreting Graphics** In Figure 26-2A, what is the event occurring at stage C? Explain why there are two possible outcomes (stage D and stage E).

75. **Drawing Conclusions** Relate two differences between the life cycles shown in Figure 26-2 that will allow you to conclude which star will be longer lived.

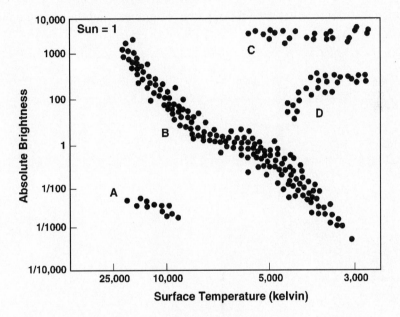

Figure 26-3

76. **Inferring** Suppose two stars are located in region A of the H-R diagram shown in Figure 26-3. Star X appears much dimmer than Star Y as seen from Earth. Which star can be inferred to be nearer to Earth, and what other factor must be considered?

77. **Applying Concepts** How would you describe the change in the properties of stars as you move from left to right along the main sequence in the H-R diagram in Figure 26-3?

78. **Interpreting Diagrams** In which region of the H-R diagram in Figure 26-3 would you find the sun?

79. **Predicting** Use the regions of Figure 26-3 to describe the fate of the sun. Where is the sun on the diagram now? How long will it be there? What will happen to the sun when this stage ends?

80. **Classifying** Describe the classification of stars shown in Figure 26-3 that begin to fuse helium nuclei. Where are such stars located on the H-R diagram?

Chapter 26   Exploring the Universe
Answer Section

MULTIPLE CHOICE

1.	ANS: D	DIF:	L1	OBJ:	26.1.1
2.	ANS: B	DIF:	L2	OBJ:	26.1.1
3.	ANS: C	DIF:	L2	OBJ:	26.1.2
4.	ANS: A	DIF:	L1	OBJ:	26.1.2
5.	ANS: D	DIF:	L2	OBJ:	26.1.3
6.	ANS: B	DIF:	L1	OBJ:	26.1.3
7.	ANS: A	DIF:	L1	OBJ:	26.2.1
8.	ANS: D	DIF:	L2	OBJ:	26.2.1
9.	ANS: B	DIF:	L1	OBJ:	26.2.2
10.	ANS: A	DIF:	L2	OBJ:	26.2.2
11.	ANS: D	DIF:	L1	OBJ:	26.2.3
12.	ANS: C	DIF:	L2	OBJ:	26.2.3
13.	ANS: C	DIF:	L1	OBJ:	26.3.1
14.	ANS: A	DIF:	L1	OBJ:	26.3.1
15.	ANS: B	DIF:	L1	OBJ:	26.3.2
16.	ANS: A	DIF:	L2	OBJ:	26.3.2
17.	ANS: D	DIF:	L1	OBJ:	26.3.3
18.	ANS: B	DIF:	L2	OBJ:	26.3.3
19.	ANS: C	DIF:	L1	OBJ:	26.4.1
20.	ANS: B	DIF:	L2	OBJ:	26.4.1
21.	ANS: A	DIF:	L1	OBJ:	26.4.2
22.	ANS: C	DIF:	L1	OBJ:	26.4.2
23.	ANS: A	DIF:	L1	OBJ:	26.4.3
24.	ANS: B	DIF:	L2	OBJ:	26.4.3
25.	ANS: C	DIF:	L1	OBJ:	26.5.1
26.	ANS: C	DIF:	L2	OBJ:	26.5.1
27.	ANS: A	DIF:	L1	OBJ:	26.5.2
28.	ANS: D	DIF:	L2	OBJ:	26.5.2
29.	ANS: C	DIF:	L1	OBJ:	26.5.3
30.	ANS: D	DIF:	L2	OBJ:	26.5.3

COMPLETION

31.	ANS: hydrogen	DIF:	L1	OBJ:	26.1.1
32.	ANS: gravity	DIF:	L1	OBJ:	26.1.2
33.	ANS: core	DIF:	L2	OBJ:	26.1.3
34.	ANS: parallax	DIF:	L2	OBJ:	26.2.1
35.	ANS: elements	DIF:	L1	OBJ:	26.2.2
36.	ANS: main sequence	DIF:	L1	OBJ:	26.2.3

37. ANS: protostar	DIF: L1	OBJ: 26.3.1
38. ANS: fusion	DIF: L1	OBJ: 26.3.1
39. ANS: mass	DIF: L2	OBJ: 26.3.2

40. ANS:
white dwarf
black dwarf
DIF: L1   OBJ: 26.3.3

41. ANS: star system	DIF: L1	OBJ: 26.4.1
42. ANS: globular cluster	DIF: L1	OBJ: 26.4.2
43. ANS: elliptical	DIF: L2	OBJ: 26.4.3
44. ANS: Doppler effect	DIF: L2	OBJ: 26.5.1
45. ANS: big bang	DIF: L1	OBJ: 26.5.2
46. ANS: dark matter	DIF: L1	OBJ: 26.5.3
47. ANS: helium	DIF: L2	OBJ: 26.2.2
48. ANS: rotation	DIF: L2	OBJ: 26.3.3
49. ANS: eclipsing	DIF: L2	OBJ: 26.4.2
50. ANS: expanding	DIF: L2	OBJ: 26.5.2

SHORT ANSWER

51. ANS: Area C is the radiation zone of the sun. Area B is the convection zone. The radiation zone transfers energy primarily by electromagnetic waves. The convection zone transfers energy primarily by moving gases in convection currents.
DIF: L2   OBJ: 26.1.1

52. ANS: 5 billion years	DIF: L1	OBJ: 26.1.2
53. ANS: the photosphere	DIF: L1	OBJ: 26.1.3

54. ANS: to determine the stars' distances from Earth
DIF: L1   OBJ: 26.2.1

55. ANS: absorption lines	DIF: L2	OBJ: 26.2.2
56. ANS: supergiants	DIF: L2	OBJ: 26.2.3
57. ANS: gravity and heat from contraction	DIF: L2	OBJ: 26.3.1
58. ANS: about 10 billion years	DIF: L1	OBJ: 26.3.2

59. ANS: When hydrogen is gone, helium fusion begins, producing carbon, oxygen, and certain heavier elements. Elements heavier than iron are created in a supernova.
DIF: L2   OBJ: 26.3.3

60. ANS: a constellation   DIF: L1   OBJ: 26.4.1

61. ANS: Globular clusters usually lack sufficient dust and gas to form new stars.
DIF: L1   OBJ: 26.4.2

62. ANS: a massive black hole   DIF: L1   OBJ: 26.4.3

63. ANS: The larger the observed shift is, the faster is the speed.
DIF: L1   OBJ: 26.5.1

64. ANS: Scientists know how fast the universe is expanding and can infer how long it has been expanding since the big bang.
DIF: L1   OBJ: 26.5.2

65. ANS: a mysterious force called dark energy
    DIF: L2   OBJ: 26.5.3

ESSAY

66. ANS: The sun's core has a high enough temperature and pressure for fusion to take place. Less massive hydrogen nuclei combine into more massive helium nuclei, releasing enormous amounts of energy.
    DIF: L2   OBJ: 26.1.1

67. ANS: The apparent brightness is how bright a star appears and varies with the distance from which the star is viewed. Absolute brightness is a characteristic of the star and does not depend on how far it is from Earth.
    DIF: L2   OBJ: 26.2.2

68. ANS: As high-mass stars evolve to the fusion of elements other than hydrogen, they create other elements, including iron. The stars eventually run out of elements to fuse. Gravity overcomes the lower thermal pressure, and the star collapses, producing a violent explosion called a supernova. The heavier elements in our solar system, including the atoms in our bodies, come from a supernova that occurred billions of years ago.
    DIF: L2   OBJ: 26.3.3

69. ANS: New stars are not forming in older elliptical galaxies because there is little gas or dust between the stars. Irregular galaxies have many young stars and large amounts of gas and dust from which to produce new stars.
    DIF: L2   OBJ: 26.4.1

70. ANS: Dark matter seems to supply most of the gravitational attraction that keeps the galaxies from flying apart. The amount of dark matter in the universe will determine if the universe will continue to expand, stop expanding, or, perhaps, increase in the rate at which it is expanding. The amount of dark energy will determine if the universe will continue to expand forever.
    DIF: L2   OBJ: 26.5.3

OTHER

71. ANS: Helium fusion would be occurring in stage G. In stage F, the star is a main-sequence star, and its energy is supplied by the fusion of hydrogen. Stage G represents the star as a red giant. As the core of the red giant collapses, it becomes hot enough to cause helium to undergo fusion.
    DIF: L2   OBJ: 26.2.1

72. ANS: Figure 26-2A; the subsequent stages of the model indicate a supernova at stage C and two possible fates at stages D and E. Low-mass stars have only one ultimate fate as a black dwarf at stage I from the white dwarf at stage H. Also, Figure 26-2A shows a supergiant, which is not a stage for a low mass star.
    DIF: L1   OBJ: 26.2.2

73. ANS: Figure 26-2B; small nebulas most likely produce low-mass to medium-mass stars because of the lower available mass in the nebula.
    DIF: L1   OBJ: 26.3.1

74. ANS: A high-mass star; a supernova results in one of two fates, depending on the star's mass. It could become a neutron star (stage D) or, for more massive stars, a black hole (stage E).
    DIF: L1   OBJ: 26.3.3

75. ANS: Figure 26-2B is a low-mass star, and Figure 26-2A represents a high-mass star. Figure 26-2A depicts the fate of the star as either a neutron star or a black hole. High-mass stars are shorter lived than low-mass stars because high-mass stars burn brighter, use up their hydrogen fuel in the core sooner, and therefore leave the main sequence sooner.
    DIF: L1   OBJ: 26.3.2

76. ANS: By the placement on the H-R diagram, we know that both stars are of roughly equal absolute brightness and surface temperature, and that both are white dwarfs. Because star X appears dimmer, it must be farther from Earth.
    DIF: L2   OBJ: 26.2.1

77. ANS: The hottest stars are blue and very bright. The coolest stars are red and have a much lower absolute brightness. They are found in the lower right of the main sequence.
    DIF: L2   OBJ: 26.2.2

78. ANS: region B, the main sequence, near the center (surface temperature of 5800 K)
    DIF: L2   OBJ: 26.2.3

79. ANS: The sun is a yellow star located in about the middle of region B, the main sequence. It will remain stable there for at least another 5 billion years. In its next stage, the sun will be classified as a red giant (region D). It will then become a white dwarf (region A).
    DIF: L2   OBJ: 26.3.2

80. ANS: As a star begins to fuse helium nuclei, its outer shell expands greatly. The outer shell then cools as it expands. The star is then classified as a red giant or a supergiant, depending on its original mass. Red giants are located in region D, and supergiants are located in region C.
    DIF: L2   OBJ: 26.3.3